THE HIGHER EDUCATION
OF WOMEN
IN ENGLAND AND AMERICA
1865–1920

WOMEN'S HISTORY AND CULTURE
(VOL. 6)

GARLAND REFERENCE LIBRARY
OF SOCIAL SCIENCE
(VOL. 661)

WOMEN'S HISTORY AND CULTURE

THE HIGHER EDUCATION
OF WOMEN
IN ENGLAND AND AMERICA
1865–1920

Elizabeth Seymour Eschbach

GARLAND PUBLISHING, INC. • NEW YORK & LONDON
1993

Library of Congress Cataloging-in-Publication Data

Eschbach, Elizabeth Seymour, 1950–
    The higher education of women in England and America, 1865–1920 /
Elizabeth Seymour Eschbach.
        p.   cm. — (Women's history and culture ; vol. 6) (Garland
reference library of social science ; vol. 661)
    Includes bibliographical references (p.   ) and index.
    ISBN 0-8240-6899-8 (alk. paper)
    1. Women—Education (Higher)—Great Britain—History—19th
century. 2. Women—Education (Higher)—Great Britain—History—20th
century. 3. Women—Education (Higher)—United States—History—19th
century. 4. Women—Education (Higher)—United States—History—20th
century. I. Title. II. Series: Women's history and culture ; 6.
III. Series: Garland reference library of social science ; v. 661.
LC2046.E83   1993
376'.941—dc20   92-31467
                                                                      CIP

Printed on acid-free, 250-year-life paper
Manufactured in the United States of America

For Phil, Philip, Anna, and Arthur

CONTENTS

ACKNOWLEDGMENTS

My interest in the history of women's education was first awakened in 1987 as I was exploring the lives of aristocratic women of the antebellum South. Of the many limitations imposed on these women, that of their educational deficiency seemed the most debilitating. "And when I looked in my own heart and saw my shocking ignorance and pitiful inferiority, I actually cried," lamented Southern diarist and journalist Sarah Morgan Dawson. This passage, written in 1862, conveyed a longing that continued to haunt me as I researched the lives of nineteenth-century women, here and abroad. Dawson's sense of intellectual deprivation, it soon became apparent, was common to many women of this time, whose letters, diaries, and memoirs speak of their unrealized potential.

"Why was I denied that education?" Dawson asked. This question, reiterated by countless other women of her time, became the focus of my research and I began, thus, to look for some answers to her question. It is my hope, then, that this study will elucidate some of these answers and, additionally, will highlight the noble efforts of those men and women who worked to uplift the intellectual dignity of women.

There are certain individuals without whose help and contributions this project would not have been completed. First and foremost is my professor, friend, and mentor Shirley Leckie of the University of Central Florida. Her excellent course on Women in American History first led me to investigate women such as Sarah Dawson and the many complexities that shaped the contours of their lives and those of our own today. I wish, therefore, to thank her for making this project possible and for continuing to be a source of inspiration and encouragement. My admiration for her as scholar, author, and teacher has no bounds.

I would also like to extend my gratitude to Thomas Greenhaw of the University of Central Florida. His fascinating lectures and love of England that he shares so enthusiastically with friends and students rekindled my love of English history and led me to include this country in my study.

Additionally, I express my appreciation to John Evans, Edmund Kallina, and Bruce Pauley of the University of Central Florida. Their friendship and interest in my work have heartened me over the years, and their scholarship continues to inspire me.

Warm thanks are also due my friends, colleagues, and students at Valencia Community College, whose interest and curiosity have encouraged me in this endeavor. In particular, I thank Carol Foltz for sharing her knowledge of this subject and her enthusiasm.

Finally, to my family I owe untold gratitude. First, to my parents, who sacrificed to assure my own education, and who have always sustained me with their love, example, and enthusiasm for my efforts, I say, once again, thank you. For my children and their understanding and special curiosity, I am fortunate. And to my husband, whose patience, reassurance, and willingness to take on additional household and family responsibilities during this time have never wavered, I offer my heartfelt thanks.

INTRODUCTION

On September 20, 1865, close to three hundred young women from across the United States made their way up the long avenue leading from the gate house to the main building of Vassar Female College in Poughkeepsie, New York. It was opening day at Vassar. It was also an important day for American women. According to one of the college's later presidents, some of the more zealous students "came as to Mecca, a holy place whose opening they had looked forward to as a sign of opportunity and progress for their sex."[1]

To contemporary ears this metaphor sounds extravagant. Nonetheless, it captured the magnitude of the moment. Vassar's first students were about to enter a phase in their lives which few women before them had enjoyed. Earlier generations had seldom granted their daughters the time, the money, or the privilege of pursuing the higher levels of classics, mathematics, and science now accorded this group.

Some of the less ardent young women arriving at Vassar that day might have trembled at the implications of their presence and their work at this institution. In nineteenth-century America, well-educated women were neither extolled nor championed by society. Rather, intellectual women were considered odd, out-of-place, and suspect in all but the rarest of social circles.

Still, these women in Vassar's first class would hardly be ignored or dismissed as insignificant. They and the new college just opening invited a great deal of attention. "The eyes of the world," noted the *New York Tribune*, "and many precious hopes are turned towards it."[2] As this group of young women proceeded through their years at Vassar College, their now highly visible lives would be closely scrutinized for data that would boost the arguments of both those who ardently approved of the path they had set out upon and those who vehemently disapproved.

A few months earlier the eyes of the world had been focused upon another event important to the lives of women. In England John Stuart Mill, just elected to Parliament by the voters of Westminster, reiterated in his election address his conviction that the Parliamentary franchise should be extended to women. His country was not ready to open a college such as Vassar that purported to offer women anything resembling a man's education. Nonetheless, the climate, as evinced by Mill's speech on behalf of women, was becoming favorable for at least discussing such ideas.

A small group had already begun meeting in Kensington in May 1865 to talk about issues concerning women, including the question of higher education. One of the group's long-term goals was the admission of women to English universities, still decades away. The year 1865 was not without achievement in this respect, though. As Vassar College admitted its first class of students, Cambridge University decided to grant young English women permission to sit for its local examinations, a tool devised by English universities to measure the degree and quality of education received in the secondary stage.

It is unlikely that many Cambridge dons recognized the significance of their institution's small concession to women. For those to whom the ideal of higher education for women was vital, however, obtaining the right to take local examinations was a strategic step.

In the entire configuration of women's concerns, articulated and defined in nineteenth-century England and America, the question of higher education stands out in importance. But the issue is not an easy one to follow, for differing views and intentions among the supporters and pioneers of women's education cloud the picture. Unlike the feminists working towards women's political emancipation, those struggling for women's intellectual emancipation could not easily agree on their ultimate goals nor the purpose of these goals.

Most advocates believed that education was necessary in order for women to become more effective wives, mothers, and teachers, enabling them to better fulfill the nineteenth-century ideal of true womanhood. To this end these supporters welcomed most educational advances. "We want true women trained to the full arc of their powers of mind, heart, and soul, and taught to devote all to their duties as women; then the world will be better as well as wiser," wrote Sarah Josepha Hale (1788-1879), editor of *Godey's Lady's Book*, to Matthew Vassar upon news of his plan to open his college. Hale envisioned this great experiment as a step forward in the civilizing, cultivating mission that was women's destiny in the crass world of nineteenth-century America.[3] Only a few saw higher education as the means by which dramatic changes might take place in the lives of women, professionally, psychologically, and socially, so that they might reach their potential as full individuals, regardless of their sex.

It was hard in 1865 to say where the doors just beginning to open would lead. In America it seemed that the opportunities for women pursuing a higher education would soon be limitless: Vassar was opening, other women's institutions of similar calibre were being considered, and universities in the West were becoming coeducational. In England little was offered women desiring higher intellectual stimulation in 1865. But the moment seemed promising: Mill was bringing women's issues before the public, the desire for educational reform was growing, and a small but necessary victory had been won when girls gained the right to take local examinations issued by Cambridge University.

The year 1865 was a landmark year. But steps that would lead to the important developments of this time date back to the eighteenth century. Here amid a social, religious, and political milieu that accorded little faith in women's mental capacity, individuals and groups initiated ideas and institutions to help ameliorate women's educational deprivation. These precedents, along with early nineteenth-century trends, will be examined in order to clarify women's academic status in nineteenth and twentieth-century England and America.

On the surface the women's education movements in these two countries appear distant and unrelated. A closer look, however, reveals relationships between the two with often similar patterns, problems, and tendencies. In examining these movements side by side, the connections as well as the distinctions become obvious. By drawing the two together, moreover, one gains a clearer picture of the advances and losses incurred by women seeking acceptance, recognition, and equality within the halls of higher learning.

The path towards intellectual emancipation was not a smooth one in either country. With each step new obstacles arose that had to be overcome. By the turn of the nineteenth century, however, America could boast of an array of heterogeneous institutions offering a variety of curricula that seemed to hold out tremendous promise for women. American society, it seems, now rooted in materialism, recognized not only the cultural, but also the monetary value of educated women. Many sources of support, therefore, both public and private, though paltry relative to the resources offered men, would open multiple channels for the training of women. In England the weight of tradition and a more rigid definition of women's place in society combined to restrict their educational advancement. While opportunity appeared abundant in America, English women were compelled to take slow, deliberate, but forceful steps to participate in higher education.

But as decades passed and new arguments were raised and old ones resurrected against women's aspirations to participate in academe, the story took unexpected turns. The promises that seemed inherent in the proliferation of educational channels for women in nineteenth-century America were not unconditionally fulfilled in the early twentieth century. Rather, the arguments that initially had limited women's access to education served now to strictly define and delineate the curriculum within higher education, especially coeducation, as women entered the halls of academe in great number. In England, by contrast, where every step seemed small by American standards, pioneers in women's education labored to establish a firm foundation upon which the ideal of an equal education for women would more readily be achieved. This task was slow and tedious by American standards, the lack of resources seeming insurmountable. "Not a penny could be spared for 'amenities'; for partridges and wine, beadles and turf, books and cigars, libraries and leisure," reflected Virginia Woolf (1882-1941), as she contrasted the impoverished women's colleges in England with the richly endowed men's colleges. "To raise bare walls out of the bare earth was the utmost they could do."[4] But the initial absence of public monetary support and patronage, coupled with the English ideal of education as a mark of privilege, interestingly helped to create stronger, less diluted educational programs for women within England's universities. Here their curricula would more closely resemble the full academic offering enjoyed by England's university men. In neither country, however, was the battle entirely won. By 1920 equal education remained a goal towards which women in America and England would continue to strive.

Notes

1. James Monroe Taylor, *Before Vassar Opened: A Contribution to the History of Higher Education in America* (Boston and New York: Houghton Mifflin Co., 1914; repr., Freeport, NY: Books for Libraries Press, 1972), 273.
2. Quoted in Taylor, 228.
3. Ruth E. Finley, *The Lady of Godey's: Sarah Josepha Hale* (New York: Arno Press, 1974), 209.
4. Virginia Woolf, *A Room of One's Own* (New York: Harcourt Brace Jovanovich, 1929), 23.

The Higher Education
of Women
in England and America
1865–1920

CHAPTER 1

THE EIGHTEENTH-CENTURY LEGACY

Late, when the house was still, parents and servants having retired, young Mary Somerville (1780-1872) made her solitary way by candlelight through volumes of Euclid, Virgil, and Shakespeare. Quietly, so her secret passion would not be disclosed, Mary night after night absorbed much of the scholarship that would one day enable her to become a renowned English scientist. But familial disapproval and censorship frequently interrupted her studies in this last decade of the eighteenth century, forcing her to momentarily abandon her books. Once, noticing the supply of candles dwindling at a suspiciously rapid pace, the servants were told to remove them from her room when she went to bed. "We must put an end to this," declared her father, "or we shall have Mary in a strait jacket one of these days."[1]

This did not deter Mary. Nor was she discouraged when she found herself placed in the village school to learn cookery and needlework to prevent her "wasting her time in reading."[2]

By the age of thirty-three, Mary Somerville had progressed in her process of self-education to the higher levels of mathematics, astronomy, and physics. She then began translating and publishing. Soon she would receive the first of the many stipends, awards, and honors from England and abroad by which her work would be recognized for the rest of her life.[3]

As an adult, Mary often looked back on this unhappy childhood "and the long course of years in which I had persevered almost without hope." Having embraced a life of scholarship, she realized that "concealment was no longer possible, nor was it attempted. I was considered eccentric and foolish, and my conduct was highly disapproved of by many."[4]

When she died in 1872 at the age of 92, *The London Post* proclaimed Mary Somerville "The Queen of Nineteenth-Century Science." She had become one of the foremost scientific writers of her age.

Mary Somerville's experience was both typical and exceptional. Her parents' hostility to her unrelenting devotion to learning reflected the prevalent attitude of late eighteenth-century English society toward scholarship in women. Mary Somerville, however, was an extraordinary woman. Thoroughly self-educated, she overcame parental and societal strictures to gain a place for herself in science that few women in history had been accorded. As scientist Margaret Alic notes, "It is impossible to know what the brilliant woman might have accomplished with early encouragement and training."[5]

A few decades earlier, across the Atlantic Ocean, the daughter of a distinguished South Carolina family pursued her studies with much the same enthusiasm as Mary Somerville would. Unlike Mary, however, young Harriott Pinkney (b. 1748) did not have to hide her learning in the darkness of the night. Rather, she was trained and encouraged by one of the best-educated women of the colonies, her mother, Eliza Lucas Pinckney (1722-1793), who taught her daughter Latin and French. Although Harriott had an able teacher in her mother, who had likened her own education to a "valuable fortune,"[6] Harriott lacked formal training, particularly the kind her brothers enjoyed in England. While Harriott attended her lessons in languages and plantation management under her mother's tutelage, her brothers matriculated through Westminster and Oxford University.[7] Always "fond of learning,"[8] Harriott continued to study, borrowing algebra and geometry textbooks from her younger brother.[9]

Harriott Pinckney, like Mary Somerville, was an exceptional woman. Born into an illustrious, forward-looking family that valued intelligence in their daughter, as well as their sons, Harriott proved to be an avid learner whose mind, said her mother, was "excellent soil" to cultivate.[10]

Nonetheless, the Pinckney family demonstrated a characteristic eighteenth-century distinction in emphasis. While her brothers were sent abroad to attain the best education, Harriott was kept at home. It was Harriott's father's wish that his elder son "be virtuously, religiously and liberally brought up and Educated in the Study and practice of the Laws of England," in order to "become the head of his family and prove not only of service and advantage to his country, but also an Honour to his Stock and Kindred."[11] No such imposing destiny would have been imagined for Harriott. Her life, instead, revolved around her home, her husband, and her children.

The lives of Mary Somerville and Harriott Pinckney, different in so many ways, shared the impact of common assumptions regarding the nature of women, the quality of their intellect, and the ideals of femininity. Both women were subject to the similar patterns and ideologies that shaped female behavior and destiny on both sides of the Atlantic in the eighteenth century, ideologies that precluded the opportunity for most women to gain educational advantage. The rationale behind these ideologies reached deep into the roots of western culture. Woman as wife, child-bearer, and nurturer had no need of formal education. Her energies were to be directed towards the service of husband, home, and family. Traditionally, then, education was a male preserve. The foundations of advanced scholarship in Europe, the early universities, prepared a man for a public life in theology, law, medicine, or university teaching. Woman, whose work was centered in the private realm of the home, had little use, tradition claimed, for advanced knowledge.

Contemporary eighteenth-century voices reinforced age-old practices, articulating and elaborating them. From the works of the celebrated Jean Jacques Rousseau (1712-1778) to the sermons and conduct manuals of relatively obscure preachers and doctors, English and American society bore no shortage of treatises that defined the dimensions and limitations of women's lives.

Translated into English in 1763, Rousseau's *Emile,* for example, affirmed the traditional notion of the social, political, and intellectual inferiority of women. While positing the kind of educational reform necessary to shape a male citizen for an idealized society, Rousseau provided a model of manhood based on strength, action, and intelligence gained through nature and experience. Rousseau's vision of womanhood, however, shared few of the characteristics of his ideal man. Passive and yielding, a woman, said Rousseau, is by nature weak and must follow the course nature has set for her. To aspire beyond her proper attributes by cultivating the "manly" qualities of strength, action, and intelligence would bring unhappiness. Created to provide pleasure to the opposite sex, the meaning of her life could be perceived only in relation to a man. The education of women, therefore, was in no need of reform. Governed largely by the natural cycles of pregnancy, childbirth, nursing, and child-rearing, women were already prohibited from intellectual exploration. In Rousseau's vision of men and women at home in a natural world, therefore, no educational changes in a girl's childhood were necessary. "To oblige us, to do us service, to gain our love and esteem . . . these are the duties of the sex at all times, and what they ought to learn from their infancy," he claimed.[12]

Some would shun Rousseau's views altogether; others would find fresh, stirring conceptions of family and gender relations and would follow Rousseau's visions accordingly. Generally among readers and thinkers of the time, Rousseau held a powerful influence. "Rousseau cast a spell over the foremost thinkers of Europe," wrote Dorothy Gardiner, "insisting that the birthright of women was inferiority of intellect and pettiness of soul."[13]

Less illustrious writers found audiences, as well. Following the pattern of the genre of courtesy books designed for gentlemen of the eighteenth century, advice books outlining general concepts of conduct for women were widely published in the latter half of the century in England. While focusing on aspects of proper decorum, these books inevitably addressed the question of education.

Written in an intimate, epistolary style, these manuals filled the bookshelves of families who aspired to gentility. Widely read and frequently reprinted, these sermons, letters, stories, and anecdotes defined for girls their religious, moral, and domestic duties, their recreations and amusements, and the nature and extent of their learning.[14]

One work by an English physician and moralist was especially popular in England and America. Dr. John Gregory's (1724-1773) *A Father's Legacy to His Daughters* remained fashionable until the 1870s. While similar to much of the didactic literature published in England during the last decades of the eighteenth century, this small book was famous for its often-quoted admonition to young women: "If you happen to have any learning, keep it a profound secret, especially from the men, who generally look with a malignant eye on a woman of great parts and cultivated understanding."[15]

Since wifehood and motherhood constituted a woman's prime vocation, such an exhortation was profoundly persuasive to girls and parents alike who might have otherwise considered the advantages of an education. Found in family libraries throughout England and the colonies and sometimes used as required reading in girls' schools, Dr. Gregory's book, as well as the Reverend John Bennett's *Letters to a Young Lady*, Dr. James Fordyce's *Sermons to Young Women,* and a host of similar tracts imposed restrictions not only on expressions of learning, but on any behavior that did not conform to the ideal of feminine delicacy.[16]

Throughout the eighteenth century, English writers of didactic literature increasingly idealized the sense of delicacy and sentiment in women. "The softness of manners," "the bloom of modesty," "the charms which enchant all hearts" were the qualities young women were to cultivate and the attributes society was to appreciate in the "fair sex." Any "bold action," or "difficulties and exertions," whether physical or mental, would stain a woman's femininity, the essence of her being.[17]

By implication, then, if not direct prescription, English priests and physicians, as well as a handful of women writers, informed their readers and followers of the inherent dangers of self-assertion in women. An active pursuit of knowledge or the quest for intellectual achievement were thus deprecated and discouraged. Only exceptional women such as Mary Somerville and Harriott Pinckney had the personal or familial resources to overcome the weight of such strictures. Most eighteenth-century women lacked these assets.

This "sentimental haze" that shrouded a woman's existence served, as Katharine Rogers indicates, to glamorize a woman's dependency. Delicacy became a euphemism for weakness, timidity, and subordination. Evolving during the eighteenth century as an ideal, modesty implied self-effacement and provided an effective barrier against tendencies toward self-fulfillment.[18] The Reverend John Bennett's *Strictures on Female Education,* for example, warned direly against the ills of intense study since, "The delicacy of the everlasting pea, which so happily unites elegance with sweetness, would be easily oppressed. The tender plant which is refreshed with gentle gales, would be entirely overwhelmed by a whirlwind."[19]

While exalting passivity, the haze of sentiment dampened the expressions of women's aspirations, and, as Mary Somerville knew so well, forced most women who sought knowledge to follow Dr. Gregory's advice and "keep it a profound secret." Femininity was the primary trait by which a woman's identity was fashioned in the eighteenth century, and few were willing to compromise this identity. Most women fiercely guarded it, displaying only what Frances Reynolds, sister of Sir Joshua, called "the most perfect feminine mind," which "habitually aims at nothing higher than an exemption from blame."[20]

In America writers reinforced the advice of Fordyce, Bennett, and Gregory. Magazines of the late eighteenth century carried essays idealizing the traits of modesty, delicacy, and "native Female softness."[21] A woman who maintained these qualities would be "loved, cherished, and esteemed"; should she "depart from these very amiable companions . . . satiety will give birth to disgust."[22]

Women sought then to uphold these traits of "feminine perfection" in order to maintain their identity and to preserve themselves from society's "disgust." This was not always easy, however, and as Katharine Rogers notes, even the semblance of knowledge or self-assertion could draw ignominy upon a woman.[23] The one area in which a woman could freely assert herself without sacrificing her modesty though was in the realm of domesticity. A woman could, through her domestic skills, become "notable" according to the common eighteenth-century usage of the word, and many colonial women wrote of their "longing desire" to be such. Some girls looked forward to a future delineated by domesticity as a means of happiness, and men generally regarded women's role in the home as a source of female fulfillment. One Georgian wrote his sister in 1796 that the performance of her domestic duties "should leave you nothing but . . . sensations of pleasure," while Governor William Livingston of New Jersey declared that women should find "happiness in their chimney corners."[24]

But the reality of domestic duties did not always conform to the anticipation. Many eighteenth-century women wrote of their work as narrow, humble, and little, adjectives reflecting, as Mary Beth Norton indicates, the low status of women's work in the eighteenth century. Far from a source of fulfillment, their duties were more often a cause of complaint as dullness and fatigue soon replaced the "sensations of pleasure" of the domestic routine.[25]

Some women too would find their domestic occupation a hindrance to the mental stimulation they longed for. "I find so much to do in the family that I have not all the time for retirement and improvement of my own mind in the best things that I wish," wrote Philadelphia Quaker Sally Logan Fisher (1751?-1796).[26]

Abigail Adams (1744-1818) frequently spoke of the intellectual limitations imposed by domesticity: "The Book of Knowledge," she wrote her sister, "is clearly closed against those who must fulfill there [sic] daily task of manual labour." Adams' expressions of dissatisfaction concerning the impoverished state of female learning and society's belittling attitude towards it struck a familiar and sympathetic chord in many women on both sides of the Atlantic whose domestic obligations and restricted social position barred them from "The Book of Knowledge."[27]

Such expressions indicate, nonetheless, the stirring of discontent that would lead to change in society's attitude toward learning in women. Outspoken literary figures of the eighteenth century in both England and America joined their voices with these plaints, citing the intellectual deprivation of women and urging society to consider the benefits of filling this need. In England a few writers had for decades emphasized the importance of educating women. As early as 1694, England's Mary Astell (1668-1731) had proposed the founding of a woman's college, and in 1697 Daniel Defoe (1660-1731) argued for academy education of girls equal to the public school education for boys.[28] A century later these ideas were more widely propounded as serious writers, both radicals and conservatives, publicly addressed the issue.

In America thinkers, writers, and public figures began to suggest ideas concerning women's education as a response to the unique conditions following the American Revolution. Before the revolution, the education of all children was uneven, dependent upon local circumstances and family priorities, with decidedly less attention accorded girls than boys. "If you complain of education in sons," Abigail Adams replied to John during the constitutional convention, "what shall I say in regard to daughters who every day experience the want of it?"[29]

With the revolution, however, came a tendency to view the women of the republic in a new light. The change was subtle and ambivalent. As Nancy Woloch explains, women benefited only indirectly from "independence."[30] Gaining no political privileges, women nonetheless attained broader dimensions within the scope of family and home. During the revolution, women had met the challenges of war, proving themselves patriots, competent home and business managers, and, in some cases, avid fighters. As the architects of the new republic began formulating the patterns on which they hoped to build a strong, viable society, they began to recognize more and more one of their strongest assets—the women of the republic. While these architects denied women the status of full citizenship in the republic, some nonetheless accorded them an essential role in their plan, placing them at the very foundation of their design.

Women, as wives, and most importantly as mothers, were viewed by many early leaders as the bedrock, without which the fragile structure of the infant republic might well collapse. If the young, and at this moment, malleable, society were to be fashioned into a republic of integrity, virtue, and moral strength, as the founders so desired, the family, with the aid of church and school, must rise to the occasion. And it was the mother in the family, the mother who nurtured, instructed, and cultivated her children into virtuous citizens that would guarantee the quality and success of the republic. As Linda Kerber explains, "Motherhood was discussed almost as a fourth branch of government, a device that ensured social control in the gentlest possible way."[31]

In light of earlier descriptions of women's status in family and society, the concept of republican motherhood in late eighteenth-century America constituted a dramatic reassessment. The notable housewives who often spoke of their helplessness and weaknesses were now urged to become true republican women, confident, competent, benevolent, and wise. They were given the examples of Cornelia, mother of the Gracchi of ancient Rome, Elizabeth I, and the contemporary English Bluestockings Hannah More and Elizabeth Carter. These women were not manly, indelicate, and despised, but were offered as paragons whose wisdom and strength were to be emulated by the new American woman. Author Judith Sargent Murray described her vision of the ideal new woman in these terms: "a sensible and informed woman—companionable and serious—possessing also a facility of temper, and united to a congenial mind—blessed with competency—and rearing to maturity a promising family of children."[32]

Such a vision introduced a new dynamic in both the ideas and the realities of women's education. As Ida Tarbell (1857-1944) forcefully stated over a century later, "It is not too much to say that the success of the Declaration of Independence and the Constitution depended in the minds of certain early Democrats, upon the woman . . . . This responsibility required a preparation entirely different from that which had been hers. She must be given education and liberty."[33]

While historians continue to debate the extent of women's liberty after the revolution, it is clear that a woman's preparation for her newfound place in American society took on new dimensions and importance. Opportunities in schooling for girls began to develop in profuse and diverse ways after the revolution, in response to a growing public demand.[34] Towns in New England, for example, began to keep their schools open during the summer so that girls might receive some training during this time. While the "regular" male students were working in the fields, young girls, whose tasks of spinning, dyeing, and sewing were usually conducted in the winter, in this way gained a few months of schooling.[35] Gradually these segregated summer sessions became integrated into year-round public grammar schools for boys and girls. Town academies responded as well by instituting special departments for girls and enlarging their programs in order "to comprehend the Ladies."[36] Finally, and most importantly, throughout the eastern states, academies and seminaries opened their doors one by one to daughters of middle-class families.

The size, quality, and life span of these institutions varied from one school to the next in early America. The key variable was the schoolmarm herself whose motivation in conducting a school was as likely to be her need for a livelihood as her desire to uplift female education. Operating a school was, after all, one of the few respectable ways a woman could conduct a business or create an institution in the eighteenth century.[37]

The history of advanced education for women after the revolution begins with the founding of the Young Ladies Academy in Philadelphia in May, 1786. Offering reading, spelling, writing, arithmetic, grammar, composition, rhetoric, history, and geography—a course of studies much like that given to academy boys in America—the Young Ladies Academy helped fill the academic void that had until this point characterized the upbringing of girls. The academy marked a departure in other ways, as well. Founded and directed by prominent men of Philadelphia, the academy institutionalized the enlightened thinking on the part of certain individuals of the republic who believed that women shared with men the capacity to reason. Prominent ministers, lawyers, doctors, statesmen, and educators, in their roles as visitors and trustees of the academy, helped make a virtue and a fashion of women's education.[38]

Physician, college educator, and original trustee Benjamin Rush (1745-1813), in particular, wrote and spoke of the need to gain public awareness of the advantages of women's education. "It will be in your power, Ladies," he commanded the students in 1787, "to correct the mistakes and practices of our sex upon these subjects by demonstrating that the cultivation of reason is alike friendly to the order of nature and to private as well as public happiness."[39]

To prove the potential for the cultivation of a woman's reason, the academy imitated earlier modes established for boys. As historian Ann Gordan explains, American academies were flexible institutions, and, as such, offered the founders of the Young Ladies Academy a diversity of ideas. Academies, in general, while offering advanced education, were not defined as colleges. Rather, academies offered two programs—the college preparatory track, requiring Latin or Greek in preparation for college and the learned professions—and a lesser track, a program complete in itself, usually pursued by those planning to enter a trade. It was the latter program that provided a model for the education that the founders of the Young Ladies Academy deemed suitable for girls.[40]

Significantly, then, the Young Ladies Academy did not offer needlework; nor did it offer advanced mathematics or classics. According to Rush, the curriculum was carefully formulated to suit the special needs of American society. The traditional ornamental education utilized in England and adopted in the colonies should now give way, he asserted, to a system of studies that would "accommodate" the new society. "It is high time to awake from this servility—" Rush announced, "to study our own character—to examine the age of our country—and to adopt manners in everything that shall be accommodated to our state of society and to our forms of government." Particularly, "in the education of our women," he added, should the new country "make ornamental accomplishments yield to principles and knowledge."[41] From Rush's perspective, the American woman was a new woman whose academic requirements must be expanded beyond those of her English counterparts. The higher accomplishments of "principles and knowledge" must be cultivated in her so that she might ably and confidently meet the challenges of her position.

While deploring an ornamental education so long equated with the training of girls, Rush also rejected the traditional emphasis on classics so long associated with the education of men. Again, recognizing that American society demanded more than the "servile" imitation of the British system of education, Rush advocated the elimination of classics from all curricula, male and female, on American soil. This would help close the gap between male and female education, he believed. "By ceasing to make Latin and Greek a necessary part of the liberal education, we open the doors for every species of improvement to the female part of society."[42]

But it would take time for male institutions to abandon classics as the heart of the liberal curriculum. Meanwhile, the omission of classics from the curricula of girls' institutions, in spite of Rush's quest to eliminate differences, would further delineate their education from that of boys and serve as a barrier to an equal education for nearly a century.[43] From Rush's time until the end of the nineteenth century, the study of classics remained in both England and America a central issue in the debates concerning women's education.

Rush's goal in formulating the curriculum of the Young Ladies Academy was one of "accommodation," a word he often used when describing the purposes of the academy. Since, Rush claimed, "female education should be accommodated to the state of society, manners, and government of the country in which it is conducted," then the substance and style of education offered at the academy presented no threat to the familial or social patterns now emerging in the young republic.[44] The academy had no intention of turning out intellectuals, or "unsexed, learned women." Rather, it promised each pupil an opportunity "to prepare for the duties in life to which she may be destined."[45]

In accord with the ideal of republican motherhood, these duties included assisting her husband, serving as an intelligent and agreeable companion to him, and educating the children in the ideals and virtues required by democracy. In place of educating for delicacy and dependency, the academy sought to educate for the sake of utility. The change was significant and heralded a new regard for the mental achievements of women. As Mary Beth Norton reflects, learning took on an air of fashion in post-revolutionary America. Intelligence in a woman was no longer a source of disparagement, but sometimes became a source of admiration. "The criteria upon which women judged each other," Norton notes, "now encompassed the qualities of the mind as well as beauty and personality."[46]

This was indeed the effect that author, journalist, and playwright Judith Sargent Murray (1751-1820) hoped that education would have on the status and identity of women in America. Writing a series of articles for the *Massachusetts Magazine* in the 1780s and 1790s, Murray, using the pseudonym "Constantia," saw education as the key to an elevated, dignified life for women. Through its lack, she believed, women, up to this time, were deemed inferior and inept.

Murray herself had enjoyed a stimulating education growing up in Gloucester, Massachusetts. Thanks to her parents' liberality, she was allowed to study alongside her brother, who, in preparation for a Harvard education, trained assiduously at home. Murray had also experienced falling fortunes and widowhood, two conditions that prompted her to advocate the training of women for self-sufficiency.[47] Having married at the age of eighteen, moreover, Murray further advised that girls should be imbued with self-respect so that they would not be tempted to "give themselves up to the first man who presents himself," in fear of becoming "old maids."[48]

Independence, personal and financial, and a strong sense of self were the themes Murray wove throughout her plays and essays. In contrast with Gregory and Fordyce, Murray told families to encourage their daughters to think, to aspire, and to believe in themselves. They would then develop "reverence of self . . . that dignity, which is ever attendant upon self-approbation."[49]

The key to such development, said Murray, lay in a thorough, academic education, the birthright of all humans, male and female.

The mindless pursuits traditionally imposed upon women led only to degradation. "Is it reasonable," she asked, "that an intelligent being . . . should at present be so degraded as to be allowed no other ideas than those which are suggested by the mechanism of a pudding, or the sewing of the seams of a garment?"[50] Education, Murray believed, would lift women "from the clouds which have hitherto enveloped them," and would help lead the way to "a new era of female history."[51]

Murray's optimism in a golden future and her emphasis on the personal advantages of education were occasionally reflected in the words of other educated women in the republic. A few of the graduates of the Young Ladies Academy, for example, having tasted the joys of knowledge, were not content to "accommodate" their experience to decreed social usage, but pleaded for greater alternatives upon the completion of their years at school. The graduation address presented in 1793 by Priscilla Mason attests to the resentment a growing number of educated women felt toward their limited sphere of activities. "Despot Man," she exclaimed, having denied women the right of an education, "and then reproached us for want of it," has in turn excluded women from "the Church, the Bar, and the Senate."[52] Such strong words from a woman were rare in the eighteenth century. But similar protests would be heard throughout the nineteenth century and well into the twentieth as entry into the higher professions remained distant for all but a few.

In the late eighteenth century the discontent expressed by intelligent women sprang mainly from those conditions, both domestic and social, that allowed little opportunity for "improving." But as Mary Beth Norton indicates, in just two decades, post-revolutionary America became unique among nations in ideas and efforts put forth in the area of women's education. Following the chartering of the Young Ladies Academy of Philadelphia, girls' academies opened throughout the East, offering educational options for the daughters of well-to-do and middle-class families responding to the need for the training and development of the rational, dutiful republican mother.

One of the better known was that established by Sarah Pierce in Litchfield, Connecticut, in 1792. Beginning with one pupil in her home, Pierce operated her school for forty years, educating over 1500 girls. Incorporated in 1827, Pierce's Litchfield Academy became one of the more advanced institutions of the period, aiming, as Pierce declared in typical eighteenth-century republican rhetoric, to "vindicate the equality of female intellect," through the development of a woman's powers of memory, imagination, and reason.[53]

In tune with the fashion of female education, a number of institutions opened their doors to boys and girls together. While the curriculum for girls often differed from that of boys in these academies, some, such as Westford Academy in Westford, Massachusetts, offered the same course of studies for all students.[54]

The South too gradually began to establish academies for girls in the latter part of the eighteenth century. Social and demographic conditions in this region in the eighteenth century were vastly different from those in the Northeast, and many wealthy families, dispersed throughout a wide, predominantly rural area, had imitated the tutorial system used by aristocratic families in England (see Chapter 5). Within the cities of the South, however, the academy movement soon gained popularity. Charleston, South Carolina, had several academies before the Revolution and became the site of several more afterwards. During the 1790s, newspapers in Maryland, Virginia, and the Carolinas frequently advertised academies for girls, as well as those for both "gentlemen and ladies."[55] Prominent among all the southern academies was the Moravian Female Academy in Salem, North Carolina, established in 1802. Modeled on the Moravian School in Bethlehem, Pennsylvania, Salem attracted over 3,000 students in its first fifty years of operation, offering the most advanced education of any institution for women in the South.[56]

As pioneers in the education of girls, the republican academies were bound by neither tradition nor the slavish imitation of British models, as boys' schools often were. They often exhibited, then, an "innovative, even adventurous" approach to the curriculum, as Linda Kerber illustrates. The results of this experimentation varied from one academy to another, producing diversity and uneven standards in girls' education. In certain instances, though, the spirit of adventure led to fresh ideas in education, as founders devised their own courses, methods, materials, and textbooks.[57]

But academy education for girls remained limited. For ultimately, this education had to "accommodate" society. Schools might innovate in curricula and texts, but the goal of all institutions for girls was to create sensible wives and mothers. Noah Webster (1758-1843) summed up the prevailing conservative philosophies concerning female education in 1790 when he differentiated between a proper and an improper education for women. Female education was good, he asserted, if it "rendered the ladies correct in their manners, respectable in their families, and agreeable in society." But society must be careful to restrict female education, for "that education is always wrong," he continued, "which raises a woman above the duties of her station."[58]

The academies generally succeeded in training women for their duties as republican mothers. Many indeed gave their students a sound education that was then placed at the service of their family and their country. But as Mary Beth Norton explains, there is evidence that some of the alumnae of these early institutions sought to rise above their "station" and expand the field of their "duties." Few at this time had the inclination to demand the right to personal growth, as Judith Sargent Murray had, or to demand inclusion in the Church, the Bar, and the Senate, as Priscilla Mason had. But a number of alumnae sought channels in literature, missionary work, the abolition and women's movement, and education. Some indeed achieved influence and fame.[59]

Late eighteenth-century England saw no such surge in the education of young women, in quality or numbers. No radical break occurred in the political and social order in England that would lead to a redefinition of women's role, as the revolution had so done in America. The veil of delicacy still covered the personalities and intellects of middle and upper class English women.

But interest in women's education took shape in eighteenth-century England as writers more and more voiced agreement with their American counterparts that the education of women would ultimately benefit society. "The improvement of the world depends most on education, and principally on that of princes, of women, and of the lower classes," claimed one writer.[60]

Slowly influential people in English society awakened to the notion that indeed an educated woman might not harm society, but might actually do it good. One group of individuals partly responsible for this growing awareness was the group of literary women who came to be known as the Bluestockings. Appearing in London society about the middle of the eighteenth century, this small group of women, inspired by the hostesses of the French salons, opened their homes on a regular basis for literary evenings.

Many of the prominent lettered men of the time, including James Boswell, Horace Walpole, and Samuel Johnson, frequented these discussions, enjoying the intimate, casual nature of the gatherings, where informal *bas-bleus,* or worsted blue-stockings could politely be worn in place of the traditional stockings of black silk. Although the name *Bluestockings* originally referred to the male guests, gradually the appellation came to be applied to the hostesses. The word would then undergo an evolution, becoming by the middle of the nineteenth century a derogatory term for women who affected erudition or who appeared "suspiciously unfeminine."[61] The kind of comment uttered by English author William Hazlitt was not uncommon: "I have an utter aversion to bluestockings. I do not care a fig for any woman who even knows what an *author* means."[62]

But eighteenth-century England generally paid the original coterie of Bluestocking hostesses a cordial respect. The evenings of serious conversation hosted by Elizabeth Montagu (1720-1800) and Elizabeth Vesey (1715-1791) provided the London literati a refreshing departure from the typical social fare of cards, dancing, and light entertainment. They won, therefore, a male following that recognized and appreciated their intelligence, and they helped pave the way for the acceptance of educated women in English society. Though few of the hostesses were scholars, they supported the scholarly work of certain women financially and emotionally. Elizabeth Carter (1717-1806) benefited most notably from their generosity, writing a widely acclaimed translation of Epictetus.[63]

But the aspirations of the Bluestockings were conservative. Desiring and obtaining acceptance in eighteenth-century aristocratic circles, they made no claim for a broad extension of female learning or for change in the intellectual status of women. Happy to remain within the boundaries of convention, they proposed nothing that would direct intelligent women outward toward a public life. "Women lose all their dignity when they meddle with subjects that don't belong to them," wrote one of the Bluestockings in 1775 in response to the rebellion in the American colonies. "Their own sphere offers them opportunities eno' to show their real consequence."[64]

Positing their convictions firmly within the realm of respectability, the Bluestockings rejected the extreme ideas and lifestyle of eighteenth-century England's most outspoken feminist, Mary Wollstonecraft (1759-1797). While the financially comfortable Bluestockings illustrated by example the limited avenues for intelligent women, Wollstonecraft, whose violent and impoverished family situation left her struggling for survival and independence, used her pen to condemn exploitation and injustice. Crying out against the conventions and institutions of English society that thwarted women's potential, rendering them, in her view, emotionally and intellectually disabled, she attacked the premises of Rousseau and Gregory. Agreeing with noted male writers, such as Jonathan Swift, who frequently held up for contempt the frivolity, complacency, and affectations of women, she cited in her *Thoughts on the Education of Daughters* the superficiality of girls' education as the culprit. She then urged a national system of coeducational schools, in which every boy and girl might be educated to his or her potential. Her proposal was significant, for not only did she view education as the means of uplifting women to nobler pursuits, but she advocated public schooling at a time when private education at home was the norm for girls.[65]

In 1792 Wollstonecraft published her controversial *Vindication of the Rights of Woman,* illustrating the means whereby changes in legal, economic, and educational conditions would help rehabilitate the socially useless middle-class woman and lead therefore to a better society. Wollstonecraft reiterated the need of a woman for an education equal to that of a man so that she might "mount with him the arduous steps of knowledge" and become his intellectual peer.[66] The society that she hoped to better, though, did not judge her ideas solely on their own merit. Rather, readers in England and America would associate Wollstonecraft's polemic with what they learned of her life through the memoirs of her husband, William Godwin. An affair, an illegitimate child, rejection by a lover, and attempted suicide—for these she would be remembered, leading the public to equate feminism with impropriety.[67]

While shunning the "rights of woman" idea, like so many of her contemporaries, the best-known and most outspoken of the Bluestockings, Hannah More (1744-1833), affirmed many of Wollstonecraft's theories of female education. In vivid language, akin to the passionate outpourings of Wollstonecraft, More declared, "Till women shall be more reasonably educated, and till the native growth of their mind shall cease to be stinted and cramped, we have no juster ground for pronouncing that their understanding has already reached its highest attainable perfection, than the Chinese would have for affirming that their women have attained the greatest possible perfection in walking."[68]

Because Hannah More vigorously defended the traditional qualities of piety and propriety in women, her views gained a wider acceptance in England than those of Wollstonecraft. The political climate in England at the turn of the nineteenth century, moreover, stirred by the war with France, precipitated a reaction against the ideals of the French Revolution, the same ideals that had given impetus and substance to Wollstonecraft's books. Hannah More reiterated, finally, that women were to be educated in order to be dutiful daughters, intelligent wives, and caring mothers. In the vein of Benjamin Rush, More deplored the emphasis on the ornaments, arguing that reasonable men want to marry "not merely a creature who can paint, and play, and dress and dance," but "one who can assist him in his affairs, lighten his cares, soothe his sorrows, strengthen his principles, and educate his children."[69] More's educated woman, not unlike the ideal educated woman of the young republic overseas, would now embrace a more serious calling as a rational being. Ultimately, this intellectual expansion would lead, More declared, to the betterment of herself, her family, and her country.

But England was slow to respond to the call for improved education for women. The "Spirit for Academy making" that in America seemed so "vigorous" at this time had not swept across the Atlantic.[70] The web of contradictions surrounding the question of female education in England stalled efforts to forge new avenues that advocates from the time of Mary Astell had sought. As historian Dorothy Gardiner notes, the same public opinion that mocked the ignorant woman condemned in one breath the learned woman. Jonathan Swift expressed this paradoxical position in a letter to Lady Betty Moore: "Those who are commonly called learned women have lost all manner of credit by their impertinent talkativeness and conceit of themselves; but there is an easy remedy for this," he continued, "if you once consider that after all the pains you may be at, you can never arrive in point of learning to the perfection of a schoolboy."[71]

With such attitudes endorsed by a large segment of the population, men and women alike, the outlets for female attainment remained limited. Although girls' boarding schools were an established feature of the educational system in eighteenth-century England, they enjoyed neither approval nor esteem. Essentially finishing schools, these schools offered the ornamentals, concentrating on drawing, music, a smattering of French, and above all, dancing and deportment.[72] "Adventurers of all kinds have found resources in this profession," wrote eighteenth-century novelist Clara Reeve (1729-1807). "Needy foreigners, without friends or characters; broken traders, ladies of doubtful virtue; ladies' waiting-maids; nay, even low and menial servants have succeeded in raising a boarding school." The "external accomplishments" at the expense of "the moral duties and the social virtues" were frequently decried. "We ought not to be surprised at the evils arising from them," uttered Reeve.[73]

The Spectator expressed the general consensus toward these establishments in the story of Mrs. Letitia Tattle, "who with no qualification other than her reduced circumstances," instructed young ladies in the etiquette and conversation proper to tea parties.[74] Indeed, the literacy level of many of the dames was so low, they were incapable of much beyond tea party conversation.

While such mockery was common, the voices suggesting positive solutions were few. Mary Wollstonecraft was decried with contempt and the Bluestockings did not gain the momentum to launch a national movement. The most advanced thinker who had the following and the resources to give substance to ideas was Erasmus Darwin (1731-1802), physician, poet, philosopher, inventor, and grandfather of Charles Darwin. Influenced by his acquaintance and correspondence with Jean Jacques Rousseau, Darwin formulated his views on girls' education in an essay entitled *Plan for the Conduct of Female Education in Boarding Schools*. Written on behalf of his two illegitimate daughters, whom Darwin educated and placed in charge of a school he opened for them, Darwin's plan, calling for a better system of operating boarding schools and advocating a range of scientific studies from natural history to chemistry, was advanced in the context of current English opinion. But Darwin clearly made known his purpose in suggesting "more branches . . . than is necessary for female erudition." Such endeavors, "by enlarging their sphere of taste and knowledge, would occasion them to be interested in the conversation of a greater number and of more ingenious men, and to interest them by their own conversation in return." Learning must be tempered in women, though, for "the female character should possess the mild and retiring virtues rather than the bold and dazzling ones; great eminence in almost anything is sometimes injurious to a young lady," and "is liable to alarm both her own and the other sex."[75]

For the majority of middle- and upper-class girls in the eighteenth century, education was gained at home, the fortunate ones learning from a father, a brother, or a tutor. The story of Elizabeth Elstob (1683-1756), eighteenth-century scholar of Old English, presents perhaps the most striking example of a woman who acquired exceptional knowledge, mastering seven languages in addition to English and Latin, from her brother. Orphaned as a young girl, Elstob and her brother William, a Saxon scholar in his own right, lived for thirteen years in London. Together, they copied, translated, and edited Anglo-Saxon texts. After her brother's death, Elstob supported herself by teaching small children, never again enjoying the financial freedom to work and publish as she longed to do.[76]

Few women had such capable, sympathetic brothers who would willingly devote years to a sister's scholarship. Most women who learned at home were taught by other women, often their mother, and, in more and more cases, a governess. The eighteenth-century governess, very likely a product of boarding schools and semi-literate dames, imparted to her students her own limited skills, thus in turn retarding the educational growth of subsequent generations.[77] But the governess played a central role in the history of women's higher education in England. As genteel women of England's middle and upper classes who due to the death or misfortune of supporting male relations were forced to earn their own way, they gained widespread attention. Novelists, priests, concerned members of their own class, and even painters addressed the plight of the governess. In the mid-nineteenth century, the recognition of the appalling economic and intellectual condition of most of these women would lead to the first stage in the development of the higher education of women in England (see Chapter 2).

Meanwhile, in the late eighteenth century, trends in both countries indicated that the intellectual status of women was gaining importance. The first evidence was suggested by the sheer amount of written material that offered advice on female training and education. While many of these works, especially those published in England, presented negative views of women's intellectual capacity and the position of the learned lady in society, they nonetheless point to the growing concern that the issue of women and education raised.

In America the republican ideology that ascribed new meaning to motherhood placed positive value on a certain degree of education in women. To be put into the service of teaching and purifying husbands and sons, the education of republican women was deemed important to the well-being and strength of this new nation. The growth of female academies, founded upon the goals of republican motherhood, gave American women their first institutions offering a fully academic curriculum.

English boarding schools of the late eighteenth century fell short of the academic goals of the republican academies. Pervaded by the haze of an idealized sentiment, English mentality seemed to prefer the passive, alabaster lady sculpted in the pages of Gregory and Fordyce to the vigorous republican women across the sea. An academic education, then, with its implication of not only a more active intelligence, but a wider role in society, would come more slowly for English women.

Finally, though, the tendency of more and more women in eighteenth-century America and England to voice awareness of themselves as intelligent beings indicates the beginning of change in both countries. Before the revolution, many colonial women deplored their lack of time and resources for self-improvement. After the revolution, some would join Judith Sargent Murray in the realization that their intelligence could be applied to tasks beyond the mechanisms of puddings and seams. In England the Bluestockings proved to themselves and to many intelligent men that the expression of intelligence did not render them monstrous. "I was intensely ambitious to excel in something," wrote Mary Somerville as she reflected on her intellectual path, "for I felt in my very own breast that women were capable of taking a higher place in creation than that assigned to them in my early days, which was very low."[78]

Perhaps it was this recognition of self in a few individual women, obscured as it might have been by ideologies on both sides of the Atlantic, that constituted the true source of energy leading to intellectual development in women.[79] This, in turn, would give impetus to nineteenth-century pioneers to reshape ideals and to create outlets. As Ida Tarbell noted of the republican woman in America, education and liberty became overriding concerns. "The woman saw this, and the story of her efforts to secure both, that she might meet the requirements is one of the noblest in history."[80]

Notes

1. Mary Somerville, *Personal Recollections from Early Life to Old Age of Mary Somerville*, ed. Martha Somerville (Boston: Roberts Brothers, 1874), 54.

2. Ibid., 28.

3. For details concerning these honors, see Margaret Alic, *Hypatia's Heritage: A History of Women in Science from Antiquity through the Nineteenth Century* (Boston: Beacon Press, 1986), 183-190.

4. Somerville, 80.

5. Alic, 189.

6. Harriott Horry Ravenel, *Eliza Pinckney* (New York: Charles Scribner's Sons, 1909), 69. Ironically, Eliza Lucas Pinckney gained her exceptional education formally in English boarding schools.

7. Frances Leigh Williams, *A Founding Family: The Pinckneys of South Carolina* (New York and London: Harcourt, Brace, Jovanovich, 1978), 20-22.

8. Ravenel, 218.

9. Mary Beth Norton, *Liberty's Daughters: The Revolutionary Experience of American Women, 1750-1800* (Boston and Toronto: Little Brown and Co., 1980), 262.

10. Ravenel, 294.

11. Williams, p. 21.

12. Jean Jacques Rousseau, *Emilius; or a Treatise of Education. Translated from the French* (Edinburgh, 1763), 74-75.

13. Dorothy Gardiner, *English Girlhood at School: A Study of Women's Education Through Twelve Centuries* (London: Oxford University Press, 1929), 453.

14. "No lady's library was complete without them, and they were sometimes used as required readings in girls' schools," indicates Julia Cherry Spruill, *Women's Life and Work in the Southern Colonies* (New York: W. W. Norton and Company, Inc., 1972), 221.

15. Dr. John Gregory, *A Father's Legacy to His Daughters* (New York: Garland, 1974), 31-32.

16. These books followed a long tradition of "advice literature" to "ladies." See, for instance, Lord Halifax, *The Lady's New Year's Gift, or, Advice to a Daughter* (London: R. and J. Dodsley, 1756). Women also penned these books. See, for instance, Lady Sarah Pennington, *An Unfortunate Mother's Advice to her Absent Daughters; in a Letter to Miss Pennington* (London, 1761; repr., New York, Samuel Marks, 1827) and Mrs. Hester Mulso Chapone, *Letters on the Improvement of the Mind Addressed to a Young Lady* (London: Printed by H. Hughs for J. Walter, 1773).

17. For a list of the qualities that expressed a woman's femininity, see W. Lyon Blease, *The Emancipation of English Women* (London, 1910; reprint, New York: Arno Press, 1977), 64-65.

18. Katharine Rogers, *Feminism in Eighteenth Century England* (Urbana, Chicago, and London: University of Illinois Press, 1982), 39.

19. Quoted in Blease, 65.

20. Ibid., 59.

21. For a discussion of these essays, see Norton, 112-113.

22. Ibid., 113.

23. Rogers, 240.

24. Norton, 4-5, 34.

25. Ibid., 36.

26. Quoted in Norton, 36.

27. It was the custom to "ridicule female learning," said Abigail Adams, one of the most outspoken critics of this time of women's restricted role. See Linda Kerber, *Women of the Republic: Intellect and Ideology in Revolutionary America* (Chapel Hill: University of North Carolina Press, 1980), 191.

28. Mary Astell, *A Serious Proposal to the Ladies for the Advancement of their True and Greatest Interest* (New York: Source Book Press, 1970). Daniel Defoe, *Essay on*

Projects, from James T. Boulton, ed. *Daniel Defoe* (New York: Schocken Books, 1965), 32-34.

29.   "If we mean to have heroes, statesmen, and philosophers, we should have learned women," Abigail added. See Norton, 263.

30.   Nancy Woloch, *Women and the American Experience* (New York: Alfred A. Knopf, 1984), 66.

31.   Kerber, 200.

32.   Judith Sargent Murray, *The Gleaner, A Miscellaneous Production,* Vol. 3 (Boston: I. Thomas and E.T. Andrews, 1798), 191.

33.   Ida M. Tarbell, *The Business of Being a Woman* (New York: The Macmillan Co., 1912), 75.

34.   Institutions of secondary learning had existed for girls prior to the revolution. The Moravians and Quakers had led the way in establishing respected academies. The Moravian Academy in Bethlehem, Pennsylvania, for example, was considered "unrivalled in the United States as a place for female education." See Norton, 283.

35.   This system was doubly expedient, for women teachers could be hired during the summer for half the salary of male school masters. See Kerber, 201. The inequity of remuneration is a continuing theme in the story of women and education.

36.   Ibid., 201.

37.   Ibid., 201-202.

38.   Ann D. Gordon, "The Young Ladies Academy of Philadelphia," in Carol Ruth Berkin and Mary Beth Norton, *Women of America: A History* (Boston: Houghton Mifflin Co., 1979), 70-72.

39.   Benjamin Rush, *Thoughts Upon Female Education, Accommodated to the Present State of Society, Manners, and Government in the United States of America, in Essays on Education in the Early Republic,* ed. Frederick Rudolph (Cambridge, Mass.: The Belknap Press of Harvard University Press, 1965), 23.

40.   Gordon, 72.

41. Rush, 27.

42. Benjamin Rush, *Essays, Literary, Moral and Philosophical* (Philadelphia: Thomas and William Bradford, 1798), 44.

43. Unintentionally, then, Rush contributed to the development of a separate curriculum "suited" for girls. The more girls' schools emphasized the special suitability of their programs, the more, says Nancy Cott, "the predominant philosophy of female education encouraged women to understand gender as the essential determinant of their lives." See Nancy Cott, *Bonds of Womanhood* (New Haven, Conn.: Yale University Press, 1977), 123.

44. Rush, *Thoughts,* 27.

45. Quoted in Kerber, 228.

46. Norton, 281.

47. This was often the pattern of the lives of women who became ardent supporters of advancements in women's education in America. Two notable examples are Sarah Josepha Hale and Lydia Maria Child. See Angela Howard Zophy, *For the Improvement of My Sex: Sarah Josepha Hale's Editorship of Godey's Lady's Book, 1837-1877* (PH. D. Dissertation, Ohio State University, 1978) and Louis Filler, "Child, Lydia Maria Francis," in *Notable American Women* (Cambridge, Mass.: Belknap Press, 1971), 330-332.

48. Judith Sargent Murray, "Desultory Thoughts upon the Utility of Encouraging a Degree of Self-Complacency, Especially in Female Bosoms," *Gentleman and Lady's Town and Country Magazine* 1 (1784), 253.

49. Quoted in Woloch, 93.

50. Judith Sargent Murray, "On the Equality of the Sexes," in *The Feminist Papers: From Adams to de Beauvoir,* ed. Alice S. Rossi (New York: Columbia University Press, 1973), 21.

51. Quoted in Norton, 295.

52. Quoted in Gerda Lerner, *The Female Experience: An American Documentary* (Indianapolis: Bobbs-Merrill Co., 1977), 213-214.

53.   Emily Noyes Vandepoel, *Chronicles of a Pioneer School From 1792 to 1833* (Cambridge, Mass.: University Press, 1903), 177-178.

54.   Thomas Woody, *A History of Women's Education in the United States,* Vol. 1 (New York: Science Press, 1929; reprint, New York: Octagon Books, Inc., 1966), 341.

55.   Woody, 1: 295-300.

56.   Ibid., 380-381.

57.   Sarah Pierce, for example, wrote a world history in dialogue form and Emma Willard wrote some of the first history and geography textbooks. See Kerber, 215.

58.   Noah Webster, "On the Education of Youth in America," in Frederick Rudolph, ed. *Essays on Education in the Early Republic* (Cambridge, Mass.: The Belknap Press of Harvard University, 1965), 70.

59.   Norton, 287.

60.   Quoted in Alice Browne, *The Eighteenth Century Feminist Mind* (Detroit: Wayne State University Press, 1987), 114.

61.   J.R. Brink, editor, *Female Scholars: A Tradition of Learned Women Before 1800* (Montreal: Eden Press Women's Publications, 1980), 5.

62.   Ibid.

63.   Bonnie S. Anderson and Judith P. Zinsser, *A History of Their Own: Women in Europe from Prehistory to the Present,* Vol. 2 (New York: Harper and Row, 1988), 112.

64.   Quoted in Blease, 48.

65.   Mary Wollstonecraft, *Thoughts on the Education of Daughters with Reflections on Female Conduct in the More Important Duties of Life* (London: J. Johnson, 1787, repr., New York and London: Garland, 1974), 8-41.

66.   Mary Wollstonecraft, *Vindication of the Rights of Woman* (the 1792 Text), ed. Miriam Brody Dramnick (New York: Penguin Books, 1978), 160.

67.   Anderson and Zinsser, 125.

68.   Hannah More, *Strictures on the Modern System of Female Education,* Vol. 2 (New York: Garland, 1974), 28-29.

69.   More, *Strictures,* 1: 86-87.
70.   This description of the young republic's enthusiasm in founding academies was made by the Reverend Ezra Stiles. See Norton, 272.
71.   Quoted in Gardiner, 380.
72.   Rogers, 28.
73.   Clara Reeve, *Plans of Education with Remarks on the Systems of Other Writers* (New York: Garland, 1974), 134-135.
74.   Quoted in Gardiner, 334.
75.   Erasmus Darwin, *A Plan for the Conduct of Female Education in Boarding Schools* (Derby, 1797, repr., New York: Johnson Reprint Corporation, 1968), 24, 40-44, 10.
76.   Mary Elizabeth Green, "Elizabeth Elstob: The Saxon Nymph," in Brink, 144-145.
77.   Wanda Fraiken Neff, *Victorian Working Women: An Historical and Literary Study of Women in British Industries and Professions, 1832-1850* (New York: AMS Press, Inc., 1966), 152.
78.   Somerville, 60.
79.   "For reasons that are still quite unclear, toward the end of the 18th century, individualism, consideration of one's own interest, began to be taken up by women," says Carl Degler, *At Odds: Women and the Family from the Revolution to the Present* (New York: Oxford University Press, 1980), 189.
80.   Tarbell, 75.

CHAPTER 2

EARLY STEPS TO HIGHER EDUCATION

The legacy of women's education in eighteenth-century England and America was ambivalent and strewn with ironies. Judith Sargent Murray and Mary Wollstonecraft had argued for radical change so that women might more closely realize their potential. But most reformers were less provocative, insisting, like Benjamin Rush, that a woman's education should accommodate the needs—not of the individual—but of the greater society. The goal of individual fulfillment, they believed, was secondary to the higher purpose of intelligent wifehood and motherhood.

One of the results of this popular rationale was an unsettled, sometimes confusing sense of identity in those women who had been educated, whether at home or school, often leading to a feeling of malaise and inertia. "With neither college nor a public career in the offing and without objectives beyond immediate studies, the joys of intellectual awakening were difficult to sustain," writes Mary Kelley of women writers of this time. "At times intellectual curiosity and excitement foundered in frustration and were undermined and distorted by a concern for questions of legitimacy."[1]

But the nineteenth century would prove that an academic education, whatever the purpose, could have unexpected results, and that a little learning could indeed be "dangerous," leading to demands for higher education and an expanded role in public life.

The story of women's education in early nineteenth–century America illustrates this theme. The academies of the post–revolutionary era had emphasized academic studies over the ornaments, thus producing a cadre of educated women whose quality and quantity surpassed that of any earlier moment in history. While most academy graduates fulfilled their designated female role, a select number gained enough knowledge, determination, and ingenuity to push beyond the limitations of academy education. The most determined of them went on to devote their lives to the creation of educational movements and the founding of institutions, primarily in the Northeast, for higher academic training.

One of these was Emma Willard (1787-1870), whose work is believed to have stimulated a revolution in America's attitude towards women's education in the early nineteenth century.[2] Though her academy training was limited to two years at Thomas Miner's Academy in Berlin, Connecticut, her delight, years later, in studying her nephew's mathematics and philosophy texts from Middlebury College, Vermont, brought home the pleasures of higher education and the inadequacies of the academies to provide it.[3] Willard then embarked upon a scheme that would have enduring consequences for women. Drawing "official" attention to the poor state of female learning, she appealed to the New York state legislature in 1819 to adopt and fund a new plan. Protesting the attitude of governments who "undervaluing the importance of women in society, neglect to provide for their education and suffer it to become the sport of adventurers of fortune who may be both ignorant and vicious," Willard proposed a seminary properly housed and equipped, offering advanced instruction, and blessed by government patronage. The New York legislature rejected her plan, but Willard kept her ideas before the public by publishing her proposal at her own expense.[4]

In 1821 the citizens of Troy, New York, acted upon her suggestions, giving Willard land and buildings to put her plan in motion. There, for three generations Troy Seminary flourished, offering its students a liberal arts curriculum that included subjects previously believed beyond their capacity, such as trigonometry, physiology, chemistry, and natural philosophy.

Through her seminary Emma Willard hoped to produce educated women who would in turn teach other young women and eventually raise the standards of female education on a broad basis. Similarly, Mary Lyon (1797-1849), a dynamic, determined, far-sighted alumna of three republican academies, inspired by her own training and encouraged by the results at Troy, devoted her life to the creation of a comparable institution. She too hoped to train teachers, raising their professionalism as well as the level of education in the lower schools.

Lyon's effort proved to have lasting significance. In 1837 she opened Mount Holyoke Seminary, the first fully endowed female institution and the first private school designed to educate girls from "the common walks of life." By 1888 Mount Holyoke had proved so successful that it became Mount Holyoke College.

Lyon's inspiration may be traced to her years in the 1820s as a student at the Female Academy in Byfield, Massachusetts. Under the tutelage of Ralph Waldo Emerson's brother, the Reverend Joseph Emerson, the students were given faith in their intellectual capacity and those of high caliber were taught collegiate subjects. An early friend of the higher education of women, Emerson spoke of his hope that soon institutions for women would be "as important as are now our colleges for the education of our sons."[5]

Mary Lyon shared Emerson's hopes and with her friend, Zilpah Grant, set out to found just such a place. But Lyon recognized that schools for women, in order to become as important as those for men, must first gain the financial viability that male schools enjoyed. At the time, no institution for women had an endowment. Female seminaries and academies generally came and went according to the life spans and fortunes of the individuals running them, whereas male academies and colleges achieved permanence and stability by virtue of grants and bequests.

The story of Lyon's efforts to gain an endowment for her proposed seminary was one of struggle and triumph. With organizational talent matched only by her enthusiasm and a powerful personal presence, Lyon tirelessly traveled, spoke, distributed circulars, and organized networks of support. Beginning in Ipswich, Massachusetts, where she had successfully taught and raised funds for the Ipswich Female Seminary, Lyon walked from door to door asking for donations. Here her quest was more than successful, for she "held before them the object dear to her heart—the bringing of a liberal education within the means of the daughters of the common people, till it loomed up to them, for the time, as it did before her eyes." Women of average means gave her "five or ten dollars of hard-earned money, collected by the slow gains of patient industry."[6]

The women of Ipswich provided models of generosity that would inspire women beyond the little Massachusetts town. Soon Lyon embarked on a series of journeys throughout New England. Speaking to women of many towns, she kindled "the spirit of emulation by holding up the example of the Ipswich ladies."[7]

It was not only the ladies of Ipswich that motivated others to contribute, but the personal presence and reputation of Lyon herself. Lyon's biographer, Elizabeth Alden Green, notes the powerful effect Lyon had on people of modest means who had precious little to give to such an enterprise. One woman of Heath, Massachusetts, wrote of Lyon's ability to stir enthusiasm, saying, "I do not believe another individual in the country could procure as much as Miss Lyon did." The little town of Heath gave $1200, a substantial sum for a time when money was so scarce.[8]

Lyon also engendered the support of a number of energetic, enthusiastic men who valued her vision and had a large share in seeing it realized. Some were powerful men of broad reputation, such as Edward Hitchcock, professor and later President of Amherst, who defended her from attacks against her femininity and educational qualifications, and the Reverend Theophilus Packard, who won for her an endorsement from the local Association of Ministers. Packard's devotion to Lyon's cause was complete. His "whole soul is enlisted," she wrote. "It is his first and great object, occupying his time by day, and many of his thoughts by night."[9]

Men of humbler ranks provided ample resources, skills, and funds, not only during the fund-raising stage of Mount Holyoke, but for decades after its opening. Among these were Joseph Avery, farmer, Andrew Porter, cotton mill proprietor, and Daniel Safford, blacksmith, all self-educated and self-made men who thus admired Lyon's energy, drive, and longing to reach out to "the adult female youth in the common walks of life." Becoming prosperous in their respective fields, all three would assure the success of Mount Holyoke by purchasing supplies and food, overseeing maintenance, and providing continuing funds and guidance as trustees as long as they lived.[10]

Though suffering setbacks from time to time, Lyon pursued her work with an optimism and sense of purpose that motivated the women and men whose generosity and work made her institution possible. But the work, she predicted, "will not stop with this institution." Rather, the founding of Mount Holyoke marked only the beginning of "an era of female education."[11]

In their urgent quest to lift women from the bonds of ignorance, Mary Lyon and Emma Willard were not so distant from Judith Sargent Murray and Mary Wollstonecraft. Their rhetoric and the image they promoted, however, were more acceptable and therefore more persuasive. "By being enlightened . . . in that which teaches the operatives of the mind," Willard assured the New York legislators, "females would be enabled to perceive the nature and extent of that influence which they possess over their children . . . and to watch the formation of their characters with unceasing vigilance."[12] Formulating their goals in the spirit of the republican academies, Willard and Lyon helped open the attitudes and pocketbooks of Americans to the cause of women's education.

Their rhetoric, nonetheless, was deceptive. Defining their mission in language that allayed the fears of their would-be opponents, they urged their students to master the "masculine" subjects of mathematics, science, Greek, modern languages, and philosophy. They also encouraged them to pursue a career. But this was not publicly evident. Rather than advertise the fact that the education they were offering would inculcate a sense of independence and professional worth in young women, they simply stated that it would create better wives and mothers, "with the prospect of doing more good through life."[13] As Anne Firor Scott has noted, Willard's language reveals how "she deftly combined an appeal to the prevailing view of women with a revolutionary emphasis upon women's intellectual capacities and with an innovative proposal for broadening 'woman's sphere' to include professional work." Gradually Willard's pupils began to disseminate her ideas throughout the country as they married, took teaching posts, or both, "often setting an example by their interest in study and learning."[14]

A number of courageous women working for women's education in the early nineteenth century met with less success, but made notable attempts, nonetheless. One of these was Prudence Crandall (1803-1890), a young woman who operated a school for girls in Canterbury, Connecticut. When she admitted a black girl to her fashionable school in 1833, her fortunes soon turned. As her white students were pulled from the school by irate parents, Crandall tried to keep the school open, operating it for black girls only. But suffering harassment, violence, and even imprisonment after the state legislature enacted a law against the school, Crandall moved on. A group of Canterbury residents then burned her school in 1834.[15]

Fortunately, the work of Willard and Lyon left an enduring legacy. One of Emma Willard's admirers would later recall the significance of her work in raising the standards of women's education: "It was with the high ideal of preparing women for their distinctive duties as chief ministers of the family state," she wrote, that Mrs. Willard demanded intellectual progress for women. The writer was Catharine Beecher (1800-1878), and her metaphor exalting women as "chief ministers of the family state" captures not only her vision of women's place in the universe, but indicates too the distinctive role Americans began to accord women in the early nineteenth century.[16]

When Emma Willard and Mary Lyon began their work in women's education, the nation was in the midst of vast economic and social changes. Industrialization, urbanization, and improvements in transportation were transforming the way many Americans led their lives, as movement—from country to city, from home as a work place to factory, and from east to west—became a national trend.[17] Life in

America was propelled by social as well as geographic mobility. The burst of economic activity in early nineteenth-century America beckoned those with initiative and ambition to take commercial risks, and some climbed quickly to the top of the economic ladder while others plunged to the base. In a society that valued drive, hard work, and success over birth and family name, those who survived the commercial ventures profited not only economically, but socially, as well. Out of this emerged a dynamic, expanding middle class, whose membership, though fluid, made a solid impact on the young nation. Deriving a sense of identity not only from commercial achievement, but from their social values, the middle class imprinted a well-defined pattern of family relations and gender roles on the fabric of society. The view of woman as "chief minister of the family state" was at the heart of this deeply woven pattern.

This "elevation" of woman contrasted with earlier periods in America when the home and family state were guided by the firm hand of paternal authority. In a time when most of the population lived in a rural environment, the home itself was a center of production. All family members, including women and children, worked together at producing, whether farming, skilled labor, or cottage manufacturing, all under the supervision of the father.

In the commercial centers of the Northeast that developed in the early nineteenth century, men left the home to work, now spending most of the day at the office, factory, or shop. As the locus of work changed, a dichotomy began to emerge, marking a strict division between the home and the work place. Instead of the common arena of living and working, separate spheres now sharply defined the work of men and women. The work place—active and public—was the realm of the male; the home—quiet and private—was the preserve of the woman. Inside the home, middle-class women, now more and more released from the spinning wheel, the loom, and the dairy, attended the necessary domestic chores, raised, guided, and taught their children, and created for their husbands a moral atmosphere and comfortable refuge from the harsh, exacting world of public affairs.

Catharine Beecher believed that women's special place in the home held positive value for themselves and society. Reiterating her conception of woman as the head of the family state, Beecher wrote extensively on the feminine virtues of purity and piety. Motherhood and domesticity were sanctified by Beecher's pen: "The duties of the woman are as sacred and important as any ordained by man," she claimed.

Beecher's affirmation of the importance of woman's sphere led her to embark on a personal crusade to extend the training of women. Fulfilling the duties of womanhood required a pragmatic education, she believed, rooted in domestic economy, without deference to the needless ornaments. Thus Beecher founded two secondary schools for women—the Hartford Female Seminary in Connecticut and the Western Female Institute in Cincinnati.

These schools were short-lived, but with their demise, Beecher launched a wider crusade to continue "the elevation of my sex," this time "by the opening of a profession for them in the education of the young."[18] Beecher's use of the word *profession* is interesting. A significant aspect of women's domestic vocation had always been the training of children. Impecunious women had society's blessing in opening dame schools, and gradually educated women came to be administrators and teachers in female academies and seminaries. Now, too, communities began to realize that they could benefit economically by hiring women to teach at half the cost of male schoolmasters.

But Beecher wanted more. She sought an outlet for women who, for whatever reason, needed to work outside the home. This work would be more than a bread ticket for the impecunious; it would confer the same distinction that the higher professions conferred upon men. The teaching profession, in turn, would provide the means by which the piety and benevolence of middle-class women would be extended across the country to the western frontier, through all levels of society. Defining teaching as an extension of women's proper nurturing role, Beecher planted her goal of a suitable female profession within the boundaries of woman's sphere. The boundaries were stretched by Beecher's work, however, as she opened to women an avenue whereby they might extend their special gifts to society at large.

Beecher quickly gained support for her cause. Tirelessly crossing the country, holding meetings, writing prodigiously, and raising money, she soon gathered businessmen, clergymen, and prospective teachers intent on activating her plans. Two groups that she founded, the Board of Popular Education and the American Women's Educational Association, gave organized identity and visibility to her crusade. In a number of cities, moreover, she mobilized volunteer societies to recruit teachers. In 1847, seventy young women from New England travelled westward to teach, enduring primitive conditions, minimal pay, unruly students, and sometimes hostile communities. Soon about four hundred women went west. In her endless crusade, Beecher also founded teacher training schools in the West, though few survived.

But the influence of Catharine Beecher survived well into the twentieth century, lending continuing irony to the struggles of aspiring women in America. Like Willard and Lyon, Beecher wanted women to have the opportunity of a professional education. Beecher's vision of the professional woman, though, was an ambiguous image, for in her view, women's highest goals were always to be set within the framework of domesticity. While she sought, then, to open professional channels for women and worked to lift feminine esteem and consciousness, Beecher did not directly challenge the doctrine of woman's sphere. Rather, she broadened the dimensions of domesticity, offering avenues whereby women might extend themselves altruistically to an expanding, urbanizing, and industrializing society, which she believed to be more and more in need of their finely tuned sensibilities and talents.[19]

America was not alone in this process of urbanization and industrialization in the early nineteenth century. England had led the industrial revolution, and its effect on gender roles in the middle class was equally, if not more, pronounced. As in America, the pre-industrial home in the middle classes had been a highly organized unit of production. Work was heavy, sometimes burdensome, but for the housewife, was varied and often required high degrees of skill and administrative ability.[20]

As the Industrial Revolution in England progressed in the first half of the nineteenth century, the middle-class home, as in America, gradually ceased to be a locus of operations. Gender roles became more differentiated, crystallized by a growing class consciousness among commercially successful members of the middle class. By the time Victoria ascended the throne in 1837, the middle-class wife was well on her way toward becoming the "Victorian lady," she whom art critic and writer John Ruskin (1819-1900) would describe as "the centre of order, the balm of distress, and the mirror of beauty."[21] Her existence, then, was more and more bound by a rigid code of behavior. Like her American counterpart, the parameters of her life were defined by the outer walls of the home. But the limitations imposed upon the activities of the English lady were more severe than those in America, for entwined within domestic ideology was the belief that idleness on the part of a woman was a prestigious attribute. Influenced by the misguided fantasy that aristocratic ladies were idle ladies, middle-class families in early Victorian England sought to imitate their social superiors. The more leisured the ladies seemed, the more successful, industrious, and wealthy appeared the gentlemen. A wife of leisure became "the middle-class man's status symbol."[22] For such women to engage in domestic chores was "to lose caste" according to the mores of many socially mobile families in nineteenth-century England. Servants were hired, sometimes an entire domestic staff, for this kind of work.

As historians are more and more careful to point out, caution should be steadily applied to generalizations concerning the Victorian lady. Recent inquiries into Victorian family life have replaced the popular stereotype of the vapid female swooning on the sofa with a complex picture of a multifaceted existence where leisure was a dream, not a reality.[23] As British historian Margaret Bryant indicates, "The myth of the idle middle-class woman often related more to aspiration than to reality, and for all but the more wealthy levels in this section of society remained unrealized."[24] Women of the lower levels of the middle class did not have the resources to hire a retinue of servants and while a wife may well have had some assistance in her domestic work, she was still burdened with the physical labor of cleaning, cooking, washing, shopping, and sewing, as well as educating the children.[25]

But for many middle-class women, the aspiration to become the leisured lady was very real, and as superficial and contradictory as it might seem, was powerful enough to deter many capable women from setting higher goals. And while historians continue to debate the validity of ascribing the mode of leisure to the lives of middle-class women during this period, believing the evidence to rest too heavily upon literary sources rather than primary documents, nineteenth-century writers addressing the question of women's education in England frequently referred to the problem of enforced idleness. As early as 1810, for example, the Reverend Sydney Smith declared education to be as good an answer as any to the problem of leisure: "There are, perhaps, 50,000 females in Great Britain who are exempted by circumstances from all necessary labour; but every human being must do something with their existence, and the pursuit of knowledge is, upon the whole, the most innocent, the most dignified, and the most useful method of filling up that idleness."[26] Activists working for women's greater participation in intellectual life would continue throughout the nineteenth century to see the aspiration of idleness as one of the greatest threats to women. "The injunction to 'make themselves happy' in luxurious idleness, is as much a mockery to them as to Rasselas and Neyakah in the Happy Valley," complained women's education pioneer Emily Davies. "To such happiness, unblessed of God and unhonoured of men, may they never learn to reconcile themselves."[27]

In America the idea of enforced leisure was generally repugnant. To a certain extent the aristocracy of the antebellum South subscribed to the ideal of the leisured lady. But as historians of the South have pointed out, rarely was a plantation lady free from her endless duties, despite the espoused goal.[28] Woman's work in America in the early to mid-nineteenth century, although limited to the home, was demanding and important work and was viewed as such by both men and women. To vibrant Americans the image of a woman lounging on a sofa all day gossiping or embroidering was considered a symptom of a decadent, class-conscious society. American men and women of the middle class seconded Julia Ward Howe's dictum that "a respect for work lies at the foundation of a true democracy."[29]

The education of women in America, then, became a vital issue as women's work assumed new importance. The Second Great Awakening, moreover, had lent a sense of moral urgency to women's high calling in this brash, materialistic age. Now beckoned "to pour balm into the wounds of bleeding humanity, to still the storm of social passions, to impart popularity and confidence to virtue," women were given permission to fortify their minds and hearts with a certain amount of education.[30] Additionally, the spirit of Jacksonian democracy helped produce a climate more conducive to the betterment of those elements of society traditionally excluded from such privileges as education. Women would be among the beneficiaries of this change.

Now the question of whether or not to educate women was replaced with a debate concerning to what extent to educate women. As Janet James has noted, "every man and his neighbor felt qualified to speak. Homilies, witticisms, and old saws about the female mind and how to form it became a staple of magazines, novels, plays, and polite conversation, while the pious and learned discoursed at length in weightier essays and books."[31]

Americans generally agreed that a girl's learning should supersede the ornamental accomplishments. How much of the solid academics should be included became the center of the new controversy, most arguing that the rigors of a classical education were unnecessary and unfeminine, and perhaps even dangerous. The first institutions of higher education in the United States that educated women were careful, therefore, to claim that their curricula were fitting for women and their special calling.

America's first coeducational institution of higher learning, Oberlin Collegiate Institute in Ohio, initiated a system for women students that would find acceptance as coeducation developed in the United States in the second half of the century.[32] Founded in 1833,

Oberlin opened its doors to women, black and white, offering to prepare them "for any position of work to which they may be properly called."[33] To train them for their proper work, Oberlin designed the Ladies' Department, known intramurally as the "female appendage." With their own curriculum, which excluded the Greek, Latin, and calculus demanded of men students, and required separate lessons in French, drawing, and essay-writing, Oberlin's women, also subject to stricter rules of conduct, retained a singular, anomalous position in the college.

It seems that a multitude of purposes were served under the guise of coeducation. For one, the "female appendage" was asked to cook, sew, and wash for the men students, "the leading sex." On Monday there were no classes so that women could tend to the laundering and mending of the men's clothes. Their own laundry, however, had to be done during their spare time in the evenings.[34]

Other, more subtle agenda were fulfilled by the "female appendage," as well. The gentlemanly conduct of male students, for example, as well as their enhanced sense of social grace, proved the advantage of the feminine presence, Oberlin's President James Fairchild claimed. This was important, since most young men of Oberlin entered the clergy. Furthermore, coeducation provided a ready pool of young women who could become pious, refined, well-trained wives for the graduates.[35]

But some of the young women had their own goals in mind. In 1837, four ambitious coeds challenged the separate, diluted course of studies reserved for the "female appendage," and asked for entrance into the full college course. They were accepted, and women were thereafter given their option of the two tracks, the majority choosing the Ladies' course. Monday was still wash day, however, even for those who followed the full degree program.[36]

Whatever its motives in offering coeducation, Oberlin represents a landmark in the history of women's education in America. In 1841 Oberlin graduated three women with degrees certifying that they had completed a full collegiate course formerly reserved for males only. The numbers seem slight and insignificant. But by 1866, eighty-four women had been granted this degree.[37]

In England the intellectual poverty of women gained a certain amount of attention in the 1830s, particularly in reference to that figure immortalized in English fiction—the governess. Apparently, the capable, well-instructed Jane Eyre type was a rarity. More often chosen for their gentility than their knowledge, governesses as a whole were unsuited to the task of teaching. Most governesses were at best undereducated; at worst, they were illiterate. "What can governesses teach?" asked one English writer. "What do they know? They themselves will answer—in all humility and truthfulness—'Nothing.'"[38]

The intellectual poverty of these women was usually matched by their material poverty, which forced them into governessing. The only socially acceptable profession open to English gentlewomen in the first half of the nineteenth century, governessing was the sole recourse of single or widowed women whose fortunes had fallen.[39] "Take a lady, in every meaning of the word, born and bred, and let her father pass through the gazette, and she wants nothing more to suit our highest *beau ideal* of a guide and instructress to our children," wrote Elizabeth Eastlake (1809-1893) in 1848.[40] Given the precarious nature of middle-class prosperity during this stage of England's Industrial Revolution, the sudden impoverishment of dependent women and girls, whose men had "passed through the gazette," was not uncommon.

Stories of exploitation and degradation in nonfiction magazines, as well as novels, abounded: on one hand were the girls, some as young as sixteen, forced into a lonely existence, and whose only companions were the children;[41] on the other were elderly women, some supporting aging, sick relatives, impoverished and still trying to governess to keep alive.[42] "A private governess has no existence," confessed Charlotte Brontë (1816-1855), knowing from experience of what she wrote, and "is not considered as a living rational being except as connected with the wearisome duties she has to fulfill."[43]

The recognition of the plight of governesses, as well as their poor performance as teachers, prompted some reform-minded individuals to try to ameliorate their conditions. Discovering what

Margaret Bryant has called an "abyss of destitution," among this class of women, the Christian Socialist Frederick Denison Maurice (1805-1872) organized the Governesses' Benevolent Association in 1841. Founded initially as a relief program to provide funds and housing for unemployed governesses, the Association then attempted to provide a system of certification guaranteeing the proper qualifications for their work to enable them to compete with qualified French and German governesses. With this endeavor, the organizers of the Association discovered an "abyss of ignorance so profound that qualifications had to be replaced by an attempt to provide the teachers with teaching."[44]

Thus was born in 1848 the first institution in England that aspired to provide advanced education for women, Queen's College, London. Under the guidance of F. D. Maurice, Queen's was founded with the intention of remedying the educational deficiencies of governesses and all teachers of the young. Graduates, he hoped, would be sufficiently trained in order to fulfill their pedagogical duties and in turn would demand greater respect and remuneration.

Like Troy, Mount Holyoke, and Beecher's Hartford Seminary in the United States, Queen's offered women professional training. Recognizing that some women not only needed to work, but were entitled to participate in the public sphere, these schools sought to enable them a degree of proficiency in the one vocational option that was open to them. But the similarities ran deeper, revealing a common religious current in American and English society that propelled the movement for advanced education of women in the first half of the nineteenth century. In America the religious awakening of the first decades of the nineteenth century posed a new dynamic in the lives of American women. Providing an impetus and an outlet for activism, the awakening led women to apply their cooperative efforts for religious, charitable, and reform purposes. The female benevolent associations that grew in size and numbers during the 1830s began to exert an influence on society. One of the beneficiaries of women's benevolence was education. Initially directed toward the higher education of men, the Female Auxiliary Education Societies that flourished in the East proved to be valuable resources when Mary

Lyon and Catharine Beecher began their work. "Was it a wonder," asked Lucy Stone (1818-1893), abolitionist and suffragist, "that as young women drew the needle they also drew the conclusion that if education was so necessary for men it must be valuable for women who were to stay at home?"[45]

Gradually, influenced by the eloquence of women's educators such as Lyon, the societies and sewing circles took up the cause of women's education. "Those who had sewed and spent time, strength, and money to help educate young men," added Stone, "dropped the needle and toil and said 'Let these men with broader shoulders and stronger arms earn their own education, while we use our scantier opportunities to educate ourselves.'"[46]

While prompting organizational support of women's education, awakened religion in America gave young women the means, the courage, and the direction to take educational and vocational steps in the larger world. Often entering New England schools, "thoughtless and bent on pleasure," many young women gained a sense of mission, and "returned home serious and bent on doing good."[47] Those with this mission and religious commitment were given courage to act upon their ideals. In 1832 Mary Lyon emboldened her students with advice to go forward, "taking the Bible for your guide, and asking God to enlighten your mind. . . . You may see but one step where you can place your foot; but take that and another will then be discovered, and if you can see one step at a time, it is all you ought to ask."[48]

By comparison, the drive towards women's advanced education launched in England in the 1840s with the founding of Queen's College cannot be separated from the religious motivations of the pioneers. As in America, English Evangelicals, driven by a dynamic, urgent benevolence, condemned ornamental education and insisted on dignity and purpose in the training of women. The work of F. D. Maurice hinged upon this conviction. Ridding women of ideas which rob them of their self-respect, he declared during his inaugural address at Queen's, was what the business of education was all about. "Colleges for men and women . . . exist to testify that opinion is not the God they ought to worship," he claimed.[49]

Maurice, in turn, inspired other nineteenth-century figures whose names would become synonymous with the movement for the higher education of women in England. His "disciples" included the notable Dorothea Beale (1831-1906), Maria Grey (1816-1906), Emily Shirreff (1814-1897), Elizabeth Garrett (1836-1917), and importantly, Emily Davies (1830-1921), the founder of the first true college for women in England, Girton College, Cambridge. As members of Maurice's London congregation or as social and educational associates, these individuals were swayed by Maurice's belief in the mental and spiritual equality of all human beings and came to share his vision of the enhanced participation of women in academic and public life.

Through all the trials and obstacles in their efforts to win for women a position of intellectual dignity, these people, with few exceptions, were carried by their fervent religious convictions. Though doctrinal differences existed among them, the distinctions were slight in relation to their common religious values. Their "passionate attempt to give meaning to life, to rescue women from their unloved, unapplied existences, to give personal authenticity, the liberation of truth, and to assert the broad and practical doctrines of what is today called Christian Stewardship," were common goals among the English reformers, notes Margaret Bryant.[50]

In many cases, the Christian reformers concerned with women's educational and economic deficiencies did help rescue women from their "unapplied existences." Maurice and Queen's College initiated the process, training notable educators who dedicated their lives to improving girls' secondary education, such as Frances Buss (1827-1894), founder of the North London Collegiate School, and Dorothea Beale, who later elevated Cheltenham College into one of the foremost girls' schools in England. Additionally, Queen's College gave educational opportunities to a broad spectrum of young women who had no intention of teaching. The poets Jean Ingelow (1820-1897) and Adelaide Anne Proctor (1825-1864), writer Julia Wedgwood (1833-1913), and England's first woman physician to win her degree in England, Sophia Jex-Blake (1840-1912), were just a few who received training and purpose at Queen's. "Oh, if there is an elysium on earth, it is this," wrote Jex-Blake with her distinctive exuberance. "Work and independence. What can be more charming?"[51]

While called a college, Queen's fell on the borderline of secondary and higher education. Professors from nearby King's College, London, lent a collegiate air to the school, offering the students of Queen's demanding courses in English, theology, history, geography, Latin, mathematics, modern languages, natural philosophy, music, and fine arts.[52] It would be another decade, however, before plans were put into motion to create a truly collegiate institution.

But the success of Queen's and the demand for this kind of education for young women led to the opening of Bedford College in London in 1849. Founded by sixty-year old Elizabeth Reid, who had always regretted her own lack of advanced training, Bedford made claims toward collegiate education, but offered academic programs almost identical with those of Queen's. Bedford, however, was nondenominational and governed by a board of men and women, whereas Queen's, under the guidance of the Church of England, was governed solely by men.

Although it initiated the women's education movement, Queen's, as one of its prominent alumnae would later reflect, "became conservative, and it did not grow."[53] Bedford would expand and intensify academically, becoming a member college of the University of London.[54]

Even with the founding of Queen's and Bedford in the mid-nineteenth century, the very discussion in England of advanced intellectual channels for women was received with ridicule and scorn by the general public. Deeply embedded in the minds and hearts and culture of English men and women was the idea that university life was the time-honored privilege of men alone. Since the founding of Oxford and Cambridge Universities in the twelfth and thirteenth centuries, these institutions, whose names had become synonymous with erudition, had been male preserves. Ironically, as Josephine Kamm indicates, the founding of the English universities in the Middle Ages represented the decline of institutional education for women in this country. Whereas Anglo-Saxon women had among them many notable scholars and were encouraged through their religious houses not only to attain intellectual standing, but, in turn, to offer training to both men and women, the later medieval women of the Norman period enjoyed fewer educational options. As more and more male scholars entered Oxford and Cambridge, scholars who centuries earlier might have entered a monastery, corresponding in Latin with their female counterparts in convents and encouraging their intellectual endeavors, the doors of institutional education were closed to women. As the locus of higher education moved from the monastery to the university in the High Middle Ages, Oxford and Cambridge would offer no sister institutions for women as convents had stood for centuries in relation to monasteries.[55]

Despite the English University tradition, a few undaunted pioneers of the mid-nineteenth century recognized that the opening of a full university education for women was imperative. In 1858 Emily Shirreff, educator, publicist, and future mistress of Girton College, Cambridge, published a book entitled *Intellectual Education and Its Influence on the Character and Happiness of Women.* Shirreff introduced a subtle change in the tone of the arguments concerning women's education. Whereas earlier proponents in England had concentrated on the value of an educated woman for home and society, Shirreff dismissed the issue of "worldly utility" as irrelevant. Echoing the sentiments of Republican America's Judith Sargent Murray, Shirreff asserted that the purpose of education was the development of the individual. "The human being remains a mutilated creature if the capacities of his mind are left dormant," she wrote.

A group of determined women shared Shirreff's views and sought ways to implement the goals she articulated. On March 2, 1859, they were prompted to act when Elizabeth Blackwell (1821-1910), the first woman to receive a medical degree in America, presented a lecture in Marylebone Hall in London. In her lecture Blackwell described her education, her work, and the suitability of the medical profession for women.[56] Blackwell's words inspired those present, and before her speech was finished she led one young woman, later to become the first licensed woman physician in England, to consider a medical education.[57]

Blackwell afterwards recalled the interested, appreciative audience, some of whom were moved to tears. "But the most important listener," she added, "was the bright intelligent young lady whose interest in the study of medicine was then aroused—Miss Elizabeth Garrett, who became the pioneer of the medical movement in England."[58]

Garrett's decision to become a physician was only the beginning of a long, discouraging, and frustrating struggle to obtain a medical education. Her intense desire to pursue these studies, however, led her close friend and advisor Emily Davies to devote her life to the opening of higher education to women in England. On behalf of Elizabeth Garrett, Davies appealed to the University of London asking that women be allowed to sit for examinations and obtain degrees. Presenting memorials to the regents of the university signed by many of England's eminents, including F. D. Maurice and William Gladstone (1809-1898), Davies met with firm opposition. This initial resistance both incensed and inspired Davies. At this point she began her work to overcome the barriers thrown in the paths of aspiring women.[59]

Elizabeth Garrett's struggle for a medical degree was difficult and ultimately unsuccessful in England.[60] The interest aroused by her efforts, however, brought the issue of women's higher education before the public. In 1862 a paper written by the journalist and suffragist Frances Power Cobbe (1822-1904) and presented to the Social Science Association in London again publicized the issue. Entitled "University Degrees for Women," it argued that the time had come for women's entry into academic life.[61] As Cobbe related in her autobiography, "Every daily paper in London laughed at my demand, and for a week or two I was the butt of universal ridicule."[62] Nevertheless, her paper stimulated thought and debate among those who had heard it. At a special meeting held to discuss the matter of degrees for women, the Social Science Association resolved that "measures ought to be provided for testing and attesting the education of women of the middle and higher classes."[63] A committee to open university examinations to women was thereby formed and Emily Davies was chosen secretary.

At this point Emily Davies emerged as the pivotal figure in the movement for the higher education of women in England. Other individuals deserve credit for their efforts, but it was the unceasing, often controversial work of Davies, carried on until the end of her life, that gave the movement force and spirit.

In background, appearance, and demeanor, Davies seemed an unlikely candidate for such a demanding role. The daughter of a clergyman, she was a small, plain, "rather dim little person with mouse coloured hair and conventional manners."[64] Her education, typical of that of girls in early Victorian England, consisted of bits and pieces of learning from a few months at a day school, language lessons from a French tutor, composition from her father, and some simple instruction from her mother. Her brothers, however, were granted a full public school and university education. Given her own intellectual ambitions, Davies evidently felt keen resentment over such inequity. "Probably only women who have laboured under it," she wrote, "can understand the weight of discouragement produced by being perpetually told that, as women, nothing much is ever to be expected of them, . . . that anything like original research or profound learning is not for them to think of."[65]

An outlet for Davies' frustration and ambition opened in the 1850s when she became acquainted with a small group of London feminists working to improve women's educational, professional, and economic opportunities. At the heart of this group lay the figure of Barbara Leigh Smith (1827-1891), a wealthy, dynamic, energetic woman whose father had encouraged education, self-sufficiency, and self-confidence from her earliest years. Around her "vital, not to say robust, and certainly uncorseted" person, a cohesive group of women began to emerge that would launch the women's movement in England. Initially meeting informally in parlors in Kensington and Blandford Square, Leigh Smith and her group founded the "Ladies' Institute" in Langham Place. Publishing the *English Woman's Journal* and operating The Society for Promoting the Employment of Women, the Langham Place ladies evolved into a highly organized, articulate group of women whose sense of purpose propelled the struggle for women's legal, political, and economic equality.[66] Emily Davies, recognizing the importance of all these concerns, "decided that the first requisite and foundation of progress must be wider and better education for women."[67] With Elizabeth Garrett's decision to pursue a professional education, Emily Davies' work began.

Envisioning ultimately the opening of full, equal university education for women, Davies carefully plotted the path that would lead to this goal. Having been rebuffed by the University of London in her efforts on behalf of Elizabeth Garrett, Davies approached the ancient universities of Oxford and Cambridge, hoping that with their stature they would not feel threatened by such an experiment as women's education. It seemed logical to begin by pursuing the opening of local examinations to girls. Instituted by Oxford and Cambridge in 1857, these were tests given locally to students in secondary schools to assess the quality of their training.[68] When introduced there had been no thought of offering these examinations to girls, who, it was believed, had no use for them. Emily Davies, with her long-range yet undisclosed plan of university education for women, saw very clearly the need. An external standard was necessary, she concluded, to raise the level of learning in the secondary schools for girls, so that they could be adequately prepared for higher education.[69]

Writing to Oxford and Cambridge, Davies asked permission to allow girls to sit for the examinations. An Oxford spokesman replied that "the University would think the examination of young ladies a matter altogether beyond its sphere of duty."[70] Cambridge University, however, after receiving a series of letters and memorials drawn up by Davies, agreed in 1863 to open the examinations to girls on an experimental basis. After two years of experimentation, "nothing alarming or scandalous occurred." Thus, in 1865, upon receiving a large memorial from Davies signed by "ladylike ladies" and educational experts, Cambridge University officially opened its local examinations to girls throughout England.[71]

Notes

1.   Mary Kelley, *Private Woman, Public Stage: Literary Domesticity in Nineteenth Century America* (New York and Oxford: Oxford University Press, 1984), 62.

2.   See, for instance, Margaret Rossiter, *Women Scientists in America: Struggles and Strategies to 1940* (Baltimore and London: Johns Hopkins University Press, 1982), 4. Also see Frederick Rudolph's essay on Willard in *Notable American Women 1607-1950: A Biographical Dictionary,* Vol. 3 (Cambridge, Mass.: The Belknap Press of Harvard University Press, 1971), 611-613.

3.   Alma Lutz, *Emma Willard: Pioneer Educator of American Women* (Boston: Beacon Press, 1964), 45.

4.   Emma Willard, *A Plan for Improving Female Education* (Middlebury, Vt.: J.W. Copeland, 1819; repr., Middlebury College, 1918), 12.

5.   Quoted in Barbara Miller Solomon, *In the Company of Educated Women: A History of Women and Higher Education in America* (New Haven: Yale University Press, 1985), 20.

6.   Kathryn Kish Sklar, "The Founding of Mount Holyoke College," in Berkin and Norton, *Women of America*, 196.

7.   Ibid.

8.   See Elizabeth Alden Green, *Mary Lyon and Mount Holyoke: Opening the Gates* (Hanover, N.H.: University Press of New England, 1979), 150.

9.   Quoted in Green, 124. Also see Sklar, 195, and Green, 122-123.

10. Green, 128-130, and 275.

11. Quoted in Sklar, 178.

12. Willard, 43.

13. Mary Lyon, *Letters and Documents,* 2 [1833], 389-392, quoted in Green, 111.

14. Anne Firor Scott, "The Ever Widening Circle: The Diffusion of Feminist Values from the Troy Female Seminary

1822-1872," *History of Education Quarterly* 19 (1979): 3-25.

15. See Thomas E. Drake's essay on Prudence Crandall in *Notable American Women* (Cambridge, Mass.: Belknap Press, 1971), 399-401.

16. See Catharine Esther Beecher, *Educational Reminiscences and Suggestions* (New York: J.B. Ford, 1874), p. 166.

17. For a discussion of the transformations these demographic changes would bring in the lives of women, see Robert V. Wells, "Women's Lives Transformed: Demographic and Family Patterns in America, 1600-1970," in Berkin and Norton, 17-33.

18. Quoted in Woloch, 130.

19. Kathryn Kish Sklar, *Catharine Beecher: A Study in American Domesticity* (New Haven: Yale University Press, 1973), 76, 155-167, 171-174, 215, 271.

20. "The housewife needed to be a highly skilled specialist and good administrator of her team of daughters, young children, apprentices, servants. The growing, marketing, cooking, preserving of food, brewing of beer or cider, distilling, boiling of soap and manufacture of other cleaning materials and the constant struggle against dirt, making, mending, washing of clothes, and even spinning and weaving of yarn and cloth, the concoction and administration of medicines, all fell to the lot of women. In addition, the housewife would often assist in her husband's business and in the frequent disaster of his death before any surviving sons were old enough to take over, such women often continued to trade in their own right." See Margaret Bryant, *The Unexpected Revolution: A Study in the History of Education of Women and Girls in the Nineteenth Century* (London: University of London Institute of Education, 1979), 28.

21. John Ruskin, "Of Queen's Gardens," in Janet Horowitz Murray, *Strong-Minded Women and Other Lost Voices from Nineteenth Century England* (New York: Pantheon Books, 1982), 38.

22.   Bryant, 29.

23.   See, for instance, Patricia Branca, "Image and Reality: The Myth of the Idle Victorian Woman," in *Clio's Consciousness Raised: New Perspectives on the History of Women*, eds. Mary S. Hartman and Lois Banner (New York: Harper and Row, 1974), 179-189.

24.   Bryant, 29.

25.   Branca, 185.

26.   The Reverend Sydney Smith, *Writings, Female Education*, (n.p., 1810), 118-19, Quoted in Bryant, 27.

27.   Emily Davies, *Thoughts on some Questions Relating to Women, 1860-1908* (Cambridge, England: Bowes and Bowes, 1910), 27. Davies' voice was only one of many that decried the ideal of leisure. See for instance, Emily Shirreff, "College Education of Women," *Contemporary Review* 15 (Fall 1870): 65; the views of Elizabeth Garrett Anderson in W. H. Davenport Adams, *Woman's Work and Worth in Girlhood, Maidenhood, and Wifehood* (London: John Hogg, 1880), 475; and Millicent Garrett Fawcett, "The Education of Women of the Middle and Upper Classes," *MacMillan's Magazine*, April 1868, 511-517.

28.   For an exposé of the realities of women's work on the plantation, see Catherine Clinton, *The Plantation Mistress: Woman's World in the Old South* (New York: Pantheon Books, 1982), 18-29.

29.   Julia Ward Howe, foreword to *Woman's Work in America*, ed. Annie Nathan Meyer (New York: Henry Holt and Co., 1891; repr., New York: Arno Press, 1972), 1.

30.   Quoted in Janet James, *Changing Ideas About Women in the United States, 1776-1825* (New York: Garland Publishing, Inc., 1981), 174.

31.   Ibid., 172.

32.   Mention should be made of Blount College in Knoxville, Tennessee, chartered in 1794. The school was unusual for its time and region in that it accepted women students. Although the claim can thus be made that Blount was the first

coeducational institution in the country, it cannot compare with Oberlin since none of the women earned a degree nor did it enjoy continuous existence. For further discussion, see James X. Corgan, "Toward a History of Higher Education in Antebellum East Tennessee," *The East Tennessee Historical Society's Publications* No. 60, 1988, p. 39-66.

33. *The Joint Education of the Sexes. A Report Presented at a Meeting of the Ohio State Teacher's Association, Sandusky City, July 8th* (Oberlin: n.p., 1852), 29; and James Harris Fairchild, *The Coeducation of the Sexes as Pursued in Oberlin College* (Hartford: Camp, 1868), 9.

34. Ronald W. Hogeland, "Coeducation of the Sexes at Oberlin College," *Journal of Social History* (1972-73): 160-176; and Jill Conway, "Perspectives in the History of Women's Education in the United States," *History of Education Quarterly 14* (Spring, 1974): 6.

35. Fairchild, 4-7.

36. Woody, 2: 233; and Conway, 6.

37. Woody, 2: 233.

38. Quoted in Josephine Kamm, *Hope Deferred: Girls' Education in English History* (London: Methuen, 1965), 170.

39. For a scholarly view of the plight of the English governess, see A. James Hammerton, *Emigrant Gentlewomen: Genteel Poverty and Female Emigration 1830-1914* (London: Croom Helm, 1979), 20-52.

40. Quoted in Bryant, 32.

41. Neff, 165.

42. Bryant, 34.

43. Quoted in Neff, 165.

44. Bryant, 22.

45. Quoted in Kathryn Kish Sklar, "The Founding of Mt. Holyoke College," 186.

46. Ibid., 196.

47. Ibid., 192.

48. Ibid., 193.

49. Bryant, 71.

50.   Ibid., 72. The work of these reformers may also be understood as a trend within the flow of reforms initiated in English society in the 1830s and 1840s, movements generally concurrent with America's Jacksonian reforms. The abolition of slavery and the Factory Act of 1833, the Poor Law of 1834, and the founding of the Chartist movement and the Anti-Corn Law League illustrate the mood of reform sweeping England during these decades.

51.   Kamm, 174.

52.   Rosalie Glynn Grylls, *Queen's College 1848-1948* (London: George Routledge and Sons Ltd., 1948), 17-24. Also see Christina Sinclair Bremner, *Education of Girls and Women in Great Britain* (London: Swan Sonnenschein and Co., Ltd., 1897), 126-130.

53.   Bryant, 77.

54.   Margaret Tuke, *A History of Bedford College for Women* (London: Oxford University Press, 1939), 24-25.

55.   Kamm, 15-19.

56.   For a fascinating account of Blackwell's struggle to obtain a medical education, see her autobiography, *Pioneer Work in Opening the Medical Profession to Women* (London: Longmans, Green, and Co., 1895; repr., New York: Source Book Press, 1970), 58-95. For a discussion of her "accidental" acceptance by Geneva Medical College, see Regina Morantz Sanchez, "The Female Student Has Arrived, The Rise of the Women's Medical Movement," in *"Send us a Lady Physician": Women Doctors in America, 1835-1920,* ed. Ruth J. Abram (New York: W.W. Norton and Co., 1985), 59-60.

57.   Jo Manton, *Elizabeth Garrett Anderson* (New York: E.P. Putnam, 1965), 50-53.

58.   Blackwell, 218.

59.   For an account of Emily Davies' work on behalf of Elizabeth Garrett, see Barbara Stephen, *Emily Davies and Girton College* (London: Constable and Co., 1927; repr., Westport, Conn.: Hyperion, 1976), 54-81.

60. She received her M.D. degree in Paris in 1869.
61. Published as Frances Power Cobbe, "The Education of Women, and How it Would be Affected by University Examinations," in *Essays on the Pursuits of Women* (London: Emily Faithfull, 1863), 216-239.
62. Quoted in Stephen, 82.
63. Ibid.
64. Louisa Garrett Anderson, *Elizabeth Garrett Anderson 1836-1917* (London: Faber and Faber Ltd., 1939), 42.
65. Davies, 131.
66. For further information concerning Barbara Leigh Smith and the Langham Place group, see Sheila R. Herstein, *A Mid-Victorian Feminist, Barbara Leigh Smith Bodichon* (New Haven: Yale University Press, 1985), 134-146.
67. Ray Strachey, *"The Cause": A Short History of the Women's Movement in Great Britain* (Port Washington, N.Y.: Kennikat Press, Inc., 1928; repr., 1969), 141.
68. For a discussion of the systems of examinations in English schools and universities, see Robert J. Montgomery, *Examinations: An Account of their Evolution as Administrative Devices in England*, University of Pittsburgh Studies in Comparative Education, no. 6 (Pittsburgh: University of Pittsburgh Press, 1967).
69. Davies rarely divulged her ultimate intentions. But in a confidential letter to a friend, she wrote, "I do not care so very much for [the examinations] in themselves . . . . It seems likely, however, that if we could get these examinations it would be a great lift towards getting the University of London." Quoted in Strachey, 132.
70. Quoted in Stephen, 84.
71. Oxford opened local examinations to girls in 1870.

CHAPTER 3

A COLLEGE LIKE A MAN'S

Cambridge University's decision to open local examinations to English girls in 1865 seemed small compared to certain events occurring in America at that time. Given the loss of over 600,000 men and the maiming of many more in the Civil War, women in America experienced a rising status and growing professional opportunities.[1] As women entered new occupations, society became more sensitive to their educational requirements.

Some individuals had perceived a growing need even before the war, and several attempts had been made to open a college "like a man's." Georgia Female College, later Wesleyan Female College, for example, was chartered in Macon, Georgia, in 1836. And Mary Sharp College, known originally as the Tennessee and Alabama Female Institute, opened in 1851 in Winchester, Tennessee. While the course offerings in these two schools exceeded those of girls' seminaries, they fell below the requirements of collegiate institutions for men. A diploma granted by Mary Sharp College in 1853, however, represents the earliest diploma known in America "issued by a woman's college, which, in form, content, and the work for which it stood," explains Thomas Woody, "can compare at all favorably with the Bachelor's degree of male colleges." The course content, Woody continues, was "narrower" than that of most men's colleges.[2] "Colleges" and "collegiate institutes" for women continued to be chartered throughout the 1850s, but most proved unsatisfactory financially and academically.[3]

In 1860, however, a wealthy brewer from Poughkeepsie, New York, childless, self-educated, and self-made, decided to establish a college which, he claimed, "shall accomplish for young women what our colleges are accomplishing for young men."[4] In 1865 Vassar College opened with an endowment greater than any previous women's college. "Considering purely material equipment, she had all that could be desired," claims Thomas Woody.[5]

Given the bleak financial record of women's institutions in the past, Matthew Vassar's (1792-1868) gift to female education was an important step. Lack of adequate funding had deprived women's schools of necessary books, facilities, and instruction. Vassar's munificence allowed his college to open with material advantages, as well as an extensive, more highly paid faculty. This included, significantly, the distinguished, prize-winning astronomer Maria Mitchell (1818-1889), one of America's first women professors of science.

Public reaction to the opening of Vassar College was, on the whole, positive. When the college was chartered in 1861, *Harper's Weekly* predicted (prematurely, as it turned out) that "the imbecile sneer at 'learned women' will sink into the proper contempt."[6] And in 1863 the *New York Tribune* called the project "one of the milestones that mark the advancement of the age."[7] *Godey's Lady's Book,* in particular, followed its opening with interest, finding fault only with the embarrassing name—Vassar Female College—and asking that it be replaced with the more dignified name of Vassar College for Women, a suggestion Matthew Vassar accepted.[8]

In England Vassar received positive press from the *English Woman's Journal.* The women of Langham Place heartily endorsed the "experiment," claiming, "This large and costly edifice is the embodiment of a new creed—the creed of woman's capability."[9] Praising Matthew Vassar for his munificence and perspicuity, the

Journal spoke of his college as a "real University for Women, intended to afford to girls just such a thorough and complete education as our own Oxford and Cambridge offer to youth of the other sex."[10] Whatever the outcome of this noble "experiment," the *Journal* concluded, Vassar would prove a "blessing to the world."[11]

With the opening of Vassar, the idea of creating a woman's college "like a man's" became an attractive idea. Some coeducational institutions were beginning to appear, but were not sufficiently widespread to accommodate all the young women now desiring an education. Sophia Smith (1796-1870) of Massachusetts heartily endorsed the ideal of equal educational opportunity for women and in her will left her fortune for the establishment of an institution "with the design to furnish for my own sex means and facilities for education equal to those which are afforded now in our colleges to young men."[12] In 1871 Smith College was chartered, opening four years later in Northampton, Massachusetts.

Thomas Woody notes that, unlike Vassar, no great fanfare accompanied the opening of Smith College, suggesting that the novelty of higher education of women had worn off by the 1870s.[13] Indeed, the first president of Smith College observed that "a new college for women excited little attention or comment."[14] But the opening of Smith was significant in two ways. It marked the first time that a woman in either the United States or England had given her fortune to create a college specifically for women. And secondly, Smith was the first women's college whose entrance standards and curriculum conformed to those of the men's colleges. Requiring Greek for admission and following the Amherst and Harvard four year course of study, Smith sought from its inception to "perfect [a woman's] intellect by the best methods which philosophy and experience suggest."[15]

Another significant step in the history of women's education was the establishment of Wellesley College in 1875. Wellesley, like Smith, claimed to offer an advanced curriculum, but did not demand the formidable subject of Greek as an admission requirement.[16]

The opening of women's colleges with the facilities, the endowments, and the ambition to give women a thorough, academic education looked promising in the decade following the Civil War. In contrast with earlier periods, this was a hopeful, expectant time for intelligent women who desired rigorous intellectual training for their sex. Upon examining the early years of collegiate education for women, however, it appears that few women attending these northeastern colleges actually received the same education as their counterparts at Amherst and Harvard. A woman's college "like a man's" was yet to come.

A look at the first class to enter Vassar College indicates the problem. Although Vassar listed advanced courses in the catalogue, only a small minority of entering students had received the secondary training necessary to pursue such courses. As James Monroe Taylor explains, "their education had been uneven, irregular, unsystematic, some unbelievably untrained."[17] While trying to maintain a semblance of its educational goals, Vassar was forced to establish a preparatory program for most of its students. Until 1888 the "regular" degree students remained a slight minority of the total number of students at Vassar. In certain years only one or two diplomas were granted, while many young women entered and left with no degree in hand.[18]

Smith College encountered similar problems with its first class a decade after Vassar opened. Requiring entrance standards as high as those of the best men's colleges and offering a "fully equivalent" curriculum, Smith, by the end of its first year, was left with only twelve students who were able to meet the requirements and follow the curriculum. Refusing to open a preparatory department, Smith in its second year of operation admitted only sixteen women.

Though noble in its efforts to maintain high standards of admission and matriculation, Smith was faced with an undeniable reality with few exceptions, such as those who had been privately tutored, young women in America did not gain enough secondary training in mathematics or classics to fulfill Smith's requirements. This fact forced the college to compromise, and Smith opened its third year with thirty-nine students, most of whom were "special students," given the option of a nonclassical course of study unlike the Amherst and Harvard curriculum.[19]

Wellesley too fell short of the standards of men's colleges, but by design as much as necessity. Founder Henry Durant made it clear in the beginning that his institution would offer its students a thorough education but not the same as men's. Rather, Wellesley chose to emphasize religion, health, and teaching skills, as well as academics. Not embarrassed by its abundance of preparatory students, Wellesley in its first year had only 30 out of a student body of 314 who were prepared to follow the college course.[20] In 1870 student Mary Elizabeth Stillwell wrote home, "Wellesley is not a college. I came here to take a *college course,* and not to dabble." The college seemed not to care "whether the Latin, Greek and Mathematics are well learned or not."[21]

As President Taylor of Vassar noted, the education of girls in America, even those who sought a higher education, was "uneven." Certainly there were good schools in the country for girls in 1865. Emma Willard and Mary Lyon had created two in the 1830s. A significant obstacle in the path of women's higher education in America, however, was the lack of required standards in secondary programs. Although colleges such as Vassar and Smith earnestly desired to offer women an education equal to that of the young men of Harvard, they could not do so until girls' education had advanced sufficiently. America provided no external test for secondary schools that would motivate them to maintain a certain quality. Not until the 1880s would those women's colleges that aspired to equal men's colleges be able to rid themselves of preparatory programs.[22]

In England in 1865 the existence of a woman's college "like a man's" existed only in the minds of Emily Davies and her associates. Davies, however, had won a victory in establishing for girls a means by which their preparation might be measured. The local examinations given by Cambridge in 1865 and later by Oxford pointed out the weaknesses in girls' education before women's colleges were created, thereby challenging the secondary schools to strengthen their curricula.

The creation by Parliament of the Schools Inquiry Commission, or the Taunton Commission, led to further improvements in female education. Organized in 1864, the Commission was assigned the task of investigating secondary schools across England and publishing its findings. At first, plans called for the commission's report to include only boys' schools, since girls' education was considered negligible. But after receiving letters and memorials from Emily Davies urging the consideration of girls' education, the Commission agreed to include girls' schools in the inquiry.

The Commission's report, issued in 1868, called attention to the weaknesses in girls' intellectual training, as had the local examinations. While noting that schools provided training in the "accomplishments" in order to raise a girl's social standing, the commissioners found little evidence of the kind of rigorous learning that would inspire a girl's intellectual capacity.[23] One commissioner concluded his investigation by stating, "The mental training of the best girls' schools is unmistakably inferior to that of the best boys' schools."[24]

As a result of these findings, which cited defective teaching, poor parental attitudes toward educating daughters, and lack of money as the culprits in girls' education, the Endowed Schools Act was passed in 1869. In this act Parliament assented to the proposal that "provision shall be made as far as conveniently may be, for extending to girls the benefits of endowments."[25] This legislation, then, led not only to the increase of endowed schools for girls throughout England, but also generated an increase in funds for girls' scholarships.

The Schools Inquiry Commission and the Endowed Schools Act seem small in comparison to the opening of endowed colleges for women in America. But they were significant steps for English women. By stimulating interest in the quality of secondary education for girls, they helped to provide a firmer foundation on which to build academic programs for women. As Josephine Kamm explains, "The Endowed Schools Act has rightly been called 'the Magna Carta of girls' education, the first acknowledgment by the State of their claim to a liberal education.'"[26]

While England's secondary schools for girls were evaluated and improved in the late 1860s, efforts were also underway at this time to open educational opportunities for women. In 1867 an organization with the tedious name of the North of England Council for the Higher Education of Women was created to arrange lectures for women in large towns around the country. In the absence of other channels of higher education for women, excepting Queen's and Bedford in London, the lectures proved popular and helped to alleviate the void.[27]

In conjunction with their lectures, the North of England Council considered establishing an examination for women over the age of eighteen. The idea of special lectures and examinations for women received support and soon "Ladies' Education Associations" proliferated throughout England. Although these special lectures gained the approval of men and women who viewed such programs as an advance, those who sought equal education for women, particularly Emily Davies and her committee, claimed that ultimately such schemes would "keep down the level of female education."[28]

Fearful of their popularity, Davies was "unhappy to see the Ladies' Lectures, Ladies' Educational Association, etc., spreading. It is an evil principle becoming organized, and gaining the strength which comes from organization," she wrote.[29] Skeptical of all schemes that funneled women into educational programs designed to suit "their needs," Davies envisioned a plan that would ultimately channel women into a position of equal status at Cambridge University. Davies then set in motion her plans to found and operate a college for women near the ancient, seemingly congenial walls of Cambridge. As Davies planned it, there would be nothing "special" about this college. Rather, it would offer a full university course to students who would work toward the same examinations and degrees as the young men of Cambridge University.

In 1867 Davies proposed to Barbara Leigh Smith that they gather a committee to raise money and public support for a women's college at Cambridge. Chosen carefully to allay suspicions of feminism and to win the confidence of "ordinary people," the members of the committee were noted for their "respectability," by the [London] *Times*. But behind this curtain of respectability stood the shadows of those whose feminism or public reputations required "private" support. George Eliot (1819-1880), for one, offered to Davies her blessings, her books, her advice on curriculum, and fifty pounds. Davies would make no public mention, however, of this vital connection with the novelist, who was now living with a married man.

Barbara Leigh Smith, too, gave generously her advice and her money during these formative years. Due to her association with the women's rights agenda, her contributions, like Eliot's, were made anonymously.[30]

In October 1869, thanks largely to Leigh Smith's support, five students moved into a rented house overlooking the village of Hitchin, just one hour's train ride from Cambridge. There they began their studies, studies which marked the first instance of university education in England for women. Unlike the opening of Vassar in 1865, the founding of the first full-fledged college for women in England was not met with fanfare or favorable press. One disgruntled clergyman sniffed contemptuously at that "infidel place" as he passed Hitchin by train,[31] but the world at large took little notice of those five young women taking lodging in this house marked by "plainness and solidity" a respectable distance from Cambridge. This was as Davies wished, for discretion was part of her plan.

Within the unremarkable walls of Benslow House, as it was called, was a certain Victorian comfort, restrained by formality and dignity. Davies, anticipating Virginia Woolf, recognized the importance of privacy in the lives of her young scholars, who had rarely enjoyed a moment alone in the midst of family, and provided each of them with her own bedroom and sitting area. "Of all the attractions offered by the college life, probably the opportunity for a certain amount of solitude, so necessary an agent in the formation of character, will be the most welcomed by the real student," a Cambridge alumna would later note.[32]

On the ground level of Benslow House was the "library," serving also as a common room and lecture hall. In the basement was the "dining hall," designed to mirror those of the colleges of Cambridge. It was a "bare, ugly room with two tables at one of which we students sat, while the mistress and her friends sat at the 'High Table' alongside," wrote Louisa Lumsden (1840-1935), one of the original five. "It needed an effort of imagination," added another, "to recognize Dons and high table and undergraduates all complete, though as it were in embryo."[33]

For Emily Davies, there was nothing laughable in her attempt to reflect the atmosphere and traditions of Cambridge. Behind the display lay a calm and serious purpose, one that was soon adopted by the students themselves, the first women of Cambridge. "There was not one of these first women who was not weighted with a sense of responsibility for the new start," emphasized student Emily Gibson.[34]

In spite of their sense of purpose, these students operated under trying conditions. Finances for Davies' project were thin, and the college lacked laboratories, equipment, and books. Support in kind, however, was soon forthcoming. Once or twice a week, depending on the train schedule, four willing lecturers from Cambridge traveled to Hitchin to share their knowledge in classics, English, and mathematics, imparting, it seems, considerable enthusiasm in addressing this experimental group. George Eliot and critic George Lewes (1817-1878) donated books from their personal collection to the library. And Barbara Leigh Smith offered paintings and furnishings, saving Benslow House "from being ugly or depressingly commonplace," wrote Davies.[35] Finally, the students, it seems, brought a sense of mission, urgency, and joy that helped them overcome material disadvantages. "The extraordinary happiness of that first year at Hitchin is a thing that cannot come twice in a lifetime," wrote student Constance Maynard (1849-1935).[36]

With all their exuberance, the women of Hitchin soon found that there was one seemingly insurmountable disadvantage that they would have to conquer. Like their American counterparts, England's earliest female college students were less prepared for full college work than male students. But ambition and determination overcame these academic limitations. When the time arrived to pass their first hurdle, an examination in classics required of all second-year students at Cambridge University, the early women of Hitchin made their preparation. Popularly known as the "Little Go," the so-called "Previous" examination was often an obstacle for the most advanced Cambridge students. For this small group at Hitchin, then, whose secondary preparation was decidedly inferior to that of the men of Cambridge, the "Little Go" was faced with uncertainty and apprehension.

Davies allowed no special dispensation for her students, however, despite their "colossal ignorance of the special subjects required."[37] In October 1870 she applied to the university for permission to take the examinations. With characteristic ambiguity, the authorities announced that the delivery of the examination to the women of Hitchin was beyond their scope, but there was no reason a private arrangement might not be made with the examiners. The examiners, whose generosity might well have been alloyed with a sense of curiosity and caprice, agreed to question the women and read their papers.

By the end of the October term, all Davies' students had successfully completed their first trial. Their victory and their celebrations reverberated well beyond the prim walls of Benslow House. *Punch,* for one, recorded the event in typically playful fashion, adding, "It is gratifying that out of all those flowers of loveliness, not one was plucked. Bachelors of Arts are likely to be made to look to their laurels by these spinsters."[38]

In 1873 the second major ordeal loomed ahead for the Hitchin "spinsters" in the form of the Cambridge Tripos Examination. Named after the traditional three-legged stool on which the candidates in the early centuries of the University sat while being questioned, the Tripos examination provoked the same fear and foreboding at Hitchin as the "Little Go," if not more. Originating in the eighteenth century as a comprehensive examination in mathematics, the Tripos was the oldest and most noted written examination in England. In 1824 a

Tripos was added in classics. Because of the rewards associated with the successful completion of the Tripos in mathematics and classics, the pressure not only to pass the examination, but to rank highly was intense. A superior mark assured a college fellowship and academic distinction for the graduates of the colleges of Cambridge University. But success required enormous preparation, as well as precision and stamina during the week of the examination. For all Cambridge students, the Tripos represented the greatest challenge in their academic career.[39]

When Emily Davies approached the university once more, asking permission for her women to take the Tripos, the officials again refused. But a number of individual examiners, as before, agreed to issue and read the papers. With its long-standing reputation as England's most formidable examination, the Tripos seemed, at the time, the ultimate test in Davies' plan to prove the intellectual equality of women. In 1873 three of the Hitchin women sat for the Tripos, two in classics and one in mathematics. Again, the women triumphed. "We have just heard that Miss Cook's translation of Aristotle was the best in the Tripos examination," wrote Davies ecstatically to a friend, "and the two Examiners who looked over it are rapturous. Miss Lumsden's paper on Roman History was 'one of the prettiest shown up.'"[40] While no degree or fellowship followed for these women, much had been gained by their successful completion of the "Little Go" and the Tripos. Ill-prepared for the high standards of Cambridge, the Hitchin women had nonetheless within the same time frame mastered the same material offered their male counterparts, who had been well-trained in England's secondary schools for boys and endowed with all the material and academic advantages of the university. Davies' goal was slowly being realized.

As the college grew in size and distinction, Davies and her committee decided in 1873 to relocate it to the village of Girton, two miles from Cambridge. The move was significant, for having proved that women could follow the course work and succeed in the examinations of Cambridge University, the college would now gain physical as well as academic proximity to the university. Here, Davies was certain again to provide her scholars with their private space. "To have a study of my own and to be told that, if I chose to put 'Engaged' on my door, no one would so much as knock was in itself so great a privilege as to hinder me from sleep," wrote alumna Helena Swanwick.[41]

The same year, another door to higher education for women opened as twenty-two of the thirty-four Cambridge professors offered Girton students admission to their lectures. Usually sitting separately from the men and always chaperoned, the young women were regarded initially as an amusing and somewhat bizarre novelty. The Girton women inevitably maintained their sense of dignity, strongly imposed by Davies, not even flinching when a specimen of a human brain was passed around in a science lecture. By the time the specimen reached the gallery where the women were secluded with their chaperones, the men in front had all turned around, anticipating a loss of composure among the women. They were disappointed.[42]

The chaperones themselves, though, could sometimes cause the women discomfort. "My chaperone was an incurably unpunctual person; a decayed gentlewoman with the poorest sort of twittering manners," remembered Helena Swanwick. Waiting for her to arrive, Swanwick became "the butt and mockery of a certain type of undergraduate, until my silly guardian chose to turn up, out of breath and apologetic."[43]

Laboratory work presented another obstacle for the Girton women, since propriety would not allow them to work side by side with men. Philip Main of St. John's College temporarily solved the problem, however, by taking the women early, before breakfast, in a special session. Main was only one example of the faculty support that enabled Girton College to succeed. "There is a long list of 'Benefactors' to whom the cause of women's higher education owes its existence, and the professors who refused fees for teaching the girls, or returned them into the college funds, and those who gave their time and leisure to the work of establishing the new venture stand high upon it," wrote Ray Strachey (1887-1940), a participant and witness of the women's movement of the late nineteenth century.[44]

While Davies and her experiment at Girton were proceeding with success, there were other trends occurring in women's higher education in England. From the lecture series of the 1860s evolved a movement to found residential halls within England's universities where women might to a greater extent share in academe. In 1871 Newnham Hall opened in Cambridge, followed by two halls in the late 1870s at Oxford.

Like Girton College the halls maintained an unofficial relationship with their respective universities. Accessibility to lectures and the right to sit for examinations were dependent solely upon the good will of individual professors. Unlike Girton, however, the founders of the ladies' halls chose in the beginning to concede to the current dictum that women's educational needs and abilities were different from men's. Davies saw this as an unfortunate compromise and one that was potentially damaging to women's full academic development. Thus in the 1870s Girton stood alone in its approach to women's higher education, differing from the halls in curriculum and philosophy.[45]

But the individuals who founded Newnham had their own clear-cut agenda. They were among a number of Cambridge dons who valued the entry of women into academe as a welcome change in what they perceived to be an outworn, encrusted, and increasingly irrelevant university system. In the mid-nineteenth century, these men, who were among the younger of the Cambridge dons, began to question the practices of centuries that continued to govern the academic life of Cambridge. The monastic ideal of celibacy, imposed on Cambridge Fellows, and the traditional emphasis on mathematics and classics to the exclusion of the "new" disciplines of science, modern languages, and modern history came more and more under attack by a new group of dynamic, forward-looking individuals.

Notable in this reform-minded group was Henry Sidgwick (1838-1900). Arriving at Cambridge as an undergraduate in 1855, Sidgwick spent the remaining forty-five years of his life there as a student, Fellow, Professor of Philosophy, activist, and finally founder of Newnham College for women. Influenced by the writing of John Stuart Mill (1806-1873), as well as the work of friend and colleague

F. D. Maurice, Sidgwick, in his quest for positive change at Cambridge, turned his attention more and more to the education of women.[46]

In 1869, as Emily Davies began her experiment, Sidgwick found himself among the supporting Cambridge faculty who weekly took the train to Hitchin to share their knowledge. In the same year, Sidgwick opened another avenue for women's higher education by initiating a lecture series for women at Cambridge. Recognizing the popularity of lecture series elsewhere in the country, Sidgwick felt it imperative to begin such a program within the walls of England's ancient seat of learning.

Sidgwick's proposal gained initial support from a number of influential individuals, including J. S. Mill and Cambridge Professor Henry Fawcett (1833-1884) and his wife, Millicent Garrett Fawcett (1847-1929), sister of Elizabeth Garrett and future President of the National Union of Women's Suffrage Society. These supporters welcomed Sidgwick's plan as the most effective means of opening university education to women throughout England. As women, not only from Cambridge, but from distant areas, converged to hear the presentations of Cambridge dons, the need arose to establish a permanent structure to house these "external students," as Sidgwick referred to them.[47] A site was chosen in the district of Cambridge known as Newnham, and in October 1875 "Newnham Hall" opened its doors to thirty students. No longer "external," these thirty were now fully embraced within the heart of Cambridge.

Thus was born the second institution for the higher learning of women in England, but one quite different from Davies' Girton. Sidgwick envisioned his college for women as an experiment designed not only to open a channel for women within the university, but to revitalize the entire university system. Conceived, then, as an institution that would lead the way in educational reform, Sidgwick did not subscribe to Davies' imperative that women students follow the same classical course, with its compulsory Greek and Latin, and the same examination schedule as the men of Cambridge. Like Benjamin Rush in eighteenth-century Philadelphia, Sidgwick hoped to avoid a "servile imitation" of the classical education, which he believed had a "mischievous effect on education." Rather, he guided his students toward the newly emerging disciplines in science, philosophy, economics, and history. He also allowed admission to students who did not intend to stay for a complete program of studies or to sit for examinations.[48]

Similarly, Oxford opened two residential halls for women in 1879. While Cambridge had been the first of the ancient universities to allow women entry to lectures and examinations, a small but active group of men and women began in 1872 to extend similar opportunities to women at Oxford. It was at this time that Oxford fellows were given permission to marry after centuries of monastic celibacy. With the presence, then, of bright, reform-minded couples, the move to share the academic gifts of Oxford began. A group of young faculty wives, including the writer Mrs. Humphrey Ward (1851-1920), first organized lectures for women presented by sympathetic men of Oxford whose names to this day elicit admiration. Among them were Mark Pattison (1813-1884), Arnold Toynbee (1852-1883), and John Ruskin. Though he later seemed to enjoy his new role as lecturer to women, John Ruskin initially balked. "I cannot let the bonnets in on any conditions this term," he protested. "The three public lectures will be chiefly in angles, degrees of colour-prisms . . . and other such things of no use to the female mind, and they would occupy the seats in mere disappointed puzzlement." Soon Ruskin and "the bonnets" established a mutually agreeable rapport.[49]

In 1878, as the demand for these lectures grew, it was decided to establish a residential hall for women at Oxford. A year later two residential halls actually opened, due to conflicting opinions concerning religious affiliation. Lady Margaret Hall, named in honor of Margaret Beaufort (1443-1509), the brilliant mother of Henry VII and patron of Oxford and Cambridge, was organized and developed under the guidance of the Church of England. A similar, yet nondenominational institution was soon founded and named in honor of Mary Somerville. Both Oxford halls, like Newnham across the way, allowed women from around England to come hear lectures without the pressure of working as hard as the men.[50]

With the rise of halls and colleges for women within Oxford and Cambridge in the 1860s and 1870s, a new chapter in the education of women began. Arising as an intrinsic part of the reform movement sweeping Oxford and Cambridge in the mid-nineteenth century, these institutions would recharge these stagnant, complacent communities. But Emily Davies' Girton College stood alone and aloof from the other three, maintaining an unwavering curriculum and philosophy. The founders of the ladies' halls chose in the beginning to accept the age-old belief that women's educational needs and abilities were different from men's and that they would therefore benefit from less stringent demands. Henry Sidgwick, too, viewed the flexibility and innovation that Newnham embraced as a positive step toward reform in the university at large. For him, Davies' vision was impractical and obsolete.[51]

But Davies, who had for so long envied her brother's university education, viewed Sidgwick's goals with contempt and fear. Her plan to prove that women were fully capable of following the same intellectual course as men necessitated a common standard. Girton students, protesting Davies' intransigence as they labored to follow the traditional pattern of examinations, later endorsed her principles. "I am heartily glad she carried her point," said Louisa Lumsden, one of the original five. "The sacrifice of the individual was thoroughly worthwhile."[52] While the other plans offered possibilities for women, Girton College, singly, in a small quiet fashion, opened the doors of equal education.

By examining the women's colleges in America and England from 1865 to 1879, certain similarities become visible. In both countries the existence of residential colleges for middle-class women from the age of eighteen offered an attractive and viable alternative to domesticity. Although the lives of women in colleges on both sides of the Atlantic were governed by strict rules and regulations, their personal and certainly their intellectual freedom within the college was generally greater than at home. A taste of independence, an opportunity to use one's time and intellect in study, and a pioneering spirit guided the early students of the women's colleges.[53]

Common problems are also obvious on both sides of the Atlantic. The most apparent was the academic deficiency of women entering the colleges. In America this problem necessitated the creation of preparatory departments or the admission of "special students." In England, with the exception of Girton College, women were offered a special program in consideration of their special needs. The lack of adequate secondary preparation for girls was more acute in America, however, for in England significant efforts through the system of examinations were begun in the 1860s to improve the girls' background. The matter was publicly addressed, moreover, through the report of the Schools Inquiry Commission issued in 1868.

One major reason for the poor preparation of girls in both countries was the dearth of financial resources in these schools. This inadequacy extended through the college level in both countries, as well. Although certain women's colleges in America, beginning with Vassar in 1865, enjoyed munificent gifts from generous individuals, these gifts proved inadequate in meeting all the needs of the respective institutions. Monetary problems were not reserved for women's colleges alone in America; lack of funds plagued all institutions of higher learning. Women's colleges, however, received less financial support than men's.[54]

Likewise, Girton, Newnham, Lady Margaret Hall, and Somerville all suffered from want of resources. Their irregular relationships with the ancient universities placed them outside the standard channels of beneficence, and the struggling young institutions relied solely on the generosity of the friends of women's education, a relatively small group in mid-Victorian England.[55] Financial problems continued to burden women's colleges in England, even as they grew in stature and numbers. Somerville College, for instance, ultimately became "like the better of the men's colleges [at Oxford] in most respects, but unlike in one," observed Professor Gilbert Murray (1866-1957). "They all have large endowments or foundations, while Somerville . . . has practically none."[56]

Despite the similarities, important differences stand out between the women's colleges in America and England. The colleges for women in northeastern America, though professing to offer an education "like a man's," were separate institutions, independent from the best men's colleges that they strove to emulate. The founder of Girton and the halls for women in England, however, deliberately chose to attach their schools to Cambridge and Oxford. Although the status of these schools remained irregular for years before the governing boards of the universities granted them recognition, the college and halls benefited from their proximity to the universities. After all, Cambridge and Oxford attracted the best minds in the country, many of whom were pleased to share their knowledge with women students. And though the use of laboratories was initially forbidden to women students, the university libraries and lectures were gradually, if unofficially, opened to them.

Women's colleges in America, due to low funding, were often limited in resources, including libraries, laboratories, and quality teaching. While a few instructors, such as Vassar's Maria Mitchell and Wellesley's Alice Freeman, stand out in eminence, the faculties of the women's colleges were not strong in the opening years. Smith College, for example, had only one full-time instructor, Professor Josiah Clarke, who taught Greek and Latin. Instruction in other areas was provided by the President, the director of social life, etc. As President Seelye of Smith admitted, "The early faculty was not an imposing body."[57] Independence, nonetheless, gave the students of America's women's colleges certain benefits, particularly those working toward degrees. While women in England were allowed to attend Girton, Newnham, Lady Margaret Hall, or Somerville only through the good will of their universities, women in America could attend colleges with full rights and with the opportunity, if they were prepared, of pursuing a full collegiate course followed by a degree. It would be decades before the women of Oxford and Cambridge would attain this goal.

Notes

1. The effects of the Civil War on women's opportunities, however, should not be overrated. Occupations for women were still few. See Mabel Newcomer, *A Century of Higher Education for American Women* (New York: Harper and Row, 1959; repr., Washington, D.C.: Zeager Publishing Co., 1975), 17.

2. Woody, 2: 172-173.

3. For a discussion of these colleges and seminaries, see Woody, 2: 137-148. The expression, "a college like a man's," originated with Lucy Downing, a member of Plymouth Plantation, who in 1636 wrote to Governor Winthrop suggesting the creation of such a college for women in New England. See Woody, 2: 137.

4. Ibid., 148.

5. Ibid., 179.

6. Quoted in Taylor, 210.

7. Ibid., 228.

8. "Female! What female do you mean?" raged Sarah Josepha Hale of *Godey's* in indignation. "Not a female donkey?" See Finley, 208. The trustees did not approve the name change until 1867.

9. "American University for Women," *English Woman's Journal* (September 1864): 45.

10. Ibid., 43.

11. Ibid., 47

12. Quoted in Clark L. Seelye, *The Early History of Smith College* (Boston: Houghton Mifflin Co., 1923), 224.

13. Woody, 2: 149.

14. Seelye, 7.

15. From an early Smith catalogue, quoted in Newcomer, 55.

16. Woody, 2: 182.

17. Taylor, 281.

18. Elaine Kendall, *"Peculiar Institutions," An Informal History of the Seven Sisters Colleges* (New York: G.P. Putnam's Sons, 1976), 106.

19. Ibid., 118-119.
20. Newcomer, 21-22.
21. Quoted in Kendall, 123.
22. For a discussion of and statistics related to the preparatory departments, see Newcomer, 21-23.
23. For extracts from the Schools Inquiry Commission, see Maria Georgina Grey, *On the Education of Women* (London: W. Ridgway, 1871), 40-63.
24. Ibid., 11.
25. Quoted in Kamm, 212.
26. Ibid., 23.
27. Study Clubs, similar to the lecture series in England, proliferated in the United States from the 1860s to the 1890s, providing the only intellectual outlet many middle-class women could enjoy in the absence of widespread opportunities in higher education. Additionally, such self-improvement programs appealed to conservative, sometimes older women with families and children, who dared not consider such a radical step as collegiate education. The study groups in America, however, rarely invited outside speakers. An exception was the Saturday Morning Club of Boston, founded in 1871, which routinely heard lecturers such as Oliver Wendell Holmes, Sarah Orne Jewett, Henry James, etc. See Theodora Penny Martin, *The Sound of Our Own Voices: Women's Study Clubs 1860-1910* (Boston: Beacon Press, 1987).
28. Quoted in Stephen, 193.
29. Ibid., 194.
30. Upon the death of Barbara Leigh Smith in 1891, the college would benefit from the 10,000 pounds she bequeathed. See Herstein, 177-180.
31. M.C. Bradbrook, *That Infidel Place: A Short History of Girton College, 1869-1969* (London: Chatto and Windus, 1969), 3.

32.   Quoted in Sandra J. Peacock, *Jane Ellen Harrison: The Mask and the Self* (New Haven and London: Yale University Press, 1988), 35.

33.   Quoted in Stephen, 220-221.

34.   Ibid., 221.

35.   Ibid., 218.

36.   Ibid., 223.

37.   Quoted in Stephen, 231.

38.   Ibid., 239.

39.   Sheldon Rothblatt, *The Revolution of the Dons: Cambridge and Society in Victorian England* (New York: Basic Books, Inc., 1968), 181-183.

40.   Quoted in Stephen, 276.

41.   Helena Swanwick, "Memoir of Girton," in Murray, 241.

42.   Stephen, 287.

43.   Swanwick, 242.

44.   Strachey, 249.

45.   Edward W. Ellsworth explains that "Within a generation of its foundation Girton emerged as a dynamic focal point of female higher education and something of a symbol of women's campaign to play an enlarged role in public life." *Liberators of the Female Mind: The Shirreff Sisters, Educational Reform, and the Women's Movement* (Westport, Conn.: Greenwood Press, 1979), 141.

46.   Arthur and Eleanor Sidgwick, *Henry Sidgwick: A Memoir* (London: MacMillan and Co., 1906), 205.

47.   Ibid., 207.

48.   Gradually the two colleges became nearly identical in curriculum and examination policy. See Olive Banks, *Faces of Feminism: A Study of Feminism as a Social Movement* (New York: St. Martin's Press, 1981), 41-42.

49.   Vera Brittain, *The Women of Oxford: A Fragment of History* (London: George G. Harrap and Co., Ltd., 1960), 39.

50.   For accounts of the early years of women's education at Oxford University, see Annie M.A.H. Rogers, *Degree by Degrees: The Story of the Admission of Oxford Women*

Students to Membership of the University (Oxford: Oxford University Press, 1938), 3-26; and Brittain, 21-65.
51. Peacock, 35; Strachey, 162-163.
52. Stephen, 280.
53. For an understanding of the sense of mission, fulfillment, and freedom the pioneers enjoyed, see Janet E. Courtney, *The Women of My Time* (London: Lovat Dickson, Ltd., 1934), vi; Muriel St. Clare Byrne and Catherine Hope Mansfield, *Somerville College 1879-1921* (London: Oxford University Press, 1922), vii., 15; and Louise Schutz Boas, *Woman's Education Begins: The Rise of the Women's Colleges* (Norton, Mass.: Wheaton College Press, 1935; repr., New York: Arno Press, 1971), 264-265.
54. Newcomer, 24-25.
55. For a discussion of the problems caused by the severe lack of finances in these colleges, see Martha Vicinus, *Independent Women: Work and Community for Single Women 1850-1920* (Chicago and London: The University of Chicago Press, 1985), 123-124, 130.
56. Preface to St. Clare Byrne and Mansfield, v.
57. Seelye, 36-37.

CHAPTER 4

REACTION TO AN EDUCATION LIKE A MAN'S

In her book, *The College, the Market, and the Court,* published in 1867, American author and reformer Caroline Dall (1822-1912) claimed, "Any woman who will do *good* work may feel sure of honest appreciation. If she does poor work, she will only the more provoke the enemy."[1]

In her struggle to gain a medical education, England's Elizabeth Garrett, in accord with Dall's encouraging maxim, believed her good work would elicit admiration. She studied and worked diligently and through her quiet perseverance gained entry to lectures and examinations at London's Middlesex Hospital. Manifesting supreme self-confidence and an impressive knowledge of the subject matter, she soon became a source of irritation to her male peers. When certain test papers were returned, moreover, indicating that hers were superior to those of her colleagues, the men gathered a petition against her and forced her exclusion from further lectures. The "enemy," it seems, had been provoked. But the provocation was aroused not because of poor performance. Rather, it was Elizabeth Garrett's "good work" that brought fear, opposition, and very little "honest appreciation."[2]

By the 1870s more and more English and American women expressed an interest in collegiate education. A few also proved they were capable of the highest standards demanded of men. But with this trend, "the enemies" became troubled. As some institutions in America espoused the ideal of equal education and as a few English women scored brilliantly on Honours examinations, opponents of higher education for women sought new arguments to bolster their position.

The medical profession provided opponents with the most convincing arguments, designed effectively to deter the advance of women into full collegiate life by detailing the debilitating physical and societal consequences of such a step.[3] Basing their assertions upon the "limited energy" theory of English philosopher Herbert Spencer (1820-1903), physicians claimed that serious mental effort in women depleted the reproductive system of vital energy. Since nature provided a sufficient, but fixed amount of energy within the body, they argued, strong exertion in one area would reduce the supply of energy in another. Rigorous mental stimulation, therefore, would take its toll on another physiological process in the system. Intellectual endeavors were especially dangerous, physicians claimed, during menstruation, when, it was then believed, ovulation occurred. In severe cases of overstimulation of the brain, a girl's reproductive capacity might well be permanently impaired.[4]

In America the most famous and effective attack was delivered in the form of a treatise entitled *Sex in Education*. Published in 1873 by Dr. Edward H. Clarke (1820-1877), an eminent Harvard Medical School professor, this book was widely read, going through seventeen printings. Though ridiculed and refuted by prominent women's educators, feminists, and female physicians in speeches, magazine articles, and books, Dr. Clarke's thesis received serious consideration.[5]

Ironically, Dr. Clarke claimed to be promoting, as the subtitle of his book indicates, "a fair chance for the girls." Having purportedly studied the cases of seven students from Vassar College, Clarke concluded that a young woman could not exert the mental effort required to win an equal education and "retain uninjured health and a future secure from neuralgia, uterine disease, hysteria, and other derangements of the nervous system."[6] Women could study and learn, Clarke added, but their education must be limited and carefully paced according to the rhythm of their physical cycle. An excess of mental exertion, especially during that critical week of every month, would compromise their reproductive capacity and would thus deprive society of the biological function of intelligent, upper-class women.[7] Ultimately, he concluded, higher education for women would result in horrors, producing "monstrous brains and puny bodies; abnormally active cerebration and abnormally weak digestion; flowing thought and constipated bowels."[8]

Clarke's professional status and his claim that his conclusions were based on scientific evidence lent credibility to the book and reinforced the nineteenth-century suspicion that women were not suited physically or mentally for intellectual challenges. In 1874, just one year after the publication of *Sex in Education,* Clarke wrote another treatise with slightly moderated views. While still expressing concern for the health of young women in school, he no longer promoted "special education" for women.[9] The damage, however, had already been done. Many people, from both the lay population and the medical profession, readily accepted his original conclusions, finding "scientific proof" for their long-held prejudices regarding women and higher education.

One of these was the English "mental specialist," Dr. Henry Maudsley (1835-1918), who in 1874 wrote an article entitled "Sex in Mind and Education," in which he reiterated Dr. Clarke's assertions concerning the delicate interaction of mind and reproductive function in women. Dr. Maudsley cautioned his English audience that excessive mental application might "arrest the development of the reproductive system" in English women, just as it was obviously doing in American women.[10] But the ill effects would not stop there, for an imperfectly developed reproductive system through mental stimulation would serve in turn to "unsex" a woman. "The result," he concluded, "may be a monstrosity--something which having ceased to be a woman is yet not a man."[11]

Advocates of women's education, fearing that the English public would accept Dr. Maudsley's dreadful vision, felt compelled to answer. Dr. Elizabeth Garrett Anderson, now married and pregnant with her second child, responded the following month. As a medical doctor, she argued that the number of cases used to support Dr. Clarke's opinions were small compared to the thousands of young women "in which the break-down of nervous and physical health seems . . . traceable to want of adequate mental interest and occupation in the years immediately succeeding school life."[12] There were many women who were indeed "morbid, self-absorbed, or even hysterical." The cause, however, lay not in demanding intellectual work, but in lack thereof.[13]

Similarly, Julia Ward Howe (1819-1910) noted that while there were health problems among young middle-class women, they could hardly be attributed to education. They were due instead to restrictive clothing and the lack of fresh air and physical exercise that boys so freely enjoyed. In her rebuttal to Dr. Clarke's assertions, she cited untrained muscles, "kept inactive by the corset, weighted by the heavy skirt, and drawn upon by the violent and unnatural motion of the dancing at present in vogue," as the source of female complaints. One remedy that "again and again proved successful," she emphasized, was a vigorous athletic and physical exercise program "identical with that usually given boys."[14]

Opponents relentlessly continued the attack, especially in pseudo-scientific journals. In the 1880s Dr. William Hammond (1828-1900), a New York neurologist, published a series of articles in *Popular Science Monthly* attempting to prove that the brains of women were smaller and weaker than those of men. The implication was that an equal education was useless, ineffectual, and stressful. Feminist Helen Hamilton Gardener (1853-1925), with the help of another New York neurologist, Dr. Edward Spitzer, refuted Hammond's ideas in her article, "Sex in Brain." The difference in size was very little, she argued. Furthermore, the connection between brain weight and intelligence had yet to be established.[15]

In America the most effective antidote to Clarke and Maudsley was the award-winning thesis written by one of America's outstanding women physicians of the late nineteenth century, Dr. Mary Putnam Jacobi (1842-1906). Recipient of Harvard's Boylston Prize for the best scholarly manuscript of 1876, Jacobi's book, *The*

Question of Rest for Women During Menstruation, destroyed the myth that menstruation disabled women physically and intellectually. Written in response to Clarke's assertion concerning the delicate interaction between mind and reproductive functions, Jacobi found that "college-bred women were in nowise incapacitated for their habitual mental exertion."[16] Jacobi, like Garrett Anderson, moreover, provided a living refutation of Clarke's thesis. Wife, mother of two, author, and physician, she asserted and proved by personal example that higher education, professionalization, and motherhood were not only compatible, but increased the vitality of healthy women.[17]

Some influential physicians continued though to advise parents not to send their daughters to college or else their health might fail. S. Weir Mitchell (1829-1914), for example, a leading Philadelphia physician in the late nineteenth century specializing in "women's problems," prevented "many Philadelphia girls from coming to Bryn Mawr College," wrote M. Carey Thomas (1857-1935), future president of Bryn Mawr. Known extensively for his "rest cure" as a prescription for wide-ranging diseases in women, including neurasthenia and depression, Mitchell was responsible for sending many women to bed, sometimes for weeks or months, without books, visitors, or stimulation of any kind, serving ultimately to further debilitate them. One of his more famous patients, writer, philosopher, and feminist Charlotte Perkins Gilman (1860-1935), was led to the brink of insanity by his "rest cure," an event reflected in her classic short story, "The Yellow Wallpaper."[18] No woman, Dr. Mitchell told Carey Thomas at a dinner party, could study and remain healthy. "He admitted I looked well," Thomas reminisced, "but said he was convinced I had some secret disease that must show itself sooner or later."[19] As more and more women completed vigorous academic study, the medical establishment succeeded in planting the fear in English and American society that educating women like men would result in weakening them and ultimately sterilizing them. For women, anatomy was destiny, claimed Mitchell with the blessing of many in the medical establishment, and the consequences of defying this dictum would be disastrous.

While the question of whether a higher education was good for women was debated back and forth across the Atlantic, the underlying question of whether an educated woman was good for society was actually the issue. Opponents claimed that educated women would be a liability, particularly to the fundamental unit in Victorian society, the family. Since women who sought a higher education were those who fell within the "marriageable age," opponents saw their decision to pursue learning at this point in their lives as a direct challenge to the primary importance of women's domestic role. Oxford Professor Goldwin Smith (1823-1910) underlined the gravity of this issue for Victorian society when he warned the members of the American Social Science Association that the question of extending higher education to women should be approached with circumspection. "A false step in anything affecting the family," he cautioned, "is more serious than anything affecting politics."[20]

Parents, in this sense, were often the worst enemies of higher education for their daughters, fearing that an education would diminish their chances of marriage. Not only would their minds be tuned to ideals other than that of matrimony during this critical stage of their lives, but their intellectual accomplishments would render them unattractive. In England one writer's response to the first students at Hitchin in 1869 was typical: "There is no doubt that this sort of woman will not be popular with men." The new college would have his approval, he added, only "if the students were taught to sew, teach, keep house, read aloud, make their own dresses, etc."[21]

In America Annie Nathan Meyer (1867-1951), founder of Columbia University's Barnard College, recalled with deep sadness her father's reaction when as a young girl she announced her scholarly ambitions. "You will never be married," he told her. "Men hate intelligent wives."[22]

Likewise, English mothers, under heavy social pressure, harbored an intense fear of educating their daughters. Their plaints to those who sought higher education for young women in place of light instruction in the accomplishments became almost a cliché: "Now Miss _____, you must not make Augusta a blue[stocking]!"[23]

Should their daughters succeed in marriage, parents then argued, the time and money spent on their education would be wasted. Sending their daughters to college was not without cost. Far better, many concluded, to invest in training a daughter in the social graces with the goal of luring her a husband.[24]

Such parental attitudes were devastating to the cause of women's education, supporters complained. As one member of the Schools Inquiry Commission noted, "Although the world has existed several thousand years, the notion that women have minds as cultivatable and as well worth cultivating as men's minds is still regarded by the ordinary British parent as an offensive, not to say revolutionary paradox."[25]

In England conservative clergymen of the Church of England joined doctors and parents in condemning higher education for women. Any action on the part of a woman that distanced her from the sanctity of the family was viewed as unchristian. Thus in sermons and magazine articles members of the ministry exhorted women not to aspire to a university education, but to seek only spiritual enlightenment. "The mind of woman cannot be trained and perfected except by the education of the higher faculty of her spirit, which rises upward to communion and union with God, the fountain of all Truth and Love!" exclaimed one Anglican priest.[26]

The founding of the colleges and halls at Cambridge and Oxford, therefore, was a controversial step from the clergy's point of view, despite Newnham's and Lady Margaret Hall's affiliation with the church. In the words of Oxford theologian Henry Liddon (1829-1890), the founding of Lady Margaret Hall was "an educational development that runs counter to the wisdom and experience of all the centuries of Christendom."[27]

Opponents of women's higher education concurred in this assessment. Training at home remained the only valid answer to the question of female education. In England this view was expressed in the popular novels and tracts of Charlotte Yonge (1823-1901). An educated, cultivated woman, Yonge was representative of the conservative Anglican position and claimed home education was "far more valuable both intellectually and morally than any external education." Besides, she added, "superior women will teach themselves and inferior women will never learn more than enough for home life."[28]

Indeed, as M. Jeanne Peterson has found, many English women, primarily those of the upper class, enjoyed extensive training at home. Benefiting from their fathers' libraries, they studied an array of subjects from history, philosophy, literature, and science, to art and music, reading this material frequently in other languages.[29] But lack of systematic training and the freedom to pursue only the interests of the moment led some women, author and ethnologist Mary Kingsley (1862-1900) for example, to complain of having gained a disorderly, chaotic education.[30]

Later, in her book *Womankind,* Yonge said that if women were to be educated outside the home, then one should avoid educating them in proximity to male students. "There is a tendency," she explained, "in their large masses to rub off the tender home-bloom of maidenliness, which is a more precious thing than any proficiency in knowledge."[31]

Even supporters of women's education felt obliged to qualify the extent of training they believed should be granted. Schools Inquiry Commissioner Sir Joshua Fitch (1824-1903), who had attacked the wretched condition of girls' schools in 1869, voiced this tentative position: "If women asked for a system of mixed education, for admission to academic lectures, to the Bar, to the Church, or the Legislature," he warned, "the reply to such demands would be very simple. We cannot imperil the social order."[32]

Americans expressed similar views and sought ways to limit women's education. As late as 1874 at an anniversary celebration of the founding of Mount Holyoke Seminary, educator William Tyler affirmed that a woman "must be educated largely at home."[33] Like Yonge, Tyler emphasized that it was a woman's purity that was at risk: "Woman's person must be protected, her virgin purity preserved, and her womanly delicacy cultivated and cherished with the most sedulous care. Hence there should be less of publicity, more of retirement and seclusion in her education than in that of the other sex."[34]

To counter the long-held beliefs that tied women firmly to the home, American and English pioneers of higher education moved cautiously. They carefully fashioned their rhetoric in order to allay rather than kindle their opponents' fears. And above all they sought always to project conventional virtues and appropriate attitudes and behavior.

Advocates argued then that learning would make women better wives and mothers, thereby strengthening rather than weakening the family unit, as well as society. "The richness of resource, the discipline of temperament, the breadth and tolerance that makes the college graduate an efficient mother and a valuable social influence" are the true reasons behind a higher education, assured one proponent in America.[35] College girls, wrote another, will mold minds, modify manners, and help raise the moral tone of men and women. America, in particular, was in need of educated women, she added, for "the daughter of a mechanic frequently becomes in this country the mother of our most distinguished citizen. College, then, should turn her out 'fit' for whatever life shall bring."[36]

In England girls' educator Maria Grey argued that society was plagued with greater ills in the nineteenth century due to women's weakened influence. In order to effect positive changes, women's moral authority, enhanced by the enlightenment of higher education, was more necessary than ever. In its absence there was no way to "rescue men" from the crass materialism which "threatens to lower the tone of national character and to make us really what the first Napoleon accused us of being, 'a nation of shopkeepers.'"[37]

Women students and their female supporters in Victorian America and England remained, nonetheless, particularly vulnerable to allegations that their intellectual pursuits rendered them manly, indelicate, and unsexed. To deflate such attacks, they consciously maintained a demeanor of femininity and delicacy. The effectiveness of such behavior became apparent to Emily Davies and her friends when they reported on the inadequacies of female education to the Schools Inquiry Commission in 1865. Speaking before a group, especially one composed solely of men, was considered unseemly in Victorian England. But their soft-spoken and decorous testimony, especially that of Davies' colleague, Frances Mary Buss, made a lasting impression on the commissioners. One recalled, "We were all so much struck by their perfect womanliness. Why there were tears in Miss Buss's eyes!"[38]

To help project an air of "perfect womanliness," these pioneers paid scrupulous attention to their dress and appearance. Elizabeth Garrett, during her temporary internship at Middlesex Hospital in London, was particularly sensitive to this, due to her awkward position as the only woman student. In a letter to Davies concerning a mutual friend, she wrote, "She looks awfully strong-minded in walking dress . . . she has short petticoats and close round hat, and several other dreadfully ugly arrangements. . . . It is abominable, and most damaging to the cause." Later she concluded, "I feel confident now that one is helped rather than hindered by being as much like a lady as lies in one's power."[39]

Davies agreed. She would go to great length to avoid unwanted appearances. Finding once her five ladies engaged in a game of football on the lawn in front of Benslow House in Hitchin, she strictly forbade a recurrence, fearing that "football for ladies would shock the world, if it were known."[40] After all, wrote Constance Maynard, an early student of Girton and founder of London's Westfield College, "the conventionalities of the age . . . were the best possible shelter for the new aspirations."[41]

All students, therefore, were strictly inspected for the proper dress and chaperoned when attending university lectures or social events. It was imperative, explained a founder of Lady Margaret Hall, Oxford, that nothing happen to feed the prejudice against "the supposed 'blue-stockings' who were invading Oxford. For several years," she continued, "the education of us elder ladies should have been greatly improved by the number of lectures we had to attend as chaperones."[42]

Equally strict in terms of decorum were the women's colleges in America. A pamphlet filed in the Vassar collection of memorabilia indicates the duties of the Lady Principal. She was to judge the propriety of her students' social calls and guard against "coarse or insipid frivolities of rustic and fashionable talk."[43] A special platform was placed in her quarters so that the proper length of students' skirts could be assured before they left the dormitory.[44] As Inez Irwin explained (1873-1970), "The eyes of the world were upon them; and all Vassar, faculty and students alike, found it incumbent to adopt a painfully ladylike attitude."[45]

Smith students, likewise, were warned to desist from any impropriety. Visits from friends at Amherst were forbidden, as were walks "merely for pleasure." Sunday strolls, the students were instructed, were allowed only if they led to the church.[46]

To avoid further arousing the vociferous opposition, pioneers in women's education in the 1870s in both America and England addressed the question of women's suffrage with ambivalence. For some college women, supporting women's enfranchisement seemed too radical a step to take. For many, however, the cause of women's suffrage was valid and worthy of attention, but too risky at this stage in the development of women's higher education to promote. "Few women," Elaine Kendall explains, "could afford the luxury of advocating two causes, and the right to education was still too fragile to jeopardize."[47]

In America the administrators of the women's colleges, as well as the majority of students, dissociated themselves from the issue of women's suffrage, Vassar even forbidding its discussion. Although a few Vassar students, such as Harriet Stanton (1856-1940), daughter of Elizabeth Cady Stanton, campaigned among students on behalf of the franchise, most remained neutral, if not opposed, throughout the late nineteenth century.[48]

The response among English women in higher education was similar. Emily Davies, an avowed feminist and early supporter of the Parliamentary vote for women, chose in 1867 to withdraw completely from suffrage activities. While she disapproved of the "radical" elements entering the suffrage movement, it seems that Davies' main concern was the success of her plan for women's education. Determined to achieve her goal, she allowed nothing to interfere.[49] Davies never lost interest in the question of the franchise, however, and by the turn of the century began again publicly advocating the cause and writing on its behalf.[50]

Other women educators in England, such as William Wordsworth's niece, Elizabeth Wordsworth (1840-1932) of Lady Margaret Hall, and A. J. Clough (1820-1892) of Newnham, chose to ignore or oppose the issue of the Parliamentary vote for women. Instead, they focused their efforts on the single cause of women's intellectual liberation. Believing this to be the key to women's larger role in society, most pioneers pursued a quiet activism within the walls of academe.

Notes

1.   Caroline Dall, *The College, the Market, and the Court; or, Woman's Relationship to Education, Labor, and Law* (Boston: Lee and Shepard, 1868; repr., New York: Arno Press, 1972), 42.

2.   Manton, 96-111.

3.   By the nineteenth century the practice of medicine in both countries had become a male profession. In America this represented a transformation from the colonial period when, in the new, unstructured society, women's work had included the healing arts, notably midwifery. Women's participation in medical practice did not last long, however. By the early nineteenth century, medicine in America was becoming a "learned profession," as it had been for centuries in England, and hence by definition open to men only. Gradually, with professionalization, obstetrics too--certainly in urban, middle class communities--came to be dominated by men. With professionalization of the healing arts, women were considered effective as nurses, but unfit to be physicians. Those who challenged this presumption, such as Elizabeth Blackwell and Elizabeth Garrett, therefore met severe hostility. The medical practitioners, moreover, who opposed women's participation in higher education, often describing the ill effects in macabre, if not gothic tones, were men. See *In Her Own Words: Oral Histories of Women Physicians,* eds. Regina Markell Morantz, Cynthia Stodola Pomerleau, and Carol Hansen Fenichel (Westport, Conn.: Greenwood Press, 1982), 3-21.

4.   For a full discussion of the many arguments concerning women's education and reproductive health, see Joan N. Burstyn, *Victorian Education and the Ideal of Womanhood* (London: Croom Helm, 1980), 84-98.

5.   Edward H. Clarke, *Sex in Education; Or, a Fair Chance for the Girls* (Boston: James R. Osgood and Co., 1873; repr., New York: Arno Press, 1972). For responses to his book,

see Julia Ward Howe, ed., *Sex and Education: A Reply to Dr. E. H. Clarke's "Sex in Education"* (Boston: Roberts Brothers, 1874; repr., New York: Arno Press, 1972).

6. Clarke, 17-18.
7. Ibid., 134-161.
8. Ibid., 41.
9. Edward H. Clarke, *The Building of a Brain* (Boston, 1874). See Elizabeth K. Helsinger, Robin Lauterbach Sheets, and William Veeder, *The Woman Question: Defining Voices, 1837-1883* (New York and London: Garland Publishing, Inc., 1983), 88-89.
10. Henry Maudsley, "Sex in Mind and Education," *Fortnightly Review,* April 1874, 476.
11. Ibid., 477. Joan Burstyn has noted an interesting coincidence concerning Clarke and Maudsley: "In the same year that each man wrote against women undertaking higher education, his institution agreed to allow women, for the first time, to take examinations under its auspices: the Harvard Corporation, in 1873, agreed to a request from the Women's Educational Association of Boston that women be permitted to take examinations similar to the Oxford and Cambridge local examinations, and University College London, in 1874, agreed to grant certificates, on the results of examinations, to women students attending courses at the college." See Burstyn, 85-86.
12. Elizabeth Garrett Anderson, "Sex in Mind and Education: A Reply," *Fortnightly Review,* May 1874, 590.
13. Ibid., 590-591.
14. Howe, *Sex and Education,* 29. To counter the attacks by the "friends of the female sex" who envisioned a "host of broken down women," colleges for women without exception instituted vigorous physical education programs. "A gymnasium, if not the first thing provided, was soon added, as a precaution against ill health," states Woody, 2: 116-117.
15. Helen Hamilton Gardener, *Facts and Fictions of Life* (Boston: Arena Publishing Co., 1895), 96-125.

16.   Mary Putnam Jacobi, *The Question of Rest During Menstruation,* quoted in Joyce Antler, *The Educated Woman and Professionalization: The Struggle for a New Feminine Identity 1890-1920* (New York: Garland Publishing Inc., 1987), 31.

17.   *In Her Own Words,* 20.

18.   Mitchell's rest cure had its ill effects on other famous women, including Jane Addams (1860-1935). See Woloch, 256 and Ann Douglas Wood, "'The Fashionable Diseases': Women's Complaints and Their Treatment in Nineteenth-Century America," in Hartman and Banner, 1–22.

19.   Marjorie Housepian Dobkin, ed. *The Making of a Feminist: Early Journals and Letters of M. Carey Thomas* (Kent State University Press, 1979), 304.

20.   Goldwin Smith, "University Education," *Journal of Social Science* 1 (June 1869): 54.

21.   Quoted in Bremner, 131.

22.   Annie Nathan Meyer, *Barnard Beginnings* (Boston and New York: Houghton Mifflin Co., 1935), 16.

23.   Quoted in Grey, 18 and Menella B. Smedley, "The English Girl's Education," *Contemporary Review* 14 (Spring 1870): 31.

24.   For the prevalence of this attitude on the part of English parents, see Grey, 19. Women, she complained, "are not educated to be wives, but to get husbands."

25.   Ibid., 17.

26.   Christopher Wordsworth, *Christian Womanhood and Christian Sovereignty* (London: n.p., 1884), 39.

27.   Quoted in Brittain, 50.

28.   Quoted in Stephen, 167-68.

29.   M. Jeanne Peterson, *Family, Love, and Work in the Lives of Victorian Gentlewomen* (Bloomington and Indianapolis: Indiana University Press, 1989), 187.

30.   Ibid., 41. Self-education has always been an option for truly resourceful, aspiring women. Certainly some of America's most gifted women benefited from self and home

education. Late nineteenth-century feminist Charlotte Perkins Gilman and reformer Florence Kelley (1859-1932) are two notable examples.

31. Quoted in Stephen, 204.

32. Quoted in Blease, 109.

33. William S. Tyler, "The Higher Education of Women," *Scribner's Monthly,* February 1874, 458.

34. Ibid.

35. Kate Holladay Claghorn, *College Training for Women* (New York: Thomas Y. Crowell and Co., 1897), 252.

36. Mary Caroline Crawford, *The College Girl of America and the Institutions Which Make Her What She Is* (Boston: L.C. Page and Co., 1905), ix.

37. Grey, 26.

38. Quoted in Stephen, 137.

39. Ibid., 59.

40. Ibid., 225.

41. Quoted in Sara Delamont, "The Contradictions in Ladies' Education," in *The Nineteenth Century Woman: Her Cultural and Physical World,* eds. Sara Delamont and Lorna Duffin (London: Croom Helm, 1978), 147.

42. Gemma Bailey, ed., *A Short History of Lady Margaret Hall 1879-1923* (Oxford: privately printed, 1923), 50-51, quoted in *The Nineteenth Century Woman: Her Cultural and Physical World,* 147. For amusing anecdotes concerning the system of chaperones at lectures in the early years of the women's colleges, see Brittain, 75, 92. Cambridge women, in often subtle ways, chose to express their disdain for society's constricting prohibitions on female behavior. The women of Newnham College, for example, challenging Victorian England's negative regard for Euripides and the forces of chaos and irrationality he exposed, overrode the principal's veto and defiantly performed *Electra*. Fearing a public reaction, Anne Clough attempted to halt the performance. The students persisted, perhaps, as Sandra Peacock suggests, to defy convention and through the

matricide theme, to defy their surrogate mother on campus. Peacock, 45.

43.   Quoted in Kendall, 107.
44.   Ibid., 107.
45.   Inez Haynes Irwin, *Angels and Amazons: A Hundred Years of American Women* (Garden City, N.Y.: Doubleday, Doran, and Co., Inc., 1933; repr., New York: Arno Press, 1974), 122.
46.   Kendall, 113.
47.   Ibid., 126.
48.   Solomon, 111.
49.   Herstein, 166.
50.   For her views on women's suffrage, see Davies, 201-207.

CHAPTER 5

THE PROMISE OF EQUAL EDUCATION IN AMERICA

As interest in women's higher education began to grow in post-Civil War America, separate women's colleges gained public support and acceptance, largely since these schools upheld the ideal of separate spheres. Many of these colleges, especially those in the Northeast, claimed to offer an education equal to that of the best men's colleges. But a number of advocates of women's education argued that separate was not equal. Though improving academically and gradually phasing out their preparatory programs and "special" students, these separate institutions were dismissed by proponents of equal education as petty and temporary.[1] Demanding that men and women study the same curriculum under the same professors and "contend together for the same rank and honours," outspoken reformers such as Susan B. Anthony (1820-1906), Lucy Stone, Elizabeth Cady Stanton, and Julia Ward Howe prescribed coeducation as the only means of reaching the ideal of equal education.[2] Countering the traditional arguments that mixed education would compromise a woman's sense of modesty and place in the social order, as well as diminish her feminine appeal, supporters of coeducation argued that this system would relieve the sexual tension engendered by cloistered institutions and would promote wholesome, positive interaction between men and women. Elizabeth Cady Stanton summarized these convictions by claiming, "If the sexes were educated together we should have the healthy, moral and intellectual stimulus of sex everquickening and refining all the faculties, without the undue excitement of senses that results from novelty in the present system of isolation."[3]

But coeducation, especially in the South and the elite male institutions of the Northeast, was slow to evolve. In those institutions where it was adopted, moreover, coeducation did not always mean equal educational opportunity.

The development of coeducation in America can only fully be understood in light of the changing nature of American universities in the nineteenth century. Like Cambridge and Oxford, many colleges and universities across the United States found themselves in a state of flux, increasingly challenged by society to undergo reform and revitalization. The United States had inherited its intellectual tradition from England, with its fixed curriculum of Greek, Latin, mathematics, logic, and moral philosophy. The time-honored classical education, considered the proper training for clergymen, statesmen, and gentlemen, had been adopted by America's early institutions of higher education.

But as Laurence Veysey points out in *The Emergence of the American University,* the classical course of training was perceived more and more as an archaic relic in the dynamic, unintellectual, and increasingly materialistic population of nineteenth-century America. And in place of growing strength and numbers, American colleges experienced diminishing influence and static enrollments from the Jacksonian period until the 1870s.[4] The popular caricature of the "rumpled professor" secluded in his ivory tower, out of touch with mainstream America, reflected the common view of academic life during this era. Nineteenth-century colleges were generally small, isolated from bustling commercial centers, and, as late as 1870, attracted just over 1 percent of the traditional college-age population.[5]

Part of this decline may be attributed to the traditional link in America between higher education and the ministry. America's first colleges and universities had been founded by the established denominations—Presbyterian, Congregationalist, and Episcopalian-for the intended, if not expressed, purpose of training the clergy, the most learned and revered profession in seventeenth– and eighteenth–century America. In the nineteenth century, the shift in the cultural climate towards a commercial, competitive, individualistic society rendered the formerly respected, intellectually elite ministry less prominent, forcing them to adopt the non-intellectual ecclesiastical style of the now-booming Methodist and Baptist populations. The dwindling stature of the established clergy signalled, then, the loss of intellectualism as a cultural force in America.[6] Ironically, the rise in materialism in the United States and the concomitant decline in intellectualism would lead to a new perception of the role of the university in American society, a role that would increasingly include the participation of women.

In the 1850s and 1860s a new breed of academic leaders emerged that would guide institutions of higher education into this new phase. As knowledge began to expand at a rapid rate during these decades, the old curriculum remained only a small portion of the ever-widening fields of inquiry. The new disciplines of biology, physiology and hygiene, chemistry, physics, astronomy, geology, modern languages and humanities, engineering, and agriculture were soon integrated into the university, and for the first time laboratory work began to accompany classroom instruction.[7]

A new vision of the university began gradually to take shape, then, in the second half of the nineteenth century, a vision which entailed, according to Veysey, three specific conceptions, namely practical public service, research, and the educational ideal of culture, borrowed from England and Germany.[8]

Political efforts in Washington supported these new goals, particularly that of practical education. In 1862 President Lincoln signed the Morrill Land Grant Act to promote "the liberal and practical education of the industrial classes in the several pursuits and professions of life."[9] Under the Morrill Act, the federal government made public lands available to states that created universities offering agricultural and mechanical programs. The second Morrill Act of 1890 stipulated that federal funds be divided fairly between blacks and whites. Both acts, without specific mention of women, significantly relaxed the barriers of class and race that had fortified the gates to higher education. Taking advantage of the drive to expand the college population, as well as the introduction of "practical" studies that would lead to "public service," women benefited from the reforms that swept the halls of higher education in the second half of the nineteenth century.[10]

The changing profile of the college student of the nineteenth century first became visible at Oberlin College in 1837, as women and blacks entered the halls of "God's College." Women, however, did not always partake fully of the curriculum required of Oberlin's men, following instead the less demanding Ladies' Course.[11] In 1857 the coeducational Antioch College was founded in Ohio under the guidance of Horace Mann (1796-1859). Unlike many educators of the mid-nineteenth century, Mann had no hesitations concerning the ability of women to gain an equal education or the importance of such a step. Envisioning his college as a "Grand Experiment," Mann required women and men to take the same classes and to recite together.[12]

In spite of his ideal of equal education, Mann increasingly expressed the fear of misconduct and impropriety that was potentially present in a mixed group such as Antioch's. This fear led Mann to place restrictions on the social contact between the men and women of Antioch. The behavior, therefore, of the women was under intense scrutiny as they functioned within the strict limitations of the Antioch social code.

Mann frequently expressed ambivalent opinions concerning the purposes of education for men and women. Although both followed the same curriculum, Mann often referred to the divergent paths that each would follow upon graduation. Women, he explained, were to be educated to perform the duties of their sphere, in the home and the classroom. While outwardly offering equal education, Antioch in its early years devised a "hidden curriculum" that directed women towards their traditional roles.

Many of the women who eagerly sought to participate in Mann's "Grand Experiment" found themselves at odds with the administration. Rejecting the limitations placed upon their social lives, their educational activities beyond the classroom, and their professional expectations, some women expressed their discontent. Upon hearing the protests against the narrow definitions of women's roles, Mann and his administrators reacted with shock. If women expected their education at Antioch to release them from the domestic sphere, then the "Grand Experiment" was a failure from Mann's point of view. Should he believe that education would lead a woman beyond her traditional role, he told one student, then "he was doing very wrong in remaining at the head of a coed school." Understandably, Antioch alumna Olympia Brown "wondered much that a professed advocate of coeducation was so disinclined to face its obvious results."[13]

Before the Civil War certain state universities in the Midwest stated that they too would admit women, but only the University of Iowa did so at this time, opening in 1855 with four women in the collegiate department. As Mabel Newcomer notes, Iowa has the longest record of coeducation among state universities.[14] But the record was not always one of harmony and sympathy. In 1858, for example, the Board of Directors adopted a resolution "excluding females from the university after the close of the term."[15] Although rejected, the resolution illustrates the undercurrent of resentment women encountered at Iowa.

Historians agree that economic reasons provided the impetus for admitting women to state universities during and just after the Civil War. The decline in enrollment brought by the war "weakened resistance," as Newcomer explains, and forced universities to admit women in order to survive. By 1870 eight state universities had allowed women entry, but as Iowa had demonstrated, their presence, especially in large numbers, was not always accepted.[16]

The University of Wisconsin, for instance, having opened the collegiate course to women in 1863, established a separate women's college four years later with limited course offerings. In 1869, when six women had completed the requirements for a degree, Wisconsin's President Chadbourne exclaimed he would not "be guilty of the absurdity of calling young women bachelors." He acquiesced, however, when informed that one definition of "bachelor" was "a young unmarried woman," and granted the women their degrees.[17] In 1873, after a boycott by women, Wisconsin recognized the inconvenience and expense of maintaining the separate college and again became coeducational. The spectre of separation would rise again in 1906, however, when the number of women rose to 50 percent of the student body. After a decrease of 10 percent in the male population, Wisconsin's president tried to institute separate classes. A protest among alumnae prevented this action.[18]

At the University of Missouri women entered full academic life in stages. Admitted to the normal department in 1870, they spent one probationary year proving they would do "no manner of harm." The president then "cautiously admitted them to some of the recitations and lectures in the university building itself, providing always they were to be marched in good order, with at least two teachers, one in front and the other in the rear of the column as guards."[19] Even more time passed before women could attend the library and chapel in the presence of men without rigid supervision.[20]

The story of the University of Michigan's admission of women began with its original 1837 charter, which called for a female department. No funds were appropriated for the department, however, even though petitions were presented to the university throughout the 1850s to open it. It was not until $100,000 had been raised in 1870 by women lobbyists as an incentive to honor the university statutes that Michigan softened its resistance to women. The resignation that year of President Henry Tappan, a staunch opponent of coeducation, also helped break the barrier. In the next administration, the University of Michigan became, in the words of Barbara Solomon, "one of the most desirable academic places for women to study."[21]

Another coeducational college opening in the 1860s was unique among all those of this time. In March 1867 President Andrew Johnson signed a bill to incorporate Howard University in the District of Columbia and by April the university opened, serving black men and women, as well as whites. The first women to enter Howard, interestingly, were five white women who matriculated through the normal department, or teacher training program. Although Howard was unusual in extending educational opportunities to such a diversity of students, traditional gender patterns soon took shape as the majority of women remained in the normal department. Howard later would be noted for the women graduates, black and white, of its law school.[22]

One of the new institutions in the 1860s that also aspired to become a desirable place for women to study was Cornell University in Ithaca, New York. Its founder, Ezra Cornell (1807-1874), hoped to build a college that would "prove highly beneficial to the poor young men and women of our country."[23] But Cornell did not take women at first, having more men students than it could accommodate. President Andrew White (1832-1918) promised at opening ceremonies in 1868, however, that the university would soon admit women, saying he was "perfectly willing to undertake the experiment as soon as it shall be possible to do so."[24]

Since Cornell's president was committed to opening a university to students that were poor, female, or both, he won the support of Elizabeth Cady Stanton and Susan B. Anthony. They hoped that this university would provide a truly equal education for women, unlike others of the time. To encourage such efforts, Anthony visited Cornell in 1869 and spoke on the importance of equal education, predicting that when Cornell became coeducational, that day would become as celebrated as the Fourth of July.[25]

Astronomer Maria Mitchell also encouraged Cornell to implement coeducation as soon as possible. Although she was a professor at Vassar College, Mitchell wrote the university's founder explaining that even Vassar, the best college of its kind, was not offering women an equivalent education. Having heard from Harvard's president that it would be at least twenty years before his university would admit women, Mitchell urged Ezra Cornell to hasten the process in Ithaca.[26]

The arrival in 1870 of a young woman named Jennie Spencer forced the issue. As the recipient of a state scholarship, she was entitled to admission to the university. Unfortunately, there was no place on the Cornell campus to house her, the halls already overcrowded with men students, so she took a room in Ithaca. Spencer soon tired of the long, arduous hillside journey she had to make several times a day in long skirts and petticoats and reluctantly left Cornell.[27]

It was in this way that the practical aspects of introducing coeducation at Cornell came to the attention of Henry Sage, philanthropist and financial consultant to Ezra Cornell. A self-made businessman, Sage came from a poor family with a number of dependent women. He understood, therefore, the value of education for achieving self-sufficiency and deplored the lack of such opportunity for women. Hoping that Cornell University could help remedy this need, Sage offered the university $250,000 on the condition that "instruction shall be afforded to young women . . . as broad and as thorough as that now afforded to young men."[28]

Women were formally admitted to Cornell in April of that year. At first they profited from the same broad and thorough instruction afforded the men and were judged according to their ability, not their gender. A subtle change took place in the late 1870s, however, when Cornell experienced a decline in female enrollment and ensuing financial difficulties. The beautiful residence made possible by Henry Sage's munificence was not full as anticipated and the administration sought ways to occupy it to capacity. In 1884 the university began requiring women to live in Sage College, as it was known, rather than allowing them to choose their residence. At the same time Cornell sought to alleviate parental fears of coeducation by imposing special restrictions on female students. Surely, the administration hoped, with the new rules the enrollment would increase.

Other restrictions were imposed by male students. No longer content to view Cornell as a place "beneficial to poor young men and poor young women," they sought to transform it into Harvard and Yale's rival in academic and social prestige. The presence of female students was regarded as detrimental to achieving this objective. Women were thus excluded from social activities, organizations, and committees. Separated socially, the women of Cornell would by 1902 face academic segregation, as well. In accord with the general academic trend in America, the majority would be channeled into feminized courses of study.[29]

Cornell was not alone among the rising number of eastern coeducational universities in placing restrictions on women students. Colby College in Maine, an institution that "opened its doors to young women on precisely the same terms as men" in 1871, had by 1890 separated women into special courses and departments so that they might "cease to compete with men for scholarly position."[30] After originally offering equal education to their students, the administration and faculty concluded nineteen years later that "an ideal college course for young men would not be an ideal course for young women, any more than the training which would be most advantageous for a bass singer would be advisable for a soprano voice."[31]

A group of alumnae, protesting the action at Colby, asked in 1890 if this change in attitude would have occurred "if the young women had shown only mediocrity instead of excellence."[32] Probably not, they concluded. But by carrying away most of the academic honors under the original coeducational plan, they had made their male colleagues uncomfortable. Now that the women of Colby posed a possible threat to future enrollment, they would have to be separated.[33]

Once again, women were judged by their good work, but instead of earning appreciation, their work became a source of provocation. The growing number of women in academe and their increasing success became disconcerting on campuses like Colby that had earlier boasted of their commitment to coeducation. The fear that their institution would become a women's college led the administration of Wesleyan, another coeducational university in the East, to impose quotas on the number of women admitted. In 1900 Wesleyan's president stated that his university, while not abandoning coeducation, would consider "changes in the direction of differentiation to a certain extent between the male and female students." Wesleyan was ready, he continued, "to concede that there are sound objections to subjecting the men and the women to identical discipline in every particular."[34] The university then adopted a policy of "partial separation" of a limited number of women, hoping to restore the endowment and "confidence in the future of the university."[35]

A few of Wesleyan's male students expressed pride in their institution's progressive role in equal education. "To our University belongs the glory of having dared to test the system first among Eastern colleges," wrote one man to the student newspaper. To most of the men, however, coeducation was a source of embarrassment. In 1909 Wesleyan ceased accepting women students. Coeducation would not return to Wesleyan until 1972.[36]

Similarly, the University of Chicago forsook the ideal of full coeducation in 1901 when the administration began segregating undergraduate classes. Before this time Chicago had assumed a leading role in coeducation, actively seeking both female students and faculty. When women accounted for 52 percent of the enrollment, however, male faculty and students became concerned. Even worse, the majority of Phi Beta Kappa recipients had recently been women.

Chicago's solution was to form separate classes for freshmen and sophomores, the first step in a gradual transition. "But when it has been completed," said *The School Journal,* "men and women will never meet in class, at lectures, or at chapel."[37] The expense and organization of separate classes soon proved cumbersome and by 1907 coeducation was restored in all but the largest elementary courses.[38]

Such organizational schemes were not uncommon in colleges and universities where women threatened to equal or excel men in numbers and honors. The trend was evident across the country, from Boston to Wisconsin to California. Between 1870 and 1900 the number of women entering institutions of higher learning rose from 11,000 to 85,000, and the rate of increase of women attending college was greater than that of men. The majority of women, moreover, chose to enter coeducational universities. But these institutions preferred women in the minority. When the number of women began to match that of men, the schools attempted to enact changes in organization and policy to exclude them from full participation.[39]

The schemes were by and large impractical, as Chicago's experience had shown, and were rejected by alumnae and certain students and faculty members. The fact that plans to reverse coeducation were implemented in so many institutions originally receptive to women indicates that equal access to higher education for American women was still not a reality early in the twentieth century.

For those who could not accept full coeducation and yet scorned the weaknesses of separate women's colleges, the idea of a coordinate college, modeled after the women's colleges at Cambridge and Oxford, seemed a worthy compromise. Such was the solution offered by Harvard University when pressured to admit women. Like the women of Oxford and Cambridge, the wives, daughters, and sisters of the Harvard faculty began requesting instruction in the 1870s. Although Boston University and Wellesley College were opening nearby, women in and around Cambridge, Massachusetts, preferred the older institution. In 1874 Harvard responded to women by administering examinations to those who had received private instruction from sympathetic Harvard professors, as Cambridge had done for the women of Girton. This step led logically to a request for the entry of women to Harvard as regular students.

The university, unwilling to risk coeducation, opened the Harvard Annex for women in 1879. By 1894 the Annex had evolved into Radcliffe, Harvard's sister college. The Cambridge University example was often cited, lending validity to the coordinate plan at Harvard. Radcliffe was to be a "regularly equipped college for women in a similar relation to Harvard as that of Girton at Cambridge University."[40] But at Radcliffe, women were contained on their own campus, while men from the Harvard faculty conducted classes. The request from women's groups that Radcliffe women receive the equivalent of a Harvard degree was refused. Instead, the college was to issue its own diploma countersigned by the president of Harvard.[41]

For those seeking an equal education for women, the Harvard compromises were profoundly disappointing. President Charles Eliot (1834-1926) had inspired their hopes in 1892 when he suggested that women solicit money to make their inclusion at Harvard a realistic possibility. A group of active women, including educator and former Wellesley president Alice Freeman Palmer (1855-1902), responded to his idea by raising $250,000. The Harvard corporation, however, declined the gift.[42]

The coordinate plan provided an answer for other institutions seeking ways to avoid coeducation. Columbia University, justifying its action, like Harvard, by recalling the English precedent, chartered Barnard College for women in 1889. Barnard women, though, earned degrees bestowed by Columbia University, making Barnard unique among affiliate colleges.[43] Coordinate arrangements were also made in other schools that had begun as coeducational institutions, notably, Flora Mather College of Western Reserve University, Jackson College of Tufts University, and the Women's College of Rochester University. In New Orleans, Sophie Newcomb Memorial College for Women was founded as an affiliate of Tulane University. Newcomb, however, in contrast to other coordinate colleges, maintained its own faculty.[44]

In a few cases the inclusion of women through a coordinate compromise was not even acceptable. Such was the case at the University of Virginia. The state of Virginia was especially in need of higher education for women in the late nineteenth century, offering opportunities only at Randolph-Macon College for Women, a few state-supported normal schools, and a couple of small private coeducational colleges. None of the four state-supported colleges—William and Mary, Washington and Lee, Virginia Military Institute, or the University of Virginia—admitted women. In the 1880s, upon faculty recommendations, attempts were made then to secure female admission to the university. After their defeat a women's committee led by Mary Munford (1865-1935) submitted five bills to the legislature between 1910 and 1920 urging the establishment of a coordinate school.

Virginian Mary Munford, like many women of her time, had longed for a college education, but had been unable to overcome family resistance to gain it. After her marriage, she devoted her efforts to opening quality higher educational opportunities for women and led a highly organized movement to sway the Virginia legislature to implement her cause. But an equally effective opposition movement composed of university alumni met each of these proposals with rebuffs that resurrected all the old arguments against the education of women. A bitter controversy ensued that extended beyond the state lines, as supporters and opponents of a coordinate facility rallied their forces. In a 136-page booklet, Munford's committee published letters of support from such disparate individuals as Woodrow Wilson and the deans of the women's colleges and halls at Oxford University. Mary Munford would not live, though, to see her dream a reality. Her petition to gain women's entrance to the graduate programs at the University of Virginia, however, was granted in 1920. It was not until 1970 that the University of Virginia admitted women to its undergraduate program.[45]

Where coeducation and coordinate plans met with resistance, educated women proved adept at finding alternatives. Such steps were a necessity in parts of the South, where by 1912 only seven state universities were coeducational. In Mississippi Annie C. Peyton's agitation in the late 1870s for an institution for women resulted in the creation of the first state-supported college for women, Mississippi State College for Women. MSCW then became a model for other state colleges for women, notably Florida State College for Women and Georgia State College for Women.[46]

Despite, then, the introduction of coeducation in America in the latter half of the nineteenth century, separateness remained the trend of women's education into the twentieth century. For men and women who saw this as detrimental to women educationally and professionally, equal education would remain a distant goal.

Outstanding among those who devoted their lives to achieving equal education in the nineteenth and early twentieth century was M. Carey Thomas. Paradoxically, the greater part of her career was spent as president of a separate women's institution, Bryn Mawr College in Pennsylvania, founded in 1885. Perhaps in energy, determination, and vision, she was equaled only by England's Emily Davies, and like her, Thomas succeeded in shaping an institution where the intellectual development of women, so often impeded by the existence of ladies' programs or special female departments, reached new heights of excellence.

Under her direction Bryn Mawr became what has been described as "the most difficult school in the United States to enter and the most difficult to graduate from."[47] Requiring entrance examinations that exceeded in difficulty those given at any American men's college, Thomas also demanded unsurpassed scholarship, refusing even to institute a Phi Beta Kappa chapter since every student was expected to be deserving of such distinction.[48] It was Thomas's hope that the Bryn Mawr student would become "as well-known and universally admired a type as the Oxford and Cambridge man."[49] Indeed, the Bryn Mawr type did become known and admired across America and helped pave the way for the acceptance of women as equals in academic life.

Bryn Mawr enjoyed recognition in England, as well. English author and educator Sara Burstall (1859-1939) wrote admiringly of Bryn Mawr in her critical survey of American colleges and universities: "The faculty consists of men and women of very high standing, including graduates of the great German universities, Zurich, Johns Hopkins, Harvard, Cambridge (England), a distinguished Newnham student and the only woman who has taken the Doctor of Science in mathematics at the University of London." By way of comparison, Burstall noted that the entrance examination of undergraduates was "nearly equivalent to the matriculation examination of the University of London."[50]

Carey Thomas's interest in higher education began in her childhood. For as long as she could remember, she later told her students at Bryn Mawr, she had longed to go to college. She had even prayed to God "that if it were true that because I was a girl I could not successfully master Greek and go to college and understand things, to kill me at once."[51] Precocious and resolute, M. Carey Thomas had no trouble mastering all the subjects necessary to enter higher education, but opposition soon arose in the form of family and societal resistance to her plan. Finding her desire to go to college "as shocking a choice as a life of prostitution," the Thomas clan, with the exception of her mother, offered little encouragement.[52]

With all her fortitude, the young Thomas occasionally trembled at the prospect of becoming a college woman. As she told her students, "We were haunted in those early days by the clanging chains of that gloomy little spectre, Dr. Edward H. Clarke's *Sex in Education.*"[53] Fearfully, she paid a visit to the first "college woman" she had ever known. But "even if she had appeared in hoofs and horns," Thomas recounted, "I was determined to go to college all the same."[54]

Her determination overcame family resistance and Thomas entered Cornell University in 1876. Having rejected Vassar College as an advanced seminary, Thomas chose the coeducational Cornell as the superior institution. Though pleased with her choice, Thomas was not immune to the difficulties inherent in the role of a pioneer, for "there is much that is hard for a lady in a mixed university and I should not subject any girl to it unless she were determined to have it." She concluded, however, that even though "it is a fiery ordeal to educate a lady by coeducation . . . it is the only way and learning *is worth it.*"[55]

After Cornell, Thomas, having been denied access to graduate school in America, pursued advanced study in Europe, receiving her Ph.D. in philosophy from the University of Zurich. The first woman to earn a doctorate at Zurich, Thomas surprised herself and the institution by graduating Summa Cum Laude.[56] While winning honors in Europe, Thomas heard from her mother that family friends considered her "a disgrace" to the Thomas clan for following such a course.

As first dean and later president of Bryn Mawr College, Thomas resolved that her students should not suffer the fear, the obstacles, and the "disgrace" that she had endured. Her mission was to create a new college woman whose image would obliterate the caricature of the unsexed, monstrous learned woman that sprouted "hoofs and horns" upon entering college. Articulate and uncompromising, Thomas, through quiet talks with students, weekly chapel presentations, and her stately presence on campus, succeeded in molding her students into an ideal.[57] Long after her retirement one alumna wrote to her, "I still see you standing in chapel and telling us to believe in women."[58] By the 1890s the ideal of the Bryn Mawr student received public recognition and was celebrated in newspapers and periodicals such as *Godey's Lady's Book* and *The Home Maker.*[59]

College women throughout America benefited from Thomas's efforts, for, as Barbara Cross relates, "By the time her presidency had ended, the 'college woman' had emerged upon the scene as a distinct and privileged species of femininity."[60] By then Thomas had not only built a women's college of great distinction, but had brought educated women visibility, recognition, and respect. She had succeeded in proving that women, when given the opportunity, were capable of excelling academically and professionally. Women, she hoped, would not be the only benefactors of her work, but the entire human race, as well. "I am convinced," she wrote in 1908, "that we can do no more useful work than this, to make it possible for the few women of creative and constructive genius born in any generation to join the few men of genius of their generation in the service of their common race."[61]

Thomas's work in women's education would continue beyond the Bryn Mawr campus. Helping organize the International Federation of University Women after her retirement, she told those gathered at its first meeting in London in 1920, "The very first step that university women should now take seems to me to be the demand for unqualified, true, out and out coeducation."[62]

Thomas had devoted her years to gaining the acceptance of women in higher education. She had helped achieve this goal by creating a women's college unexcelled in academic prestige. But she looked forward to a time when there would be no need for separate colleges, "when women would gain more than they would lose by entering the more fully endowed great universities."[63] Continued separation, she argued, would bring a decline in the quality of education for both men and women. Her next step, then, through her work in the new international federation, was to help women worldwide attain the best education possible. "Only by having the schools and universities coeducational," she asserted, "can we ensure the girls of the world of receiving a thoroughly good education."[64]

Emily Davies would have agreed. Now, in 1920, at the age of ninety, she was retired in Hampstead and unable to make public appearances, such as the London conference. But her work and that of M. Carey Thomas had touched many common chords. Like Thomas, Davies had sought to shape an institution for women that in every respect was the equal of the best institutions for men. Like her American counterpart, she too had hoped that her college would produce a new woman, scholarly, refined, always "ladylike," yet equipped with the academic tools necessary to compete successfully with the best of the men students.

Indeed, her emphasis on reaching the highest educational standard for women, defined at that time by Cambridge University, which, with Oxford, constituted the age-old seats of learning for all England's eminents, had had its effect throughout England. But with her victories would come many disappointments, particularly in the final two decades of the nineteenth century. As universities in America tried to exclude and segregate women, England's ancient universities would also present difficulties. Having allowed women initial entry within their walls, the universities would then deny them the credentials they so earnestly sought, as well as the prestige and honor that should have accompanied their successful academic careers.

Notes

1. The preparatory department of Wellesley became an independent institution in 1880; Vassar closed its preparatory department in 1888. See Newcomer, 22.

2. "Coeducation of the Sexes," *Woman's Journal,* 21 September 1872, quoted in William Leach, *True Love and Perfect Union: The Feminist Reform of Sex and Society* (New York: Basic Books, Inc., 1980), 76.

3. Quoted in Leach, 77.

4. Laurence R. Veysey, *The Emergence of the American University* (Chicago and London: The University of Chicago Press, 1965), 4-6.

5. Patricia Albjerg Graham, "Expansion and Exclusion: A History of Women in American Higher Education," *Signs: Journal of Women in Culture and Society* 3 (1978): 759-773.

6. See Ann Douglas, *The Feminization of American Culture* (New York: Alfred Knopf, 1977), 22-43.

7. Leach, 73.

8. Veysey, 12-13.

9. Solomon, 44.

10. Ibid., 44-45.

11. Oberlin provided a model for other private religious coeducational institutions in the Midwest. Many black colleges opening in the 1860s also followed its example, such as Fisk, Howard, and Wilberforce. As at Oberlin, women were usually secluded in separate departments. Ibid., 50.

12. Horace Mann, Massachusetts educator and founder and president of Antioch College from 1852 to 1859, is also considered the "Father of American Public Education." Serving on the Massachusetts Board of Education from 1837 to 1848, Mann revolutionized public school organization and was instrumental in establishing the first normal school in the United States in 1839.

13. John Rury and Glenn Harper, "The Trouble with Coeducation: Mann and Women at Antioch, 1853-1860," *History of Education Quarterly* 26 (Winter, 1986): 481-502.
14. Newcomer, 12.
15. J.L. Pickard, "Historical Sketch of the University of Iowa," *Annals of Iowa* 3 (1899), quoted in Solomon, 52.
16. Newcomer, 12.
17. M. Curti and V. Cardensen, *The University of Wisconsin, A History, 1848-1925,* Vol. 1 (Madison, 1949), 371, quoted in Newcomer, 13.
18. Ibid. See also Woody, 2: 239-244 and Solomon, 53.
19. D. Read, "Historical Sketch of the University of Missouri," *Historical Sketches of State Universities* (United States Bureau of Education, 1883), 41, quoted in Newcomer, 14. The normal department was a teacher training program. For a discussion of this important aspect of women's education, see Chapter 7.
20. Solomon, 53.
21. Ibid. See also Woody, 2: 244-247.
22. Rayford W. Logan, *Howard University: The First Hundred Years 1867-1967* (New York: New York University Press, 1969), 22-36.
23. Quoted in Woody, 2: 248.
24. Quoted in Charlotte Williams Conable, *Women at Cornell: The Myth of Equal Education* (Ithaca and London: Cornell University Press, 1977), 56.
25. Ibid., 58.
26. Ibid.
27. Ibid., 65-66.
28. Sage to the Trustees of Cornell University, February 13, 1872, Department of Manuscripts and University Archives. Ibid., 74.
29. By the 1920s, Cornell was noted for its state subsidized home economics program. Ibid., 98-133.
30. These quotations are from a memorial from the alumnae to

the trustees and faculty of Colby entitled *Coeducation at Colby* (Waterville, Maine: Colby 1890), 1.

31.   Ibid., 2.

32.   Ibid.

33.   Ibid., 14-15.

34.   *Papers on the Relations of Wesleyan University to the Higher Education of Women* (n.p.: Pelton and King Print, 1900), 16.

35.   Ibid., 14.

36.   Leach, 75.

37.   Quoted in Woody, 2: 281.

38.   For a detailed discussion of the vicissitudes of coeducation at the University of Chicago, see Woody, 2: 281-290.

39.   Solomon, 58.

40.   *Education,* Vol. 1 (Boston: n.p., 1880), 62, quoted in Woody, 2: 305.

41.   Solomon, 55. For a discussion of the ambiguous attitudes concerning women's education as reflected in the Radcliffe compromise, see Eugenia Kaledin, *The Education of Mrs. Henry Adams* (Philadelphia: Temple University Press, 1981), 45-50.

42.   Solomon, 54-55.

43.   Meyer, *Barnard Beginnings,* 42.

44.   Newcomer, 42; see also Solomon, 55-56.

45.   Mary Gathright Newell, "Mary Munford and Higher Education for Women in Virginia," in *Stepping Off the Pedestal: Academic Women in the South,* eds., Patricia A. Stringer and Irene Thompson (New York: The Modern Language Association of America, 1982), 26-38. In 1944 Mary Washington College came under the control of the Rector and Visitors of the University of Virginia. But the physical distance from the university made it impossible to share facilities. Hence Mary Washington was more properly deemed a separate rather than a coordinate institution. See Woody, 2: 254-255.

46.   Solomon, 54.

47. Peter Gay, *The Bourgeois Experience: Victoria to Freud,* Vol. 1 of *Education of the Senses* (New York: Oxford University Press, 1984), 184.
48. Ibid.
49. M. Carey Thomas, "The Bryn Mawr Woman," in Barbara Cross, ed. *The Educated Woman in America: Selected Writings of Catharine Beecher, Margaret Fuller, and M. Carey Thomas,* Classics in Education, no. 25 (New York: Teachers College Press, 1965), 140.
50. Sara Burstall, *The Education of Girls in the United States* (London: Swan Sonnenschein and Co., 1894), 130-131.
51. Thomas, "Motives and Future of the Educated Woman," in Cross, 159.
52. Logan Pearsall Smith, *Unforgotten Years* (London: n.p., 1938), 89-90, paraphrased in Cross, 34.
53. Thomas, "Motives," in Cross, 162.
54. Ibid., 161.
55. Quoted in Edith Finch, *Carey Thomas of Bryn Mawr* (New York: Harper and Bros., 1947), 64.
56. Dobkin, 263.
57. Finch, 231-234.
58. From a letter read by M. Carey Thomas in her *Address at the Fiftieth Anniversary of Bryn Mawr College* (Bryn Mawr, n.d.), 54, quoted in Cross, Introduction, 37.
59. Ibid., Introduction, 36.
60. Ibid.
61. Dobkin, 16.
62. Quoted in Finch, 280.
63. Ibid.
64. Ibid.

CHAPTER 6

THE HOPE OF EQUAL RECOGNITION IN ENGLAND

In England the struggle to equalize educational opportunities for women was not as much a matter of integration and curricular substance as it was a matter of recognition. By the late 1870s in America, a young woman could choose to attend a separate women's college or a private or state-supported coeducational institution. Following either a collegiate course or a ladies' curriculum, she could then obtain a Bachelor of Arts or a Bachelor of Science degree. Several avenues of higher education were also open to English women at this time. Most accessible and therefore most popular were the lecture series that proliferated throughout the country. These, however, provided an informal mode of instruction, and while eminent scholars imparted a wide assortment of knowledge, the women who took advantage of the lectures gained neither systemized education nor enhanced status. In addition, by the late 1870s, women could enter the colleges and halls tenuously associated with Oxford and Cambridge, or they could attend Queen's or Bedford in London. None of these institutions, however, would grant them a university degree.

The question of degrees in England must be examined in order to understand the reluctance with which they were conferred upon women. Degrees in England were not bestowed lightly; only a chartered university could grant them. A small private college such as Queen's might issue a certificate to its graduates, but a Bachelor's, Master's, and Doctor's degree could be obtained only from one of England's universities.

For this reason educated people in England regarded American degrees as inferior. "The simple possession of a degree does not imply so much in America as in England," stated suffragist Millicent Garrett Fawcett. "We suspect that the comparative ease with which a small and unimportant society can change itself into a college and obtain a charter with the power of granting degrees, has deteriorated the value of all degrees."[1] British Professor Goldwin Smith concurred. While teaching in America, he noted, "The value of University degrees, and their efficacy as inducement to go through an Academical course, appear in this country to be almost irrevocably lost."[2]

In nineteenth-century America an undergraduate's performance was measured daily by attendance at class lectures, recitations, written work, and examinations demanded by the individual professors in charge of each class. By contrast, degrees from English universities were won only after a series of major examinations had been successfully completed, examinations issued, not by individual professors, but by the university at large at selected intervals. Examinations were one of the striking features of English undergraduate studies and represented the major, unrelenting obstacle in a system designed to impose a barrier, through which only the intellectual elites might pass. Whereas the newfound mission of the American undergraduate system of the late nineteenth century was to more and more provide exposure to general culture "for the average person," the English system, exemplified by Oxford and Cambridge, excluded the average person. "At no point in [an American student's] career is he expected to submit to any examination comparable . . . to the final honours examinations at Oxford and Cambridge," concluded Burstall.[3]

Additionally, earning a degree from an English university implied privileges and responsibilities beyond that of the diploma. Once a student received a degree, for instance, he became a voting member of the university, able to participate in its governance. The extent of participation varied from one university to another. Cambridge, in particular, allowed graduates considerable power in the academic and administrative control of the university. Granting degrees to women, therefore, meant granting them equal privileges, equal status, and equal voting power within the university.[4]

As English society at large remained unwilling to grant women such equality, so too were English universities, especially the venerable Oxford and Cambridge. Indeed, reports Rita McWilliams-Tullberg, "The women's degree campaigns at Oxford and Cambridge can be seen as microcosms of the national struggle for female enfranchisement."[5] The first breakthrough came at the University of London in 1878 when it was rechartered in order to admit women to all degrees, including medicine. This brought the work of Emily Davies to fruition almost twenty years after her efforts on behalf of Elizabeth Garrett. Four years later London extended voting privileges to women, thus offering them full equality.

Although London's action was significant, the nature of this university enabled these concessions to be enacted with greater ease than in other universities. In 1878 London was not a residential, teaching university. Rather, it was an examining body that conferred degrees, and it would remain so until the end of the century. Some criticized it as having only "a brass plate, a pair of swing doors, and a charter," which dated from 1836.[6] In relation to Oxford and Cambridge, therefore, it was a new university, with "no accretions of past centuries having to be broken through."[7]

In spite of the criticism directed toward the University of London, women were thankful for the opportunities it provided. "We women owe it gratitude," stated Sara Burstall, "for it received us as an Alma Mater." Women educators especially rejoiced with this breakthrough, knowing now there was an added goal to their efforts in teaching women—the university degree.[8]

While many were hopeful that London's policy would set a trend throughout England, those resisting the encroachment of women at other universities hoped that with London's concession they might be spared the task. If a woman wanted a degree, opponents at Oxford and Cambridge argued, then let her go to London to get it.[9] This, in fact, is what a woman often had to do if she planned to pursue teaching or professional work upon graduation. It was not unknown, moreover, for a young Girton or Newnham student, after passing Tripos examinations, to sit for the examinations of the University of London in order to receive a B.A. degree.[10] Without these two "magic letters" after her name, an educated woman found herself at a professional disadvantage.[11]

Gradually other universities in England began to offer degrees to women. In 1881 the University of Durham opened to women a degree in arts, but this ancient establishment remained a limited option for a period since there was no residence for women, nor access to instruction. By 1895 Durham would offer all degrees to women.[12] The university college at Liverpool, opening in 1882, admitted women from its inception and offered them full participation and degrees except in its medical school. Liverpool's beginnings reflect many of the disadvantages of England's "new" universities in industrial areas. With inadequate facilities and accommodations, students often faced grim realities. As Ramsay Muir (1872-1941) commented in his autobiography,

> When I entered it, the main part of the college was housed in a disused lunatic asylum, in a slum district, with a huge workhouse on one side. . . . Across a corner of the derelict quadrangle ran a deep railway cutting, which belched forth clouds of smoke. The street which climbed the hill from the city to the college . . . contained twenty-two public houses and a number of sordid shops; the pavements were haunted by slatternly women and barefoot street Arabs. The city abattoirs lay just behind and diffused a smell of

blood. These were sorry
surroundings for the education of
aspiring youth.[13]

These conditions did not deter women, however, who by the second session comprised over half the regular student population.[14]

The University of Manchester, somewhat grudgingly, presented its first degrees to women in 1887. The supporters of the women graduates, reportedly, gave a great fanfare. "So great was the cheering," announced a school newsletter, "that a pause was made to let the first enthusiasm work itself off before the ceremony was finished."[15] The university was less enthusiastic in allowing women their full rights, however. Although the original charter of the university in 1880 had stipulated their admission, their full participation, and the right to obtain a degree on equal conditions with men, the only constituent college, Owens College, initially refused even to allow women admission. After much debate and a three-year battle in the press between opponents and supporters, women gained access to limited classes in the Arts and Sciences for a five-year probationary period. The restrictions lay primarily in advanced science classes and laboratories, restrictions which, as one local high school teacher emphasized in the *Manchester Guardian,* dampened the enthusiasm of the better students, who would have to look elsewhere for advanced training. The period of probation ended in 1888 and with its conclusion, women entered all departments except engineering and medicine and were entitled to laboratory work. In 1900 these departments opened to women.[16]

By 1895 the new provincial universities in England, as well as those in Scotland, Ireland, and Wales, all awarded degrees to women. This brought to twelve the number of universities throughout the British Isles where women were allowed to study and receive a degree.[17]

In the minds of most English people, however, a university education meant matriculation through Oxford or Cambridge, not a new university, or a provincial university, or an examining body such as the University of London.[18] And so it was with women who sought the best in a university education. Oxford and Cambridge, the most respected universities in the country, were considered "the finishing schools," moreover, "for the nation's leaders."[19] But as England's new and provincial universities admitted women as degree-seeking candidates, Oxford and Cambridge relentlessly refused to do so until the 1920s. The struggle was disappointing, especially at Cambridge, where English women had taken their first steps toward higher education. Ironically, Cambridge was destined to become the last English university to grant degrees to women and would not concede them full privileges and membership until 1948.[20]

Throughout the 1870s Girton and Newnham had quietly expanded. The students attended lectures by dons sympathetic to their endeavor, prepared for examinations, and proved that they could meet the demands of the university. As the years passed, the quiet presence of the women became accepted as natural. In formal relations with the university, however, their position remained anomalous.[21]

In 1881 the first official link with Cambridge was forged when the university formally opened the Tripos examinations to the students of Girton and Newnham and agreed to offer a certificate upon their successful completion. This action followed the brilliant triumph of a Girton student in her yet unofficial Tripos examination in mathematics, a subject considered beyond the scope of women. While acknowledging the existence of women students at Cambridge, the certificate was bestowed as a concession on the part of the university with the hope of deflecting the desire for the degree. Some opponents of women's presence at Cambridge rightly assessed, however, that the concession was "the thin end of the wedge" and would only lead to further agitation.[22]

Such was the case in 1887 when a Girton student named Agnata Ramsey placed first in the Tripos examination in classics, another subject deemed above women's interest and ability. Having outranked the Cambridge men who took the same examination, Miss Ramsey drew positive public attention upon herself and the peculiar position of all the women of Cambridge.[23] Her victory, moreover, gave rise to the hope that the university would now consider degrees for women.

Emily Davies believed the time was auspicious and gathered a committee of prestigious individuals, including Lady Goldsmid (1818-1909) and Lady Stanley of Alderly (1807-1895), to petition the university. Their memorial requested that degrees be granted "to all, without distinction of sex, who fulfill the prescribed conditions."[24] But the time was not favorable, for opponents saw the move as "interference" in men's affairs, and the university refused to debate the question.[25]

Two years later another woman of Cambridge achieved brilliant success in her examination. Newnham's Philippa Fawcett, daughter of Millicent Garrett Fawcett and the niece of Elizabeth Garrett Anderson, placed highest in the mathematics Tripos. Outranking the highest of the male examinees, Philippa was denied the title of "Senior Wrangler," traditionally bestowed on the leading honours candidate. Instead, the title was given to her male colleague who ranked "400 marks" below her.[26] Despite such success, the Cambridge women hesitated to raise at this time the question of degrees.

In 1884 Oxford University formally offered honours examinations to women in mathematics, natural science, and modern history. Regarded as the "turning point," Oxford's gesture, like that of Cambridge, signified the official entrance of women into university life and was celebrated as a major victory among Oxford women.[27] Although the Oxford statute opening the first examinations to women passed by a vote of 461 to 321, there was reaction in certain quarters. A clergyman preaching in New College Chapel, for instance, rebuked the forwardness of the Oxford women from the pulpit, saying, "Inferior to us God made you, and inferior to the end of time you will remain. But you are not the worse off for that."[28]

Lagging behind Cambridge, Oxford did not open all honours examinations to women until 1893. In the hopeful anticipation of degrees, the leaders of Somerville College began in 1894 to require the full degree course of all their students. Like Girton, Somerville now demanded the highest academic standards from its students. Lady Margaret Hall's principal, Elizabeth Wordsworth, was confident "that if women *did the work,* that was the great thing, and that, sooner or later, they would get credit for it."[29] Soon Lady Margaret Hall joined the women's colleges in raising its standards to those of the men's colleges.

It would be later rather than sooner before the women of Oxford received degrees, but that was unforeseen in 1896 when the Association for the Education of Women at Oxford asked for the privilege. Although the women of Somerville now followed the compulsory degree course, the opposition warned that the curriculum for the B.A. degree was a "crushing force," too cruel to impose on women who were "honoured guests" of the university.[30] One male supporter, Arthur Sidgwick (1840-1920), countered, "It is not my idea of honouring a guest to make her do all the work and refuse her due recognition and rewards."[31] But the university, still unwilling to allow their guests to descend from their position of honour, refused their due recognition by a vote of 215 to 140 on March 3, 1896. In a gesture of conciliation, Oxford began issuing certificates to women specifying the number of terms of residence and the examinations passed.[32]

Women remained encouraged, though, one supporter remarking, "The novelty of the proposal will wear off and the fears, at once perfectly unreasonable, which drove many members of the university to the verge of panic, will die away."[33] Oxford, trying to stay conciliatory, continued to contemplate the degree question in the early twentieth century with the installation of the new chancellor, Lord George Curzon (1859-1925), who inaugurated a number of institutional reforms. Urging Oxford to reform itself before outside pressure was brought to bear upon the university, Curzon issued a public statement arguing in favor of degrees, citing the advantage this would bring professional women. Additionally, Oxford would benefit, he stated, by attracting England's most gifted women. In 1909, Oxford passed a resolution favoring a reflection and discussion of degrees and women. But the pause for reflection and discussion proved to be a long one, and a number of major interruptions ensued before a decision would be reached, including, most significantly, World War I.

Lord Curzon continued his campaign for reform, creating hope for Oxford's women when he appeared at Lady Margaret Hall on October 22, 1911, to open a new block of buildings. As the first official visit to a women's college by the head of the university, thhis event was important. His speech at the opening, moreover, gave the women additional optimism. "The sound of Oxford must go out into all lands," he proclaimed, "and women as well as men must bear the message."[34]

Curzon's position as an advocate of women's rights within Oxford seemed to contradict his obdurate position concerning women's suffrage and participation in the political life of the country at large. Could the reason be, speculated author Vera Brittain (1896-1970), "that this enigmatic character had three remarkable daughters and no sons?"[35]

Meanwhile, in the last years of the nineteenth century, a renewed effort to grant women degrees occurred at Cambridge. But in contrast to Oxford's relatively calm and short debate with its lingering atmosphere of hope, the issue at Cambridge grew into an eighteen-month-long dispute that disrupted the routine of university life and left Cambridge with the bitter taste of antifeminism for years to come.

When the question arose in early 1896, women and their supporters were confident that degrees would soon be awarded. A memorial circulating through Cambridge predicted success, as two thousand Cambridge men indicated their support for the proposal. By May 1897 the majority had changed their minds and the measure was defeated.[36]

Arguments in favor of degrees for women revolved around the practical and professional difficulties that resulted from their lack. For years alumnae of Girton and Newnham wrote of the disadvantages they encountered when seeking employment without the highly valued parchment. Alumna Alice Williams, who after concluding her work at Girton traveled to Ireland for her B.A., wrote that the degree, "however low from *any* university," was necessary.[37] The certificates issued by the university were no substitute for degrees, another argued, and from a distance seemed "slightly ludicrous. . . . Is it that the idea of a mere certificate has in it something of an antidote to the unsexing influence of university distinction?" she asked.[38]

Another writer countered the claims of the "unsexing influence of university distinction" by rehabilitating the old argument of women's moral influence over home and society. With the full recognition of a degree, women might extend their benevolent, civilizing purity, and actually inspire higher education:

> A belief in the equal rights and equal responsibilities of women seems to have leavened at least part of the undergraduate world; and to the same extent, and by virtue of the same causes, purity of thought and purity of speech have become the accepted rule. How much more will this be the case when women shall have a recognized place in the University . . . and the last remnants of monastic disease and mediaeval impurity shall have been purged from the statutes of the Senate.[39]

The opposition reacted to the degree proposal with memorials, pamphlets, editorials, and speeches. One of the first documents made a case for the intellectual inferiority of women. Written by Cambridge Professor Alfred Marshall (1842-1924), the pamphlet was particularly damaging since Marshall, once a supporter of women's entry to Cambridge, had taught many women over the years and had married Newnham scholar Mary Paley. Once Marshall's pamphlet appeared, the tide of opposition swelled as charges of sabotage, deceit, and manipulation were hurled against women.[40]

If women were given a Cambridge degree, there would be a "considerable defection . . . of the best youth of the country to Oxford," which had by now rejected the degree proposal. "The glorious career of this university as a producer of great men," continued a letter to the *Times,* "will receive a most serious check."[41] Selfishly, women were "seeking to force their way into everything male without, it appears, taking much thought for the interests of the institution," submitted another.[42]

Besides, it was said again, women had special needs and should therefore be educated in a separate university with its own degree. The idea of a separate university for women similar to the separate colleges in America had many supporters in England, including Oxford's Charles Dodgson, more widely known as Lewis Carroll (1832-1898), and gained additional support as the debate over degrees at Oxford and Cambridge heated. In 1897 a group of Oxford and Cambridge officials and scholars convened at a conference in London and elaborated a plan for a "Queen's University," that as it grew would be granted degree-giving powers.[43] Women's supporters countered that women themselves had no desire for such a place. Those who promoted a separate facility, one writer claimed, were "wolves in sheep's clothing," who beneath their disguise wanted a separate, second-rate standard for women. Separation, the writer added, contradicted the meaning of the word *university.* Defining a university as an institution that embodied the highest development and achievement of the mind, and represented every aspect of human thought, the idea of exclusivity by sex was not only contradictory, but fatal: "A university composed exclusively of military men, a university composed exclusively of Nonconformists, a university composed exclusively of clergymen—each of these is less anomalous than a university founded exclusively for the benefit of women."[44]

Other opponents questioned the motive behind women's struggle for degrees—was it the pursuit of knowledge or was it the urge to gain power within the university? Were the women of Cambridge, some accusingly asked, linking the degree question with the odious question of political rights for women? Anti–suffragist Alice Stopford Green (1847-1929) believed this was the case and wrote to the *Times* that women were defeating their purpose "by allowing the cause of learning to be persistently bound up in one bundle with schemes of women's rights and woman's suffrage."[45]

Green's comments, like Marshall's, were harmful to the degree cause, since she was a prominent historian and intellectual in her own right. As author of a biography of Henry II for the *English Statesmen* series, and coauthor with her husband of the *Short Geography of the British Islands,* Green represented the image of a woman who had achieved scholarly stature without the benefit of a university degree. Green was a fortunate woman, however, for under her husband, historian J. R. Green (1837-1883), she had learned historical methods and had gained prestige by association with his well-respected name.[46]

To refute the arguments of the opposition, the women's degree committee in May 1897 brought a proposal before the university asking only for degree titles. Excluded from the proposal were provisions for the official admission of women to lectures, laboratories, the library, or university membership. Stripped of all privileges, the degree title for women would add weight to their credentials in the world at large without changing their status within the university.

This compromise did not calm the debate; instead, it continued to grow more heated. "It would be difficult to exaggerate the intensity of the feeling which has been aroused by these new proposals," wrote a St. John's College don to the *Times.*[47] Professor Alfred Marshall claimed he would gladly have sacrificed a year's salary to avoid "the wear and tear of this weary year." Having such close associations with Girton and Newnham, only "unwillingly" did he bring himself "to oppose" the proposals, he added. But in order to "save the birthright of Cambridge from being sacrificed for a very small mess of pottage for a few women," Marshall urged all non-resident members of Cambridge to take the "inconvenience" to come to Cambridge to vote against the measure.[48]

The same day, the *Times* announced a special train service to and from Cambridge and published another letter urging all in opposition to take the train to vote.[49] Undergraduates, excitedly caught up in the "festive" spirit of the day, provided hackney service to the Senate House of the university where the vote was to be taken.[50]

The vote was taken on May 21, 1897. Amid banners, an effigy of a "bloomered" woman riding a bicycle, and a carnival-like atmosphere, alumni of Cambridge made their way through crowds of cheering undergraduates to mark their decision. The proposal was soundly defeated by a vote of 1,713 to 662. Afterward a riotous group of Cambridge undergraduates broke out in celebration with bonfires, rotten eggs, fireworks, and events duly recorded in a special edition of the *Cambridge Weekly News,* entitled "The Triumph of Man."[51] The following day, the *Times* ran an editorial congratulating Cambridge on its decision. "Cambridge has hitherto treated her women students with indulgence," it was said, "some may think excessive indulgence." Now "concessions must cease if it is to maintain its ancient tradition as a seat of learning based on the collegiate system and governed in the interests of men."[52]

The women had been put in their place. With such resounding defeats, they would not raise the issue of degrees again until after World War I, but would retreat quietly to their colleges and resume their academic life without recognition, awards, or honours.

Notes

1. Millicent Garrett Fawcett, "The Medical and General Education of Women," *Fortnightly Review,* November 1868, 557.
2. Smith, 47.
3. Burstall, *The Education of Girls,* 110.
4. Rita McWilliams-Tullberg, *Women at Cambridge: A Men's University—Though of a Mixed Type* (London: Gollancz, 1975), 14.
5. Rita McWilliams-Tullberg, "Women and Degrees at Cambridge University, 1862-1897," in *A Widening Sphere: Changing Roles of Victorian Women,* ed. Martha Vicinus (Bloomington and London: Indiana University Press, 1977), 118.
6. Sara Burstall, *Frances Mary Buss* (London: Society for Promoting Christian Knowledge, 1938), 62.
7. Bremner, 140.
8. Burstall, *Frances Mary Buss,* 62.
9. Rogers, 10. See also McWilliams-Tullberg, *Women at Cambridge,* 102.
10. McWilliams-Tullberg, *Women at Cambridge,* 126.
11. Ibid.; see also David Rubinstein, *Before the Suffragettes: Women's Emancipation in the 1890s* (New York: St. Martin's Press, 1986), 43.
12. Ellsworth, 144.
13. Quoted in Thomas Kelly, *For Advancement of Learning: The University of Liverpool 1881-1981* (Liverpool: Liverpool University Press, 1981), 56.
14. Ibid., 58.
15. Quoted in Mabel Tylecote, *The Education of Women at Manchester University 1883 to 1933* (Manchester: Manchester University Press, 1941), 43.
16. Ibid., 10-15, 43,44.
17. McWilliams-Tullberg, "Women and Degrees at Cambridge," 117.

18. Vicinus, *Independent Women,* 127; see also McWilliams–Tullberg, *Women at Cambridge,* 143-144.

19. McWilliams-Tullberg, "Women and Degrees at Cambridge," 118.

20. As Rita McWilliams-Tullberg notes, by 1948, Cambridge had restricted the rights of graduates in university government. Women, therefore, never fully shared in the government at Cambridge. See "Women and Degrees at Cambridge," 120.

21. McWilliams-Tullberg, *Women at Cambridge,* 70.

22. McWilliams-Tullberg, "Women and Degrees at Cambridge," 133.

23. *Punch* celebrated Miss Ramsey's success with a cartoon depicting Mr. Punch politely escorting her into a first-class train compartment designated "for ladies only." See Stephen, 327.

24. Stephen, 330.

25. McWilliams-Tullberg, "Women and Degrees at Cambridge," 134.

26. Millicent Garrett Fawcett, *What I Remember* (London: T. Fisher Unwin Ltd., 1925; repr., Westport, Conn.: Hyperion, 1976), 137-148.

27. For a sense of the enthusiasm this move invoked among the women of Oxford, see Georgina Battiscombe, *Reluctant Pioneer: A Life of Elizabeth Wordsworth* (London: Constable, 1978), 93 and Elizabeth Wordsworth, *Glimpses of the Past* (London: A.R. Mowbray and Co., 1912), 169.

28. Contemporary records indicate the congregation laughed aloud. This did not stop Dr. Burzon from publishing his sermon under the title, "To Educate Young Women Like Young Men and With Young Men—A Thing Inexpedient and Immodest." See Brittain, 69.

29. Wordsworth, 169.

30. Brittain, 107.

31. Ibid.

32. St. Clare Byrne, 65.
33. Brittain, 110.
34. Ibid., 130.
35. Ibid.
36. McWilliams-Tullberg, "Women and Degrees at Cambridge," 137.
37. Rubinstein, 202.
38. "The Education of Girls: Their Admissibility to Universities," *Westminster Review* 109 (Winter 1878): 82.
39. "Should University Degrees be Given to Women?" *Westminster Review* 115 (Winter 1881): 505.
40. McWilliams-Tullberg, "Women and Degrees at Cambridge," 137-139.
41. Letter from Adam Sedgwick, *Times,* 19 May 1897, p. 16.
42. Quoted in Blease, 149.
43. Rogers, 56. For additional information on this issue, see Burstyn, 161-163.
44. "Should University Degrees," 495-496.
45. The *Times,* 19 May 1897, p. 16.
46. Peterson, 176-178.
47. The *Times,* 19 May 1897, p. 16.
48. Letter from Alfred Marshall, The *Times,* 21 May 1897, p. 14.
49. The *Times,* 21 May 1897, p. 16.
50. McWilliams-Tullberg, *Women at Cambridge,* 137-138.
51. Ibid., 139.
52. The *Times,* 22 May 1897, p. 13.

CHAPTER 7

HIGHER EDUCATION IN THE SOUTH

While the history of higher education for American women reflects, despite many disappointments, relatively steady, if slow progress in the Northeast and Midwest, the story of women's higher education in the American South reveals a drama that fitfully unfolds against a background laden with the tragedy of war and reconstruction, poverty, and at times a pervasive hostility to the ideal of higher education. Due to the distinct cultural patterns of the American South, patterns that demarcate this region from the rest of the country, it is beneficial to separately examine women's education in the South in the nineteenth and early twentieth century.

In their history of the South, William Cooper, Jr. and Thomas Terrill note that "the history of women's education in the nineteenth-century South . . . became a story of brave beginnings and limited achievements. Ideological barriers did as much as tight finances to slow improvements."[1] Ideological barriers to education in the South were erected as early as the founding of the southern colonies in the early seventeenth century. David Hackett Fischer indicates that education in the Chesapeake Bay area, for instance, was a gift of the privileged, not to be shared with the populace. The response of Governor William Berkeley (1606-1677) in 1671 to the condition of education in Virginia illustrates this mindset: "I thank God there are no free schools nor printing, and I hope we shall not have these [for a] hundred years; for learning has brought disobedience, and heresy, and sects into the world, and printing has divulged them, and libels against the best government. God keep us from both!"[2] Education remained the preserve of the planter gentlemen and, as such, was a cherished attribute. "Better be never born than ill-bred [or unschooled]," wrote William Fitzhugh (1651-1701) of Virginia in 1687.[3]

Women, like the lower classes in the South, were neither expected nor encouraged to become educated during the time of Berkeley and Fitzhugh, a condition that Thomas Woody notes was certainly no different in the North during the same era.[4] Like their northern counterparts, southern women were believed unsuited for higher learning and simultaneously mocked for the lack of it. A century later, women were still enduring public ridicule for their ignorance. The *North Carolina Journal,* for example, ran the following:

> Woman's a book of tiny size Suited
> to catch the coxcomb's eyes; In silks
> and muslins neatly bound, And
> sometimes richly gilt around. But
> what is strange in readers' sight.
> This book oft' stands unletter'd
> quite! The *frontispiece* is gayly drest.
> *Blank paper* fills up all the rest!!![5]

As Thomas Woody notes, women's "unletter'd state" and the public response to it might well have been otherwise had the South taken note of Thomas Jefferson's (1743-1826) thoughts on education. In 1779 Jefferson introduced a bill in the General Assembly of Virginia for the founding of a system of public elementary and secondary schools and colleges, crowned with a state university. Though it had its weaknesses, Jefferson's plan was a century ahead of its time, especially in its emphasis on male and female training in the elementary years.[6] Jefferson's vision of a higher liberal education was primarily for talented men of the new republic, but he was unique in the emphasis he placed on his own daughters' intellectual development. Together, Jefferson and daughter Martha (1772-1836) prepared a list of recommended books for the education of girls, including works by Livy, Plutarch, Shakespeare, Racine, Corneille, Voltaire, Gibbon, as well as those of several women writers. The list was comprehensive and would have provided any intelligent person of the late eighteenth century with a thorough grounding in the liberal arts. Jefferson especially wanted his daughters to be educated to "enable them when become mothers, to educate their own daughters and even to direct the course for their sons."[7] Chances were "fourteen to one," he wrote a friend, that Martha would marry a "blockhead" and she would thus be charged with heading and educating her family.[8]

With the exception of the creation of the University of Virginia, the capstone of his vision, Virginia rejected Jefferson's plan, afraid, as educator A. D. Mayo (1823-1907) suggested later, of "the result of educating 'the common herd.'"[9] And, for the most part, parents ignored Jefferson's ideas concerning the education of daughters. The common response among southern families who wanted to educate their daughters from the colonial period well into the nineteenth century was to hire tutors, much as the upper gentry and the aristocrats of England hired governesses and private instructors during the same period. One of the best-documented cases of the role of the tutor in a southern family is that of Philip Fithian (1747-1776), a Princeton graduate, who joined the household of William Carter of Virginia in 1773. In his journals and letters, Fithian left an account of his day by day instruction of the five daughters, two sons and nephew in the Carter family. While the girls proceeded through elementary "ciphering," reading, and spelling, the boys tackled Roman history, Latin and English grammar, composition, and "ciphering." Music and especially dancing were deemed essential for both sexes.[10]

Wealthy southern families also took advantage of the seminaries and academies now growing in the North. Still reeling in the late eighteenth century from the massive destruction of the

Revolutionary War and with a largely rural population, the South was slightly later in founding academies (see Chapter 1).[11] But in the nineteenth century, the South began to participate in the academy "movement," giving southern families choices closer to home. One of the most reputable in the entire country, founded in 1802 by the Moravians, was in Salem, North Carolina. Others, cited by Thomas Woody, include the Edgeworth Seminary in Greensboro, North Carolina, Nazareth Academy in Bardstown, Kentucky, Knoxville Female Academy in Tennessee, Columbia Female Institute also in Tennessee, and Elias Marks Female Academy in Barhamsville, South Carolina.[12]

During the 1820s and 1830s, Georgia and Alabama incorporated school after school for women, blessing some with the designation of "college," although these were "such in name only."[13] While some of the southern academies were family owned and staffed, some of the more notable academies imported teachers and administrators from the established institutions in the North, such as Troy, Mount Holyoke, and Hartford.[14] Huntsville Female Academy in Alabama, for example, hired three teachers and a principal in its opening year in 1831 from Catharine Beecher's Hartford Female Seminary.[15]

As southern academies began to proliferate in the 1830s, the majority of Emma Willard's graduates who became teachers found positions in the South.[16] Mrs. Willard's sister, Almira Lincoln Phelps (1793-1884), after eight years as teacher and vice-Principal at Troy Female Seminary, took charge of Patapsco Institute near Baltimore, Maryland, introducing Willard's Plan into a southern state.[17] The traditions and curricula established by Willard, Lyon, and Beecher, therefore, guided some of the newly forming southern seminaries.

Some of the seminaries founded in the southern states during the 1840s and 1850s, suggests historian Fletcher Melvin Green, were created for political reasons. The planter class had sent their sons to academies and colleges above the Mason-Dixon, and daughters too were still sent northward. But as tensions rose between the North and South during these decades, southerners began to fear the "fanatical teachings" that some of their children were receiving in northern schools. Green asserts that sectionalism influenced the education movement in the South. "What is the tonic for the insidious northern influence?" asked Albert Gallatin Brown (1813-1880) in his commencement address at Madison Female College in Sharon, Mississippi, in 1859. "Let us have our own schools, academies, colleges, and universities. Let us rear and educate our own teachers." The schools that developed for such reasons, Green acknowledges, could not have contributed "to education in its truest sense."[18]

As the war raged in 1863, Edward Joynes (1834-1917), professor of modern languages at Hollins Institute (later Hollins College), one of the few institutions remaining open at this time, wrote a treatise on "The Education of Teachers in the South." Proposing that Hollins play a prominent role in this pursuit, he noted,

> Up to this time, for want of such provisions, our people have been compelled, for the most part, either to send their daughters at a premature age to boarding or other public schools, or to import female teachers from abroad—most frequently 'ready-made' school mar'ms and governesses from Yankee land. These have been often mere adventurers, unfit even for associates, much less for models for Virginia daughters; and still more frequently they have been wholly hostile to our institutions, and out of sympathy with the social and family life of our people.[19]

Seminaries throughout the American states became objects of ridicule in the nineteenth century, and certainly those in the South were no exception. Woody concludes that little of this criticism was unwarranted.[20] With few exceptions, mediocrity was the goal of the southern seminaries, which upheld the doctrine of separate spheres and institutionalized the fear of more than "a little learning" on the part of women. A line from the graduation address delivered at the Greensboro Female College of North Carolina in 1856 is revealing: "I would have you shun the one [too little learning] as the plague, and the other [too much] as the leprosy; I would have you intelligent, useful women . . . . yet never evincing a consciousness of superiority, never playing Sir Oracle, never showing that you supposed yourself born for any other destiny than to be a 'helpmeet for man.'"[21]

This passage clearly delineates the contradictions of women's education in the antebellum South. While seminaries, academies, and "colleges" for women proliferated from 1820 to 1860, the majority of advocates of women's education, including the male founders of these institutions, argued that it was primarily for man's best interest that these schools were founded. The dull, frivolous housewife with "coarse and vulgar ideas" and "low, ungrammatical language" was a drudge to her husband, not an asset. The ideal graduate of a seminary was a gracious, charming, cultivated lady. She became an ornament to her husband, her family, and the South itself.[22] A cultivated lady, however, was not necessarily an educated lady. As psychologist Christine Ladd-Franklin (1847-1930) wrote at the end of the nineteenth century in her essay on education in the South, "The women of New Orleans, and Charleston, and Richmond were often cultivated women in the best sense of the word, but of the higher education, as the modern woman understands it, very little has hitherto existed in the Southern States."[23]

The ideal of cultivation pervaded the lives of southern women, especially those of the aristocratic classes, and herein lies the basic distinction between the education of women in the South and other parts of the country during the antebellum period. As Elizabeth Fox-Genovese points out, the Northeast and Midwest gradually accepted the higher education of women in order to maintain a steady pool of well-trained, yet low-paid, teachers. The South, however, valued education in women primarily as a means of cultivation. A southern lady's education, then, more closely resembled the ornamental training of the eighteenth century.[24]

Given the lack of demanding academic programs, intelligent women in the antebellum South—both those with seminary experience and those without—were known to express their discontent. Often uttered in subtle nuances, the plaints nonetheless were audible. Deep in the heart of the diary of Sarah Morgan Dawson (1842-1909), for instance, are the following words written in 1862:

> And when I lay down and looked in my own heart and saw my shocking ignorance and pitiful inferiority so painfully evident even to my own eyes, I actually cried. Why was I denied the education that would enable me to be the equal of such a man as Colonel Breaux and the others? He says the woman's mind is the same as the man's originally; it is only education that creates the difference. Why was I denied that education?[25]

Dawson was far from illiterate. Although she had only completed eleven months of elementary schooling, she launched into a program of self-education through her constant reading in English and French and after the war became a journalist in Charleston, South Carolina. But her words echo the anguish and frustration of countless women to whom an intellectual life was denied, even forbidden.

A decade before Dawson wrote of her supposed inadequacies, one of the South's most articulate proponents of equal rights for blacks and women, Sarah Grimké (1792-1873), expressed her own dissatisfaction: " . . . the powers of my mind have never been allowed expansion; in childhood they were repressed by the false idea that a girl need not have the education I coveted."[26]

Sarah Grimké's thwarted ambitions reflect the restrictions imposed on restless, energetic women of her era and region. While she was given a seminary education in Charleston, following the traditional courses of reading, writing, arithmetic, a little French, drawing, needlework, and deportment, her longing to study Latin and, as a young woman, her intense drive to study law were not only denied, but mocked by members of her family. Later, she would describe the humility and disappointment: "With me learning was a passion. My nature [was] denied her appropriate nutriment, her course counteracted, her aspirations crushed."[27]

The ironies of her situation were not lost on Sarah's acute mind. As a child, Sarah had delighted in the purposeful transgression of teaching a slave girl to read: "The light was put out, the keyhole screened, and flat on our stomachs, before the fire, with the spelling book under our eyes, we defied the laws of South Carolina."[28] For Sarah, the message was clear. The education of her slave—and her own further education—were forbidden. The liberating light of knowledge was a dangerous instrument and would remain dim and indistinct in the distance.

Ambitious antebellum women such as Grimké and Dawson bore an additional burden, for rooted within southern culture was an ideal of womanhood that exceeded even the restrictive vision of femininity held in northern and certainly midwestern culture. In addition to the qualities of piety and purity that all early Victorian women were to embrace, the notion of indolence was an intrinsic part of southern womanhood, as it was for the English lady. Few writers—contemporary or modern—have found evidence that the image of the woman of leisure matched the actual lives of southern women in the shanty or the plantation, but the vision of the lady at ease was a powerful symbol, guiding the standards by which prosperous southern families raised their daughters. The ideal woman, diarist Mary Boykin Chesnut (1823-1886) sardonically remarked, was "soft and sweet—low-toned, indolent, graceful, and quiescent."[29] Intense demands upon a young woman's intellect, therefore, were unsuitable.

The Civil War drastically altered the lives of southern women, and the image of the "indolent, graceful, quiescent" belle vanished in the wake of necessity. The question of proper female behavior was of less importance to a society ravaged by war, and some women quickly shed the confining yoke of southern ladyhood to step into larger, more demanding roles. Now, in the absence of male family members and personnel, women managed property, nursed wounded soldiers, and volunteered in countless capacities.[30]

The postwar period found women throughout the United States in a wholly unexpected, unprecedented position. With over one million casualties of war, women were faced with the urgency of self-support. While the war created widows, spinsters, orphans, and general hardship everywhere, the economic deprivations were far worse in the South. The economic plight of the South during Reconstruction left an ambivalent mark on the destiny of its women. On the one hand, necessity drove women into the work force; in factories, textile mills, offices, stores, and schools, women now took their place as paid employees.[31] On the other hand, the dire conditions in the postwar South left few resources available for higher education. The trend towards widespread academy and seminary training for women, begun in the first half of the century, was shattered in 1861 by the war and its aftermath. It would take approximately three decades for the South to resume the development of higher education.

But the South's need for educated women had never been greater. Efforts to expand public education were magnified during the Reconstruction era, as more southerners, in spite of traditional indifference and hostility, recognized that increased education was essential for a revitalized economy. Women were thus called upon now, by society's as well as their own economic needs, to teach. Of all the jobs in which women now found themselves, that of schoolteaching was the oldest and most respectable. Women from the higher classes, therefore, chose this channel above others as a means of self-support.[32]

The Rev. A. D. Mayo, a Universalist minister who worked in the educational movement in the South, noted that a virtual "volunteer army" of southern aristocratic women filled the schoolhouses, both public and private, in the southern states. "Some of the best private and public schools of New Orleans have been and still are under the direction of ladies representing the families of Jefferson Davis, General Humphrey, Bishop and General Polk, Sargent S. Prentiss, General Beauregard, and others only less eminent," he found. In schools throughout the South, he continued, were the widows of Confederate governors and generals.[33]

Their task, however, was a challenge many felt inadequate to meet, since their own training had been so insufficient. Southern women began in the decades after the war, then, to pour into northern cities during the summers to receive advanced training. "Our great Northern cities are swarming through the summer with bright and energetic Southern teachers, often at sacrifice of time, money, and health, spending their vacation in study," noted Mayo.[34] Gradually, though, opportunities began to arise in the South. In the first decades after the war, these usually took the form of summer teacher-training institutes, summer normal schools, and even three-day institutes.

Normal schools were a distinct type of vocational training for women during this period. Established for those who intended to be teachers, normal schools were often part of a public high school, a college, university, or a seminary; frequently they were state-supported institutions developing as the demand for teachers grew. Generally in the normal schools, women reviewed their secondary subjects, studied educational theory and a few subjects of higher learning, and practiced supervised teaching. Normal schools had been prevalent in the North in the prewar period with the growth of common schools and now would begin to take on importance in the South.

In 1875 The Peabody Education Fund of Massachusetts financed a normal school in Nashville, Tennessee, which from the beginning included women students and faculty members. Soon normal schools spread throughout the South and while hardly a substitute for full collegiate training, they affected the course of the higher education of women in the South. As Anne Firor Scott notes, "The teachers trained in these normal schools began to teach in the public schools and there helped create the clientele for the few women's liberal arts colleges which were beginning to develop in the South."[35]

The development of quality liberal arts colleges, however, was slow. In 1886-87, when the United States Commissioner of Education published a report distinguishing between institutions that could rightfully be considered "arts colleges" and those seminaries and other schools of lesser status, there was not one women's school in the South that qualified for the former category. Collegiate training in the South for men, likewise, was lagging. Charles Foster Smith, in an article in *The Atlantic Monthly,* noted that

> There has been no great advance, if any, in college work in the South since the Civil War, and in preparation for college there has been a positive decline in most states. I am led to this view partly by my own experience; in six years of college work I have found few men whom I considered fully prepared both in quantity and quality of work for a good freshman class.[36]

Shortly after the commissioner's report concerning women's schools, a number of individuals began to take steps to create collegiate education for southern women. Within the next twenty-five years well over one hundred institutions bearing the name "College for Women" would emerge in the South, but still only a few met the goal. When the Southern Association of College Women published its findings on the state of women's higher education in the South in 1916, only seven institutions for women qualified as true centers of higher learning. These were Agnes Scott, Converse, Florida State College For Women, Goucher, Sophie Newcomb, Randolph-Macon, and Westhampton.[37]

A glimpse at the formative years of these colleges provides insight into the overwhelming barricades placed in the path of women's higher education in the South. Sophie Newcomb, Tulane's coordinate in New Orleans, was the first of the seven to open. In his *Brief History of H. Sophie Newcomb Memorial College,* Brandt V. B. Dixon (1850-1941), the college's first president, looked back on the opening year of 1887, recalling his frustration and discouragement. Parental indifference to educating daughters, the equating of education with ornamental accomplishments, and on-going poverty were a few of the seemingly invincible enemies of his work. His overwhelming difficulty, however, and one that was now a universal theme in women's education, was his students' poor preparation for college work.[38]

In its second year, therefore, Newcomb established a high school and by 1895 a four-year preparatory course was in place. Not until 1918 would the high school be discontinued. The development of an advanced curriculum leading to a Bachelor of Arts degree remained the goal of the college, however, even in its early period. But like its northeastern sister colleges decades earlier, Newcomb had to initially prepare its own constituents.

The first southern women's college to be recognized as fully collegiate by the Commissioner of Education in 1890-91 was the Woman's College of Baltimore, or Goucher College. Opening in 1888 with one freshman class, Goucher added a class each year, completing its organization by 1892-93. Additionally, Goucher was the first southern women's college to be recognized by the Association of Collegiate Alumnae. Perceiving itself less bound to a curriculum emphasizing primarily classics and mathematics, Goucher was one of the first women's colleges to give modern humanities equal standing with the traditional disciplines, all within a rigorous academic setting. Elizabeth Young concedes that "the education of women in the South owes to the College in Baltimore a very real debt."[39]

A year after the founding of Goucher, the Presbyterian Church of Decatur, Georgia, created a school for women called Decatur Female Seminary. Although this school initially, as the name suggests, provided elementary grammar and secondary education exclusively, within two decades, the institution attained full collegiate status as Agnes Scott College. The process of the gradual elevation of the seminary into the college was unusual and, like Mount Holyoke, represented a reversal of the trend in women's higher education whereby a college, upon inception, found that it had to downgrade its course offerings to accommodate poorly prepared students. Agnes Scott began as a grammar school, then began adding high school courses. Soon it was able to eliminate the lowest grade each year, adding simultaneously a higher grade. This continued until the grammar school was phased out and Agnes Scott Institute became a college preparatory school. At the end of the century, Agnes Scott evolved from the preparatory stage into the collegiate. By 1912-13 the preparatory school was discontinued and Agnes Scott emerged as a full-standing college with a curriculum emphasizing mathematics and Latin.

The step-by-step elevation of academic growth did not render Agnes Scott immune to the difficulties that plagued all women's schools in the South during this time. In his history of Agnes Scott, President F. H. Gaines, reminiscent of Newcomb's President Dixon, reiterated the problems the school faced as it sought yearly to upgrade: "It was a new and somewhat daring thing to undertake to maintain a high standard in education in the South. Such a school must encounter the criticism and opposition of other schools, must meet the surprise if not the opposition of the public, and could not expect to be at once popular with its pupils." The task of educating girls, moreover, was doubly arduous in the South. "Parents," Gaines continued, "would plan to send their daughters away for a year to *finish* her education. The serious, thorough education of girls was comparatively new. The movement for the college education of women had not begun, or if at all, had made very little progress in the South."[40]

Persistent lack of funds was another problem. "It was a constant struggle," recalled Gaines, "to make a small and inadequate amount of money meet pressing educational demands of laboratories, library, etc."[41] Agnes Scott was fortunate to have a solid benefactor in its early years, Colonel George Washington Scott, in whose mother's memory the school was named. But the future was confirmed in 1908-09 when the General Education Board of New York, an agency founded by John D. Rockefeller, began to take interest in Agnes Scott. Designed to promote "education in the United States without distinction of race, sex, or creed," the General Education Board focused its efforts on "the industrial and educational upbuilding of the South." Through a series of challenge grants, the agency motivated the institution to work to become financially secure, and as it did so, it reached higher academic standing, becoming a "pioneer in high grade education for women in the South."[42]

Another school that lifted the educational standards for women in the South was Randolph-Macon College for Women in Lynchburg, Virginia. Opening in 1893, the college was a member of the Randolph-Macon System of Colleges and Academies, of which the Randolph-Macon College for Men in Ashland, organized in 1830, was the parent. Like Goucher College in Baltimore, Randolph-Macon opened as a college rather than a seminary. Facing the same privation of resources that stunted all women's schools in the South, Randolph-Macon cloaked its statements of purpose in tones that soothed the potential fears of its supporters and constituents:

> We wish to establish in Virginia a college where our young women may obtain an education equal to that given our best colleges for young men, and under environments in harmony with the highest ideals of womanhood; where the dignity and strength of fully developed faculties and the charm of the highest literary culture may be acquired by our daughters without loss to woman's crowning glory—her gentleness and grace.[43]

Interestingly, Randolph–Macon sought to promote two ideals—that of southern womanhood and that of equal education, two notions that before the birth of southern women's colleges, had been perceived by southerners as mutually exclusive. But from its inception, Randolph–Macon, true to its prospectus, adopted as its academic course leading to a Bachelor of Arts a curriculum like that of its partner college in Ashland. The College for Men, in turn, had used as its model the curricular plan of the University of Virginia, whose scheme, in the words of Elizabeth Young, was recognized as "the very synonym of higher education in the South."[44]

The official rhetoric of the school, however, almost belied the rigorous academic program. As one historian of Randolph-Macon explained, the president of the college, William Waugh Smith,

> foresaw the many prejudices that he would probably encounter in the South in establishing a college for the higher education of women. He knew the great value of tact, he felt that too sudden or too radical innovations, especially in the State of Virginia would forestall the accomplishment of his purpose.[45]

To placate those who feared the "innovation" of the higher education of women, the authorities of the college sought to prove that far from producing an assertive, monstrous creature, a kind of "*superwoman, who was to equal if not surpass, in scholarly attainments the brother student at College in Ashland,*" Randolph-Macon would preserve the "Southern type of womanhood."[46]

Fiercely guarding the traditional image of the southern lady, colleges such as Randolph-Macon, responding to the threat of reconstruction and possible assimilation, attempted to uphold the separateness of the South through the separate identity of its women.

Gradually, a cadre of highly educated women emerged in the South. Though small in number, these women, educated both in northern schools and the newly emerging women's colleges of the South, effected promising changes in the educational and professional patterns of southern women. Adding solidarity to this group was the development in Knoxville, Tennessee, in 1903 of the Southern Association of College Women. Limiting its membership to women with degrees from colleges with the highest standards, the Association, citing the "deplorable" state of women's higher education in the South, strove to elevate the quality of southern women's colleges.

Instrumental in the association in the early twentieth century was Elizabeth Avery Colton (1872-1924). Colton experienced firsthand the inadequacies of women's higher education in her native North Carolina when, having completed her Bachelor's degree at a women's college in Statesville, she entered Mount Holyoke, only to spend a year in the preparatory program before gaining admission to the freshman class. Receiving her M.A. degree from Columbia University in 1905, Colton taught at Wellesley College, then became head of the English department at Meredith College in Raleigh, North Carolina.

As an organizing member of the Southern Association of College Women, Colton played a prominent role in publicly addressing the weaknesses of women's education in the South. In 1910 Colton became head of the Association's Committee on College Standards and began her painstaking task of surveying all the institutions for women in the South that called themselves "colleges." Researching in detail all the requirements, curricula, degree programs, faculty qualifications, materials, equipment, and facilities of the schools, Colton published her findings in a series of bulletins issued by the association from 1911 to 1916.

The results of her inquiries were shocking and controversial. Citing in her first study of 1911 only four out of 141 "colleges" worthy of the name, Colton uncovered the pretense and sham that marked these schools. Colton's bulletin of 1916, entitled *The Various Types of Southern Colleges for Women,* added further details to the picture of women's education in the South. Dividing the 124 colleges into six classes, Colton found seven standard colleges, eight approximate colleges, six normal and industrial colleges, thirty junior colleges, twenty-one unclassifiable colleges, and thirty-two nominal and imitation colleges, to which a list of twenty was appended which had failed to comply with her study.

Describing the grandiose claims found in the catalogues of some of the "imitation colleges," Colton revealed how "the Wellesley of the South," or the "Vassar of the South" were, at best, providing only a high school education. Because of her revelations, Colton's work did not go unchallenged. As the Southern Association of College Women mailed some 4,000 copies of *The Various Types of Southern Colleges for Women* to girls graduating from high school the year it was published, Colton became the target of protests from indignant alumnae and administrators and received threats of lawsuits from disgruntled college presidents. Only a few administrators asked the association how they might improve their schools; most simply denied the validity of the bulletins. One particularly unhappy president threatened to shoot Elizabeth Colton and "thrust his hand in his pocket apparently to make good his threat." Under Colton's "steady, honest gaze," he retreated. "Shortly afterward he closed his so-called college."

Ultimately the furor abated, and, as Colton wished, the South took positive steps to remedy its educational deficiencies. In tribute to Colton, the American Association of University Women cited her publications "as beginning a new era for the education of women in the South." True college work for college degrees was Colton's goal, "in order," she stated, "that our Southern institutions for the higher education of women will not continue to be the laughing stock of the educational world."[47]

While educated women of the South pushed to raise the quality of women's colleges in their region, other efforts were under way to open doors to those women whose economic and social standing had excluded them from any form of higher education. In the antebellum South, all forms of education were virtually denied to the majority of women. With no broadly-based common school system and with statutes in certain southern states forbidding the education of slaves, women outside the white, wealthy classes had no access to formal schooling. After the war, significant steps were taken to ameliorate the educational deprivations of black women and white women from lower economic classes, largely through the creation of vocational and normal schools.

Educational developments for black women had begun outside the South prior to the war. The first organized effort, following Prudence Crandall's courageous attempt, occurred in Washington, D.C. in 1857 when two white women, Anna Inman and Myrtilla Miner (1815-1864), founded a seminary for black women. Recalling the experience of Crandall, individuals such as Frederick Douglass (1817-1895) initially tried to dissuade Miner from opening her school. Soon, though, in spite of opposition that forced her to frequently move locations, Miner was training future teachers, six of whom by 1858 were conducting their own schools. In 1860 the fear of Douglass and others was realized when Miner's school was set afire, temporarily closing it. It reopened in 1864 as Miner's Normal School and by 1929 had evolved into Miner's Teachers College.[48]

In 1862 Mary Jane Patterson (1840-1894) from Raleigh, North Carolina, daughter of fugitive slaves, became the first black female college graduate in America, receiving her degree from Oberlin College. So important was Patterson's education to her parents, they had moved to Ohio in the 1850s so she could matriculate through this unique school. At this time thirty-one other black women were enrolled at Oberlin.[49]

With the war's end, the South became the locus of a proliferation of colleges for blacks. Prompted by the need in the region for teachers, most of the black colleges admitted women and a number of separate women's schools were founded.

The school that would gain the most prestige of the separate institutions was Spelman in Atlanta, Georgia. Founded in 1881 by two white Bostonians whose evangelical ministry led them to venture southward, Spelman Seminary was the first school for black women to claim to provide college level courses. Its primary goal, however, was to train public school teachers and Christian missionaries. As a member of the American Baptist Mission Society, founder Sophie Packard (1824-1891) enlisted the financial aid of the Baptist Congress and soon the motto of the school became "Our Whole School for Christ."

Additional support came from Laura Spelman (Mrs. John D.) Rockefeller (1839-1915), whose gifts enabled Spelman to grow and develop independently when it appeared that it would have to merge with nearby Morehouse College for men. In appreciation the school was named in honor of Mrs. Rockefeller's mother.

Offering several areas of specialty, including domestic science and nurses' training, Spelman's strength in its years as a seminary lay in teacher training. Reflecting its motto, a number of graduates embarked as missionaries to Africa. The predominantly white faculty and administration of Spelman created a curriculum and atmosphere that they hoped would inspire their graduates to "lift the masses of their people" in the home, in the school, and in distant Africa.[50] In 1927 Spelman began to evolve into a full-fledged liberal arts college, joining, as a coordinate college, the Atlanta University Group in 1929.[51]

Of the black coeducational facilities that developed in the South after the war, historian Cynthia Neverdon-Morton has noted two types: the "industrial" school and the "academic."[52] The earliest example of the former was Hampton Normal and Agricultural Institute below the town of Hampton, Virginia. Founded in 1866, Hampton became the model of other schools throughout the South designed "to train teachers for the public schools and make industrial leaders for the race," the phrase, "industrial leaders," indicating "better farmers," acknowledges Neverdon-Morton.[53]

Hampton Institute was additionally significant in that it opened its doors to Native Americans, male and female, in 1878. Coming from various tribes, the Native Americans were segregated from the black students in separate dormitories and, until 1912, in a separate dining hall. Classes, however, were integrated. The first Native American woman to earn a medical degree, Susan La Flesche (1865-1915), was a Hampton graduate of the class of 1886.[54]

Hampton underwent a series of curricular changes, adding a nursing program in 1890 and domestic science in 1898. By the early 1920s, Hampton was offering a four-year college program leading to a Bachelor of Science degree. Because of its emphasis on service and teaching, about ninety percent of its early students became teachers. This was true also of the Native Americans, many of whom returned to reservations to work. Hampton was noted, too, for the number of graduates who founded schools upon the Hampton model, most importantly, Booker T. Washington (1856-1915), who established Tuskegee Institute in Alabama in 1881. Like Hampton, Tuskegee offered instruction to black women in domestic science, teaching, and nursing. Some limited academic training was interspersed with the technical courses.

Certain black leaders and educators of the late nineteenth century argued that too much emphasis was being placed on the industrial education of black students. Advocating a strong liberal arts curriculum, black scholars such as Atlanta University's George Towns (b. 1870) and W. E .B. DuBois (1868-1963) saw fully academic programs as essential to black economic development. Atlanta University, Fisk University in Nashville, and Morgan State College in Baltimore were three black coeducational institutions that were primarily liberal arts schools and espoused this philosophy.[55] Interestingly, the story of women at these colleges presents a narrative woven with paradoxes, reflecting in some ways the gender patterns in predominantly white coeducational schools across the country, and in other ways a unique drama. Most of the women in these schools followed, like white coeds, separate courses of study, usually in the normal or domestic science departments. Women at Fisk University, no matter what their major, were required to take domestic science courses.[56] The channeling of women into these courses was propelled by the predominant argument, prevalent among educators of black women, that their students "should be trained to teach in order to lift the masses of their people and become excellent homemakers for their husbands and children," noted Jeanne Noble.[57]

Rarely were black women of the late nineteenth and early twentieth century offered or encouraged to acquire training beyond this prescribed level. Those that sought more knowledge were challenged, not only by a white society that continued to debate the intellectual capacity of blacks and women, but by blacks themselves, who came more and more to hold a rigid view of women's role and education. Suffragist, black leader, and Oberlin graduate Mary Church Terrell (1863-1954) recalled her father's belligerent attitude toward her education and professional aspirations: "He disinherited me, refused to write to me for a year because I went to Wilberforce to teach. Further I was ridiculed and told that no man would want to marry a woman who studied higher mathematics. I said I'd take a chance and run the risk."[58]

This attitude on the part of Terrell's father reflects a growing theme in black gender roles in the late nineteenth and early twentieth century. For a number of reasons, including, as historian Linda Perkins illustrates, the passage of the Fifteenth Amendment in 1870 which granted black men the franchise and hence a new sense of "apartness," black men began to change their perceptions of the role of black women. Ironically, black men began more and more to embrace white middle-class patterns of gender distinctions, expressing the desire that women stay home to be wives and mothers. "When I married my wife I married her to wait on me," explained a freedman to his former master. Black women's education, then, should be fashioned to prepare them for such a role, claimed many articles in the black press. "Shall Our Girls Be Educated?", "The Homemaker," and "Woman's Exalted Station" were the titles of some articles appearing in a popular journal published by the African Methodist Episcopal Church in the 1880s and 1890s.[59]

A rigid social code came to be forced upon the coeds, reinforced by a heavily moralistic curriculum, in black colleges and universities. As Jeanne Noble points out, administrators of black colleges were no doubt influenced by white coeducational schools whose conduct codes and academic restrictions they tended to imitate. But such limitations—social and academic—marked an abrupt change in the traditional role of black women. Having played "an equal if not dominant role in the slave culture," black college women were now placed decidedly below the men in institutions that sought to emulate white gender patterns.[60]

This treatment imposed a double handicap on aspiring black women, whose influence, emphasized distinguished black educator Anna Julia Cooper (1859-1964), was vital at this moment. It was incumbent upon black men, she stressed, to awaken to the importance of women's wider role. But sadly,

> . . . that her intermeddling could improve the management of school systems, or elevate the tone of public institutions, or humanize and sanctify the far-reaching influence of prisons and reformatories . . . that she has a word worth hearing on mooted questions in political economy . . . I fear the majority of "Americans of the colored variety" are not yet prepared to concede.[61]

Behind the excessively rigid codes for the black coed, however, may have lurked a more troubling, unnamed force, the spectre of the past with its image of the "foremother's sex role as a slave." Now, in order to eradicate the stigma of past "sins," the black woman's behavior was to be impeccable, with no suggestion of impropriety. Thus, Noble concludes, "her education in many instances appears to have been based on a philosophy which implied she was weak and immoral and that at best she should be made fit to rear her children and keep house for her husband."[62]

Nashville's Fisk University, for example, viewed the "right education" of black women as one of its primary missions. To this end, little freedom was accorded its coeds in dress, social activities, or academic choices. Such restrictions did not deter women from entering Fisk, though. So many continued to apply that hundreds of women applicants had to be refused yearly.[63]

This longing for education ran deep among black women, and by the turn of the century, they were entering not only black colleges, but were enrolled in white institutions in the North and Midwest, the

South far from integration at this point. These included the University of Chicago, Cornell, Radcliffe, Wellesley, Smith, and of course Oberlin.[64] The urgency to gain an education was tremendous for many of them, as was the pressure to succeed. Fannie Jackson Coppin (1837-1913), for example, a graduate of Oberlin's full collegiate program in 1865, reflected, "I never rose to recite in my classes at Oberlin but I felt that I had the honor of the whole African race upon my shoulders. I felt that, should I fail, it would be ascribed to the fact that I was colored."[65]

Aspiring black women, unlike their male counterparts, many of whom embraced a patriarchy and "true womanhood" within the black community, recognized the economic and social realities of the time: most black women had to work. These women believed in the value of education, therefore, not only as a means of "uplifting" themselves and their race well beyond their present station, but as a means of survival.

The majority of educated black women of the nineteenth century, again with a sense of urgency and necessity, became teachers, and some founded their own schools. Born a slave in Macon, Georgia, in 1854, Lucey C. Laney (1854-1933) became a graduate of Atlanta University and after teaching public school for a number of years established Haines Normal and Industrial Institute in Augusta, Georgia, in 1886. Offering liberal arts courses, as well as vocational, Laney taught future teachers, some of whom would in turn found their own schools, notably Charlotte Hawkins Brown (1883-1961), Janie Porter Barrett (1865-1948), and Mary McLeod Bethune (1875-1955).[66]

Mary McLeod Bethune played many roles in her life. As educator, activist, founder of organizations for women, and member of the Roosevelt administration, Bethune was a dynamic, visible star in the public, political arena of the 1930s and 1940s. It was her work, however, creating a school for girls out of a "dump heap" in Daytona Beach, Florida, that proved to be her most beloved project. Selling ice cream and sweet potato pies to raise the $5.00 down payment for a site known as "Hell's Hole," which had at one time been a garbage dump, Bethune, with courage and enterprise, built her school.

Beginning as Daytona Beach Literary and Industrial School for Training Negro Girls, the institution, under her guidance, grew to become in 1929 Bethune-Cookman, a four–year coeducational accredited college.[67]

For the most part, the education of women in the South, both black and white, was designed to uphold the doctrine of separate spheres. For white women, the institutions that strove to provide an education "equal to a man's" were the separate women's colleges that were accorded recognition by the Southern Association of College Women. Coeducation came slowly in the South, and, as will be examined in the next chapter, did little to offer the majority of women full academic programs. By 1912 only seven southern state colleges were coeducational; several of the most notable institutions of the South, such as the University of Virginia and the University of North Carolina, still adamantly refused to consider the idea of educating women. Though black women were enrolled in black coeducational schools in the late nineteenth century, they too were generally relegated to feminized programs that would lead to teaching and domestic service. Through their work as teachers, however, educated black and white women continued to struggle for the intellectual dignity of new generations of women.

Notes

1. William J. Cooper and Thomas E. Terrill, *The American South: A History* (New York: Alfred A. Knopf, 1990), 282.
2. David Hackett Fischer, *Albion's Seed: Four British Folkways in America* (New York and Oxford: Oxford University Press, 1989), 347.
3. Quoted in Fischer, 347.
4. Woody, 1: 239.
5. Ibid., 247.
6. See Charles William Dabney, *Universal Education in the South* (Chapel Hill: The University of North Carolina Press, 1936), 3-21.
7. Quoted in Woody, 1: 275.
8. Solomon, 12.
9. A.D. Mayo, *Southern Women in the Recent Educational Movement in the South,* Dan T. Carter and Amy Friedlander, eds. (Baton Rouge and London: Louisiana State University Press, 1978; reprint of the 1892 ed. published by the Govt. Print. Ofc. Washington, as Circular of Information, 1892, No. 1. of the U.S. Bureau of Education), 37.
10. Woody, 1: 277-278.
11. The South endured much greater ruin and hardship from the Revolutionary War than did the North. See Norton, 274-275.
12. Woody, 1: 384.
13. Ibid., 395.
14. Solomon, 21.
15. Woody, 1: 390.
16. Alma Lutz, *Emma Willard: Daughter of Democracy* (Boston: Houghton Mifflin, 1929; repr., Washington D.C.: Zenger Publishing Co., n.d.), 117.
17. Christine Ladd-Franklin, "The Education of Woman in the Southern States," in Meyer, *Woman's Work in America,* 91.
18. Fletcher Melvin Green, "Higher Education of Women in the South Prior to 1860," in *Democracy in the Old South and*

Other Essays, ed. J. Isaac Copeland (Nashville: Vanderbilt University Press, 1969), 210-211.

19. Quoted in Dorothy Scovil Vickery, *Hollins College 1842-1942: An Historical Sketch* (Published by Hollins College, Virginia, 1942), 16.

20. Woody, 1: 410.

21. Quoted in Ladd-Franklin, 89.

22. Genteel southern womanhood was identified with the South itself. For a discussion of this, see W.J. Cash, *The Mind of the South* (New York: Alfred A. Knopf, 1941), 85-86.

23. Ladd-Franklin, 90.

24. Elizabeth Fox-Genovese, *Within the Plantation Household: Black and White Women of the Old South* (Chapel Hill and London: The University of North Carolina Press, 1988), 46-47; 256-257.

25. Sarah Morgan Dawson, *A Confederate Girl's Diary,* ed. James I. Robertson, Jr. (Bloomington: Indiana University Press, 1960; repr., Westport, Conn.: Greenwood Press, Inc., 1972), 249-250.

26. Quoted in Anne Firor Scott, *The Southern Lady: From Pedestal to Politics 1830-1930* (Chicago and London: The University of Chicago Press, 1970), 64. The outpourings of discontent can be read in the letters and diaries of women across the antebellum South. For some examples, see Scott, 72-77.

27. Quoted in Gerda Lerner, *The Grimké Sisters from South Carolina: Pioneers for Woman's Rights and Abolition* (New York: Schocken Books, 1975), 29.

28. Ibid., 23.

29. Mary Boykin Chesnut, *Mary Chesnut's Civil War,* ed. C. Vann Woodward (New Haven: Yale University Press, 1981), 59.

30. Woloch, 224.

31. Ibid.

32. Scott, 110-111.

33. Mayo, 52.

34.   Ibid., 57.

35.   Scott, 114.

36.   Elizabeth Barber Young, *A Study of the Curricula of Seven Selected Women's Colleges of the Southern States* (New York: Teachers College, Columbia University Bureau of Publications, 1972; repr. of 1932 edition), 74-75.

37.   Ibid.

38.   Brandt V.B. Dixon, *A Brief History of H. Sophie Newcomb Memorial College 1887-1919* (New Orleans: Hauser Printing Co., 1928), 32-33.

39.   Young, 93.

40.   F.H. Gaines, *The Story of Agnes Scott College 1889-1921* (n.p., n.d.), 56.

41.   Ibid., 57.

42.   Walter Edward McNair, *Lest We Forget* (Atlanta: Tucker-Castleberry Printing, Inc., 1983), 37; Young, 102.

43.   This statement of purpose was printed regularly in the college catalogue in Randolph-Macon's early years. See Roberta D. Cornelius, *The History of Randolph-Macon Woman's College* (Chapel Hill: University of North Carolina Press, 1951), 31.

44.   Young, 109.

45.   Quoted in Young, 104.

46.   Quoted in Young, 104-105.

47.   Mary Lynch Johnson, *Elizabeth Avery Colton: An Educational Pioneer in the South* (Issued by the North Carolina Division of the South Atlantic Section of the American Association of University Women, n.d.), 3-16.

48.   See Sadie St. Clair's essay on Myrtilla Miner in *Notable American Women,* 2: 547-548.

49.   Oberlin produced virtually a "who's who" of "articulate, classically trained, race-conscious, and feminist black women during the nineteenth century." Linda M. Perkins, "The Education of Black Women in the Nineteenth Century," in *Women and Higher Education in American History,* eds. John Mack Faragher and Florence Howe (New York and London: W.W. Norton and Co., 1988), 77. See also Jeanne

L. Noble, *The Negro Woman's College Education* (New York: Bureau of Publications, Teachers College, Columbia University, 1956), 18-19.

50. Noble, 22. See also Cynthia Neverdon-Morton, *Afro-American Women of the South and the Advancement of the Race 1895-1925* (Knoxville: University of Tennessee Press, 1989), 41-52.
51. Solomon, 152.
52. Neverdon-Morton, 15.
53. Ibid., 16.
54. Ibid., 24-25.
55. Ibid, 15-40.
56. Ibid., 55.
57. Noble, 22.
58. Ibid., 23.
59. Perkins, 76-77. See also Woloch, 225.
60. Noble, 24.
61. Anna Julia Cooper, *A Voice from the South by a Black Woman of the South* (Ohio: Aldine Printing House, 1892; repr., New York: Negro Universities Press, 1969), 135.
62. Noble, 24.
63. Neverdon-Morton, 57.
64. It is difficult to assess the numbers of black women being educated at this time. Paula Giddings cites one article that claimed that four thousand women had graduated from ninety normal schools and universities by 1905. In terms of full collegiate work, however, she cites Jeanne Noble's count of 227 black women B.A.'s in 1910. See Paula Giddings, *When and Where I Enter: The Impact of Black Women on Race and Sex in America* (New York: William Morrow and Co., 1984), 76.
65. Fannie Jackson Coppin, "Training to Become an Educator," in Gerda Lerner, ed. *Black Women in White America: A Documentary History* (New York: Vintage Books, 1973), 89.
66. Giddings, 76.

67.   Rackham Holt, *Mary McLeod Bethune: A Biography* (Garden City, New York: Doubleday and Co., Inc., 1964), 57-159.

CHAPTER 8

EXPANSION AND LIMITATIONS IN THE EARLY
TWENTIETH CENTURY

After the turn of the century, Americans proudly proclaimed
their preeminence in the area of higher education for women. Citing
the advances made by the women's education movement in the
preceding decades despite the many obstacles, some enthusiasts noted
that women were now gaining from an array of notable institutions.
Indeed, reported Marion Talbot (1858-1948), Dean of Women at the
University of Chicago, the women's education movement "proceeded
with a force which marked it as one of the great characteristics of the
last century, and made it a contribution of the United States to
civilization which has aroused the admiration of the world."[1]
     Recognized as the decisive factor in women's expanding role
in public life, America's curious profusion of educational
opportunities was a source of pride for those involved in the process.
The Commissioner of Education of the United States cited in
particular America's system of coeducation as responsible for "the
freedom that women enjoy in the country with respect to the pursuit
of careers, and especially the large share which they take in the
educational work of the country."[2]
     By the last decade of the nineteenth century, college after
college door had opened to women in every region of the country,

and soon it was no longer a fearful or rare occurrence to meet a college woman. For the next two decades the movement accelerated, and by 1920 women constituted nearly half (47.3 percent) of the college population. In this year, 283,000 women were studying in approximately 1,000 institutions of higher learning across America.[3] Although women students were primarily from the higher economic strata of the professional middle class, the numbers reflected a growing democratization as scholarships, loans, and work programs enabled a wider range of the population to seek intellectual training.[4]

The rise was meteoric. Time had verified Henry Adams' (1838-1918) admission that it was "a hopeless task" to resist women's demand for education, and opponents, apart from a few feeble protests, rested their case.[5]

But as the experience of coeducation in America indicated, women's advances into the halls of higher learning were often greeted with efforts to divert their academic interest. As more and more women partook of intellectual training, efforts to channel them into separate programs, departments, and colleges prevailed. Far more debilitating than the endeavors to isolate women in separate classrooms, as the University of Chicago had attempted, were trends in academic programs within coeducational facilities that were designed exclusively for women. Normal departments, home economics programs, and gradually schools of social work (although in its early years, social work was not a feminized area) assured the continuation of "woman's place" within academe, much as the "Ladies' Courses" in the mixed schools had done a few decades earlier. Men, too, found themselves in gender-specific programs of study. As practical pursuits continued to govern the direction of higher education in America, men were concentrated in colleges of agriculture, business, and engineering.

The separation of women occurred with the most success and ease in colleges and universities that promoted a curriculum in home economics. As Margaret Rossiter indicates, the rise of home economics as a viable course of study accompanied the phenomenal rise of women students in coeducational institutions in the 1890s. By 1910 home economics had become a leading field for women.[6]

Included in the curriculum were cooking, sewing, household economy, sanitation, and child culture. For the many women who followed these courses, college ceased to provide an alternative to domesticity. Rather, college served as a vehicle that drew them securely back to the home.

Interestingly, the growth of home economics as a suitable area may be attributed to the work of a few professional women holding powerful positions far from the confines of the home, notably Ellen Swallow Richards (1842-1911) and Marion Talbot. A protégée of Maria Mitchell at Vassar and the first woman to attend Massachusetts Institute of Technology, Richards attempted to resolve the conflict of domesticity and professionalism by combining the two in academic settings. In 1890 she proclaimed the new field of domestic science before the Association of Collegiate Alumnae, saying,

> We have been greeted for some years by discussions from eminent men as to our mental ability, our moral and physical status, our predilection for matrimony, voting, or the presidency, etc.; but the kind of home we should make if we did make one, the position we should take on the servant question, the influence we should have on that centre and source of political economy, the kitchen, seem to have been ignored.[7]

Richards, therefore, devoted her career to instituting these domestic concerns, serving as professor of sanitary chemistry at MIT and professor of domestic science at Simmons College, Boston. As the chief advocate of home economics, she presented books, papers, exhibitions, and conferences, and in 1908 organized the American Home Economics Association.[8]

Marion Talbot, one of Richards' graduate students, founded the home economics department at the University of Chicago. As one of the major champions of women's entry into higher education, Talbot presents the paradox of many women academics during this era who sought the full participation of women in university life, yet who personally were forced to accept less.

Talbot came to Chicago in 1890 as assistant professor of sociology and assistant dean of women under former Wellesley president Alice Freeman Palmer. Viewing the challenging city of Chicago, with its slums and growing immigrant population, as a "social laboratory" where her students--men and women alike--might cooperatively work to help remedy the ills of modern urban life, Talbot urged President William Rainy Harper (1856-1906) to establish a department of public health. Far from a feminized program, Talbot's department would offer men and women a curriculum heavy in science, including chemistry, physics, and physiology, as well as political economy and modern languages. Together, men and women would then apply their knowledge, steeped in the sciences, to the task of urban reform, and in so doing, help eliminate the barriers that delineated the separate spheres of "feminine" and "masculine" work.

Unfortunately, due to lack of funds, President Harper dismissed Talbot's request and her vision never materialized at the University of Chicago. Instead, in 1904, President Harper appointed Talbot head of the newly created "household administration" department. Hoping to incorporate many of the ideas of her original project into this new program, Talbot worked to strengthen this field. Talbot's new role, though, placed her firmly over a specifically female area, a condition she had sought to prevent in her earlier plan for a public health program.[9]

Now, as Chicago's dean of women, Talbot endowed home economics with the stamp of academic and professional authenticity. Young women hoping for a suitable career could look to successful, visible women such as Richards and Talbot and perceive a vocational option, yet one that kept them safely anchored to the ideals of home, wifehood, and motherhood. The higher education of many early twentieth-century American women, then, was well grounded within traditional roles. As Talbot advised, "Throughout all a woman's training, there should run the idea of her high function as a wife, as a mother, as a home-maker in the true sense."[10]

In some cases the institutionalizing of home economics benefited women professionally, providing new career opportunities on faculties of coeducational universities, where women had constituted a minute, underpaid segment. With the development of this discipline, new positions as professors, department heads, and deans were generated. Women trained in the field also entered work outside universities, notably in hospitals and settlement houses.[11] Catharine Beecher's older vision of women's education as training for appropriate feminine professions thus became a reality in America as the theme of domesticity found expression within university catalogues, curricula, and syllabi.

But the path of home economics as an academic and professional alternative for women was strewn with pitfalls and often led women, not into the larger world, but back to the home. In universities the burgeoning departments served to channel numbers of women students out of the academic mainstream and into separate, feminized courses that attempted to dignify homemaking with the names of science and economics. Institutions such as Cornell, where the presence of women was deemed harmful to prestige, used the department of home economics to further isolate women.[12]

And though there were some vocational rewards for the women trained in home economics, many of the new jobs remained marginal and underpaid, serving to weaken professional status and reinforce separate spheres. On a number of faculties, moreover, women academics trained in chemistry, physiology, history, and other academic subjects, found themselves "promoted" to professorships in home economics.[13] Sophonisba Breckinridge (1866-1948), for example, with a law degree and a doctorate in political science, joined Marion Talbot on the faculty of the Department of Household Administration at the University of Chicago.[14] Women scholars, often faced with closed doors in academe, found the path to college faculties less difficult, moreover, if they entered through the backdoor of home economics. When asked by the Trustees to consider a proposal to admit women to the Cornell University faculty in 1911, members resolved that "the University Faculty, while not favoring in general the appointment of women to professorships, interposes no objection to their appointment in the department of Home Economics."[15] This trend discouraged some talented students from pursuing scientific disciplines, steering them instead into home economics programs.[16]

Teacher education programs continued to isolate women within coeducation institutions, as well. Evolving out of the normal schools of the nineteenth century, departments of education were incorporated more and more into colleges and universities at the turn of the century.[17] By this time elementary and secondary teaching were well within the domain of woman's work and pedagogy became an established department or college of most coeducational facilities as the normal schools were phased out. While women composed the majority of students in teacher training programs, interestingly they were in the minority on the education faculties. Having predominated on the faculties of the normal schools, they were soon replaced by men when these programs became part of a college or university.[18]

Domestic science and education programs were strongest in the land grant universities. The older women's colleges in the Northeast and the South, with predominantly female faculties and administrations, attempted to resist the intrusion of feminized courses in their curricula. Due to "the prevalence of the tradition that only a classical training was real education,"[19] as well as the tradition of providing women with an education "like a man's," these liberal arts schools shunned the courses related to domesticity. But their resistance was met with criticism and pressure from the outside to conform to what was considered an innovative pattern in women's education. Samuel Dike (1839-1913), for instance, in an article praising women's special affinity for social work, was dismayed to find that women's colleges duplicated the courses offered in men's colleges. The time had arrived, he said, "for an advance to the higher ground," so that education may "equip the girl for what I may call the great profession of being a woman, in her social trinity of wife, mother, and member of society."[20]

Similarly, Charles Eliot urged women's colleges to convert. Women had succeeded in proving their mastery of "men's" studies, he conceded in a speech before the Association of Collegiate Alumnae in 1908. Now women's colleges should feel free to educate their students for their special calling. "It calls, and calls loudly, and often calls in vain, for carefully trained mental power, as well as great moral power," he exclaimed. "I look forward therefore to the future of the higher education for women as a great influence in the perfecting of home life, of family life, of household joy and good."[21]

Leaders of the women's colleges, such as M. Carey Thomas and Mount Holyoke's President Mary E. Woolley (1863-1947), deplored the vision of such a future and considered the trends in feminized, specialized training disastrous to the cause of women's higher education. President Woolley fought public opinion, as well as Mount Holyoke's Board of Trustees, to prevent the intrusion of home economics courses in the curriculum. She eventually won her case and saved the college "from becoming a vocational school," remembered history professor Ellen Deborah Ellis (b. 1878).[22] But even Bryn Mawr swayed under the weight of the arguments and during the latter part of Thomas's presidency instituted a department of social work on the graduate level. Other women's colleges conformed, as well, until by 1910 most offered at least token courses in home economics, hygiene, social work, and pedagogy.[23]

The emphasis on such subjects remained slight in the leading women's colleges, however, and in 1918, the United States Bureau of Education reported that the curricula of these colleges were a "safe imitation" of those of the men's colleges.[24] But the number of women attending separate colleges in America was minuscule compared to the multitudes now entering the larger coeducational facilities that offered new "practical" training.[25]

As in America, a growing number of women entered university life in England at the turn of the century.[26] Considering the recent barriers and opposition English women faced, the educational gains in the early twentieth century were notable. Critics continued to respond with ridicule and admonitions, but, as early as the 1890s, Ray Strachey acknowledged, the "flutter of the old opposition . . . had an out-of-date flavour."[27] Gradually, as numbers increased, old assumptions faded away. "The college girl was found, on trial, to be still a normal woman, better trained, perhaps, with wider interests than her predecessors, but not more alarming, even to guardsmen, than the others."[28]

Due to the strict quota systems and to the degree controversies at Oxford and Cambridge, London and the provincial universities gained the higher proportion of students in the early twentieth century. In the newer universities women "worked with men as colleagues, sharing in the organization of teaching, examinations, and other university business, as well as the opportunities for advanced work and research.[29] By contrast, the unresolved question of degrees at the ancient universities significantly weakened their attraction, despite their quality and prestige.[30]

The demands of World War I and women's responses to them engendered throughout England a new acceptance of women as capable, industrious, and courageous human beings. The abrupt shift in public opinion was summarized by Prime Minister Herbert Asquith (1852-1928) when he paid tribute to the memory of British nurse Edith Cavell (1865-1915), who had unflinchingly faced a German firing squad in 1915: "There are thousands of such women," he admitted, "but a year ago we did not know it."[31] In 1918 the nation rewarded women for their war efforts by granting the parliamentary franchise to those over thirty. In a further gesture, Parliament passed the Sex Disqualification Removal Act in 1919, dismantling even more barriers that had blocked women's participation in professional and political life.

Accordingly, in 1920 Oxford University awarded without opposition equal status to the women of their residential colleges in all areas but theology. Women were thus accepted for matriculation and admitted to degrees "under the same conditions as regards standing, examinations, courses of study, and periods of residence as men."[32] They were also admitted to university government, faculties, boards, delegacies, and examining bodies.[33]

Cambridge, the first university to have accepted women informally, was the last to grant them equal status on a formal basis. In 1921 Cambridge agreed to issue women degree titles, as had been requested in 1897, but limited the number of women receiving university instruction to five hundred. Women of Girton and Newnham were also given the right of admission to university lectures and laboratories, privileges previously granted only by courtesy of individual lecturers. Not until 1948 were women awarded full membership in Cambridge University.[34]

While equality of recognition remained distant for the women of Cambridge, they achieved near equality in the remaining universities throughout England, as well as Scotland, Ireland, and Wales. Although degrees in divinity were reserved for men, women students partook of the same course work, examinations, and degrees as their male peers in the other disciplines. Most women in England chose to enter the Faculty of Arts, but by the 1920s they were also enrolling in Faculties of Science, Medicine, Law, and Commerce.[35]

England was not entirely immune to the influx of feminized specialties. Departments of education and hygiene did exist, as well as independent vocational schools and independent teaching colleges. These programs, however, existed outside the universities, and upon completion were not awarded with a university degree, but a certificate or diploma. The study of social science was also popular among English women, but, as in America, this new field was not exclusively feminine. Schools of social science existed primarily in connection with the settlement houses organized by the Universities of London, Manchester, and Glasgow.[36]

As of 1921 only King's College of the University of London had designed a "Household and Social Science Department." Again, a certificate was awarded to women in this field, most of whom passed through "Municipal Schools of Domestic Economy" in England's major cities or the growing number of vocational and technical schools developing in urban centers.[37]

These programs were significant, though, in terms of numbers of women. Advanced education outside England's universities attracted more and more women in the early twentieth century, especially from the lower economic groups. Here the emphasis was on gender specific vocational and domestic preparation. As Sarah Delamont notes, this represents a reversal of educational conditions of the mid-nineteenth century when middle-class girls received a smattering of instruction in the feminine accomplishments while working-class girls studied what their brothers did, however rudimentary.[38]

Now as women from professional families joined their brothers in universities across England, women of lower economic and social status entered vocational programs or schools of domestic economy.

Like the elite women's colleges in the United States, the women's colleges connected with England's great universities remained dedicated to strictly academic achievement, Newnham, Somerville, and Lady Margaret Hall having embraced, like Girton, full academic programs and examinations. Toward the end of the nineteenth century and the beginning of the twentieth century, however, a trend was underway in England to promote domestic ideology and to give it a respected position in the female curriculum. The National Association for the Promotion of Housewifery in the 1880s worked toward the goal of "removing the stigma attached by so many to domestic work, and giving it its true place in a girl's education."[39] Indeed, earlier in England, there had been a stigma attached to this kind of training. Poet Matthew Arnold (1822-1888), for one, in his education reports as school inspector in the mid-nineteenth century, denounced domestic courses in teacher training programs, arguing that intellectual training was primary and "cooking and clear starching" would be superfluous in an already overcrowded syllabus.[40]

Unfortunately, by the early twentieth century, even educated women, those who had been pioneers in the struggle to gain full academic rights in England's universities, began to promote the new tendencies. Lillian Faithfull (1865-1952), for example, an early Somerville student who succeeded Dorothea Beale as principal of Cheltenham Ladies' College, wrote, "The old 'blue-stocking' type, who prided herself on not knowing how to sew or mend, and who

thought cooking menial and beneath her, no longer appeals to anyone.
. . . We want our girls to grow up into sensible, methodical, practical
women, able to direct intelligently and practically the manifold duties
of the home."[41]

Infused, then in the curriculum of girls' secondary schools
was a stream of household-related courses. Writer Grace Foakes (b.
1901) remembered her experience at the London Board School in
1900 with nostalgia and humor. Girls in the upper grades, she
recalled, were sent to a central school for a class in either
housewifery, laundry, or cooking.

> If we did the housewifery course, we
> were taught to sweep, dust, polish,
> make beds and bathe a life-size doll.
> We had great fun on this course, for
> it was held in a house set aside for
> the purpose, and with only one
> teacher in charge we were quick to
> take advantage when she went to
> inspect some other part of the house.
> We jumped on the bed, threw
> pillows, drowned the doll and swept
> dirt under the mats. This was the
> highlight of the week, the one lesson
> that we never minded going to.[42]

Principals, instructors, and those that set curricular policy,
such as the Education Department in London, did not take domestic
instruction as lightly as Foakes and her fellow schoolmates. Instead,
England seriously set out to inject secondary schooling for English
girls with a full dose of strictly feminized training with all its
ideology of separate spheres of gender and class. Many of the girls
trained like Foakes in dusting and polishing would later find
employment in the homes of a new professional class of women
emerging from the women's colleges of Oxford and Cambridge, not
unlike the young black women trained at Hampton and Tuskegee,

who would find employment in hospitals, schools, and homes of families across the tracks from their own neighborhoods.

But these trends in secondary and vocational training would not affect the studies of women at Girton, Newnham, Somerville, Lady Margaret, or those within England's other universities. The struggle by English women to gain university privileges had been difficult and slow, particularly at Oxford and Cambridge. When the privileges were won, then, most women students chose to take advantage of a full university program, pursuing the same courses, examinations, and degrees as their male counterparts. The newer fields of social science, hygiene, and domestic science did enter the curricula in certain universities. But they were slow to do so and were not always popular, as illustrated by the experience of the hygiene department at Bedford College, London, which closed for lack of students. Such disciplines were generally reserved for technical institutions where the course of study involved less time and money for completion than university courses.[43] By 1920, despite Cambridge's obdurate position, university women in England had achieved nearly equal status in academic life.

Notes

1. Marion Talbot, *The Education of Women* (Chicago: University of Chicago Press, 1910), 18-19. For further opinions concerning America's leading role in educating women, see M. Carey Thomas, *The College Women of the Present and Future* (n.p.: McClure's Syndicate, 1901), 2-3.

2. *Reports of the Commissioner of Education of the United States, 1901,* Vol. 2 (Washington: Government Printing Office, 1867-1915), 1228, quoted in Woody, 2: 302.

3. Newcomer, 37, 46.

4. Solomon, 66-77.

5. Henry Adams, unsigned review of Edward Clarke's *Sex in Education* (1874), quoted in Kaledin, 137. Early twentieth-century arguments opposing the higher education of women cited the problem of "race suicide." It was feared by these opponents that if college women did not marry and have children, immigrant populations would soon outnumber the older American stock. See, for instance, G. Stanley Hall and Theodore L. Smith, "Marriage and Fecundity of College Men and Women," *The Pedagogical Seminary* 10 (September 1903): 375-414. Most college women did marry, but did so later than noncollegiate women. See Solomon, 121.

6. Rossiter, 65.

7. Ellen Henrietta Swallow Richards, *The Relation of College Women to Progress in Domestic Science* (Publications of the Association of Collegiate Alumnae, Series 2, no. 27, 1890), 1.

8. Rossiter, 67-69.

9. Rosalind Rosenberg, *Beyond Separate Spheres: Intellectual Roots of Modern Feminism* (New Haven and London: Yale University Press, 1982), 32-35, 49.

10. Talbot, 56.

11. Rossiter, 66-72.

12. Conable, 113-115.

13.   Solomon, 86-87.

14.   Geraldine Jonçich Clifford, ed. *Lone Voyagers: Academic Women in Coeducational Universities 1870-1937* (New York: The Feminist Press at the City University of New York, 1989), 18.

15.   Quoted in Clifford, 18.

16.   Rossiter, 70.

17.   As Geraldine Jonçich Clifford notes, it was "through the limited admission of women students into such normal courses or into summer sessions for teachers that many institutions became fully coeducational." Clifford, 19.

18.   Ibid., 19-20.

19.   Mary Roberts Coolidge, *Why Women Are So* (New York: Henry Holt and Co., 1912; repr., New York: Arno Press, Inc. 1972), 237.

20.   Samuel Warren Dike, "Sociology in the Higher Education of Women," *Atlantic Monthly,* November 1892, 673-675.

21.   Charles Eliot, *Women's Education: A Forecast,* (Publications of the Association of Collegiate Alumnae, Series 3, no. 17, 1908), quoted in Roberta Frankfort, *Collegiate Women: Domesticity and Career in Turn-of-the-Century America* (New York: New York University Press, 1977), 99.

22.   Penina Migdal Glazer and Miriam Slater, *Unequal Colleagues: The Entrance of Women into the Professions, 1890-1940* (New Brunswick and London: Rutgers University Press, 1987), 41.

23.   Frankfort, 80-83. See also Newcomer, 89-90.

24.   M.L. Robinson, "Curriculum of the Woman's College," *no. 6* ([Washington, D.C.]: United States Bureau of Education, 1918), 108, quoted in Newcomer, 87.

25.   Newcomer, 37.

26.   It can be estimated that women remained less than one-third the population in English universities. See McWilliams-Tullberg, "Women and Degrees at Cambridge," note 1, 293.

27.   Strachey, 262.

28.   Ibid.

29. Stephen, 359.
30. Ibid.
31. Quoted in Strachey, 348.
32. St. Clare Byrne and Mansfield, 68.
33. Ibid.
34. McWilliams-Tullberg, 203, 210-214. See also Stephen, 358.
35. For a description of the universities, faculties, curricula, and lecture system within Great Britain as they related to women in the early twentieth century, see Phoebe Sheavyn, *The Higher Education for Women in Great Britain* (London: International Federation of Women, Pamphlet no. 2, 1921).
36. Ibid., 15.
37. Ibid.
38. Delamont, 164.
39. Quoted in Carol Dyhouse, "Social Darwinistic ideas and the Development of Women's Education in England, 1880–1920," *History of Education* 5 (1976): 48.
40. Ibid.
41. Ibid., 53-54.
42. Grace Foakes, "A London Schooling," in Murray, *Strong-Minded Women,* 253.
43. Tuke, 232-233.

CHAPTER 9

CONTINUING HOPE AND STRUGGLE

Upon surveying the scope of university education available to women in turn-of-the-century England, educator Maria Grey optimistically announced, "The privilege is won. The door so long closed is open wide, and the ways and means of knowledge abundantly provided."[1] Grey's work spanned the era of struggle in England, and it was with a sense of accomplishment and satisfaction that she viewed the progress in her country. Likewise in America, one educator proclaimed, "Women have achieved education, the key of liberation, the tool of talent, and all careers are open.[2]

In both England and the United States the advances were significant and offered women the means to "throw off the mental and moral defects contracted during long ages of irresponsible dependence."[3] Their brief college interlude enabled them to flourish intellectually by joining others whose mutual interest stimulated their mental processes. They also experienced a sense of freedom unobtainable within the home and family.

Letters, memoirs, and speeches of women on both sides of the Atlantic attest to the sense of release and joy provided by the college alternative. Hitchin pioneer Constance Maynard, for instance, awoke there every morning "with a sort of sting of delight," writing that "at last, at last" she and her colleagues "were afloat on a stream that had a real destination, even though we hardly knew what the destination

180

was."[4] Although only a handful of women reaped the benefits of higher education in England during Maynard's years at Hitchin and Girton, supporters recognized the importance of such modest beginnings. George Eliot, for one, praised Davies for her early efforts at Hitchin, writing that she was "cheered" by the opening of the college. "I care so much for individual happiness," she emphasized, "that I think it is a great thing to work for, only to make half a dozen lives better than they might otherwise be."[5]

The joy of intellectual fulfillment was often accompanied by the pain of a growing gulf between students and their families. The exposure to new ideas inevitably raised doubts and questions in the minds of educated young women concerning the value and validity of traditional religious, political, and social tenets held by the family. Mary Paley Marshall, for example, began to doubt her "old beliefs" after a few years at Newnham College. "I never talked on these subjects with my father, but we both knew that the old harmony between us had melted away."[6]

Newnham's Jane Ellen Harrison (1850-1928), classical scholar and one of the foremost nineteenth-century authorities on ancient Greece, experienced a similar separation from her past, but one which brought elation and emancipation:

> To realise the release that Aristotle brought, you must have been reared as I was in a narrow school of Evangelicalism--reared with sin always present, with death and judgment before you. . . . It was like coming out of a madhouse into a quiet college quadrangle where all was liberty and sanity, and you became a law to yourself.[7]

As the first generations of college women matriculated, those who entered academic life professionally provided outstanding role models for the following generations. Tutors and lecturers at the women's colleges at Oxford and Cambridge, though sometimes appearing "dowdy and ineffectual in daily life," were magnetic personalities within the academic setting and bestowed on their students a sense of direction and possibility.[8] Mary Paley Marshall and Jane Ellen Harrison, who both became lecturers at Newnham, drew accolades from their students. "She is enthusiastic and simple," wrote one of Marshall's students admiringly, and has "a face one likes to watch."[9] Similarly, a protégée of Harrison's exclaimed, "You flashed into my life like some new planet . . . and taught us the thrill and passion of intellectual things. . . . What sparks you struck out of our dull clay."[10]

The college experience proved no less rewarding for serious students in America, particularly those who followed full academic courses which led them to question, probe, and debate intellectual ideas. Many concurred with Lucy Salmon (1853-1927), professor of history at Vassar, who as a student had written her stepmother in 1873, "College is such a grand place and there are such noble girls here that I am beginning to dread the breaking up in '76."[11]

Most students, like Lucy Salmon, forged meaningful relationships with other students. But college was especially rewarding if strong intellectual bonds were established with faculty members. Sara Burstall, comparing the atmosphere on American campuses with those in England, noted the warmth and friendliness between faculty and students, and "the absence of stiffness and formality."[12] For many fortunate students, concerned professors, male and female, generated a love of learning and set them on intellectual paths that they followed throughout their lives. "You did more for me than you can realize," wrote a student to the University of Minnesota's professor of rhetoric Maria Louise Sanford (1836-1920), "since you don't know how hemmed in . . . my life seemed at the time when I first met you."[13] Vassar's Maria Mitchell, Radcliffe's professor of English George Lyman Kittredge (1860-1944), and Wellesley's Mary Calkins (1863-1930) in psychology and philosophy were some of the names often mentioned by several generations of college women in letters home.[14]

Such respected professors became mentors for a growing number of women students in the late nineteenth and early twentieth centuries. Gradually, as more and more women took their places on faculties, particularly in the women's colleges, strong mentor-protégée chains developed. Women faculty, only too aware of the obstacles confronting aspiring women, solicitously encouraged promising students to achieve. In certain women's colleges, mentor-protégée chains endured generations, as women professors selected their brightest students to succeed them. Once chosen, the protégée was cultivated and supervised by her mentor, who later would help arrange the student's appointment on the faculty.[15]

The story of women's education from 1865 to 1920 in England and America is truly one of remarkable personal advances. As M. Carey Thomas exclaimed in a speech delivered in 1913, the preceding decades were years of "splendid triumphal progress." So much had been accomplished, she noted, that it was "exhilarating" from her vantage to look into the future.[16] But in the early twentieth century, the ideal of equal education had yet to be achieved. As Thomas observed in her speech, "Women have almost won the right to study what and where they please. They have to-day almost equal opportunity to study."[17] Equal education was "almost" real, but not quite.

By 1920 the word *almost* applied to the collegiate status of women in both countries. University women in England enjoyed near equality with men, but the exceptions remained, notably in the question of degrees at Cambridge University. Discrimination of a more subtle nature continued to exist in English universities, as well, where women were restricted by quotas and, constituting a minor proportion of the enrollment, remained on the periphery of university life. According to Martha Vicinus, English women maintained a marginal status in the totality of university life due largely to their own inertia. Having sufficiently silenced the opposition so that they might study and matriculate, they were hesitant to agitate for other related goals for fear of further reaction. "Hedged in on all sides by social and economic constraints," Vicinus explains, "they bought intellectual freedom at the price of political timidity, a frequent fear of change, and a dislike of innovation."[18]

In America the "almost" represented a vaster space. One British writer in 1878 had congratulated America for its "powerful educational movement." But, the writer predicted, "It is even possible that America, which was first in recognising women's claims, may be last in recognising them completely."[19] Indeed, the trend in America toward curricular segregation, apparent in coeducational facilities, served to demarcate the dimensions of women's education. The seeds planted by Catharine Beecher's gospel extolling the virtues of a practical education in domestic concerns and teacher training came to fruition throughout the broad spectrum of America's institutions of higher learning in the early twentieth century.

It was primarily the separate women's colleges in America that gave the latitude in curriculum, professorships, and status within the collegiate community sought by the proponents of equal education. These small schools primarily in the Northeast and South fulfilled to a greater degree the demand for academic parity, emphasizing the sciences and liberal arts, while shunning exclusively feminine studies. These colleges were impressive by all standards, and according to Sara Burstall, with their outstanding libraries, observatories, and equipment were "on the whole finer than anything in England." Vassar was majestic, as was Wellesley, "with its beautiful grounds, its seclusion, its art treasures, its traditions," she wrote admiringly.[20] Affecting only a minute percentage of the population of college women, however, these colleges represented a small portion of the total picture.

By the twentieth century it was the mixed institutions that attracted the greater proportion of women. At the turn of the century over 70 percent of women college students attended coeducational facilities. By 1920 this number had increased to over 80 percent.[21] And here women's position remained ambiguous. While it was not impossible for bright, serious women to pursue the "masculine" subjects of history, mathematics, classics, chemistry, and philosophy, social ideals and professional realities induced the majority of women to follow feminine courses that would prepare them for their seemingly preordained roles as intelligent homemakers and teachers.

Feminists and reformers in England and America believed that the pathway to women's emancipation was through higher education, "the keystone of the arch, without which the rest of the fabric could have neither stability nor permanence."[22] But in reality women's lives more often than not fell short of the potential higher education promised. As Ellen Fitzpatrick notes, "The great contradiction of the revolution in women's higher education was that it prepared the first college graduates for a world of opportunities that did not really exist."[23] The next logical step beyond higher education, that of higher professional life, eluded most college women. Educated women did not in great numbers race to prove that they were now, as Charles Eliot had direly predicted in 1882, "enabled to compete with men at the bar, in the pulpit, the Senate, the bench."[24] The entry into professional life remained, despite the abundance of higher education, slow and difficult.[25]

Again, it was in the northeastern women's colleges that women were urged to put their education to professional use. During the Progressive era, the women of Vassar, for example, emphasized women's work over women's rights, embracing as their "Bible" Charlotte Perkins Gilman's *Women and Economics*, which argued for the economic independence of women through gainful employment. Vassar students considered opportunities in law, medicine, journalism, and business. But the new field of social work gained the most attention among those seeking professional outlets. Guest speakers lecturing at these women's colleges on social issues, settlement houses, and the role of the educated woman in society inspired many students to engage in altruistic work. Settlement houses, in particular, gave energetic, community-minded women a mission, and, as Jane Addams had found, a sense of liberation. "I had wanted to escape from my class prison, and I did," wrote Wellesley English professor and settlement worker Vida Scudder (1861-1954) of her experience at Denison House in Boston.[26]

Similarly, in England social concerns directed the ambitions of many educated women. Philanthropic work among English women had traditionally been viewed as the one appropriate public outlet for respectable women, and throughout the nineteenth century, the vast, unpaid personnel within charitable societies were women.[27] University women, then, began moving to the forefront of public service in the late nineteenth century, working in settlement houses and campaigning for election and appointments to School Boards, Poor Law Guardianships, and factory inspection teams.[28]

Many of the jobs open for women in social service in England remained without pay, and herein lay their appeal for women--and their families--whose overriding concern was that of respectability. Indeed, philanthropic work was advocated over paid employment as a superior avenue by some of the educators of English women, including Dorothea Beale of Cheltenham Ladies' College. The question of respectability remained an obstacle well into the twentieth century for aspiring women of the middle and upper classes in England as the equating of financial remuneration of women with degradation continued to influence this society, still enthralled by the ideal of the idle lady. Sophia Jex-Blake's altercation with her father over this issue in the nineteenth century illustrates England's ambiguity. When Jex-Blake was offered a mathematics tutorship at Queen's College, her father, a prominent attorney, agreed to it only if she not accept payment. Jex-Blake, with her typical tenacity, held her position. "You, as a man, did your work and received your payment, and no one thought it any degradation, but a fair exchange," she wrote her father. "Why should the difference of my sex alter the laws of right and honour?"[29]

With or without pay, the socially conscious English woman of the turn of the century became distinct from her pious, philanthropic predecessor and often sought ways to make thorough-going changes in society. It was while serving as a Poor Law Guardian in the 1890s, for example, that militant suffragist Emmeline Pankhurst (1858-1928) reached a turning point that changed her life, as well as the course of English politics.

But many English women who set out to work could ill afford to forgo a salary for the sake of middle-class respectability. Every woman who had sought employment at the Langham Place Society for the Employment of Women in the 1860s, for example, desperately needed a paying job, but faced at once the double onus of few available positions and loss of status. The burden was especially hard for unmarried women--women who lived with the stigma of "spinsterhood," which in Victorian England represented a "failure" on their part. Not only had they failed "in the business" of marriage, which gave women status, identity, and livelihood, but "redundant women," as nineteenth-century English society labeled them, frequently faced deprivation, if not destitution.[30]

It had been the plight of unmarried, middle-class women that had initially prompted English feminists, the Langham Place Circle in particular, to push for expanded opportunities in women's employment. With a list of distinguished patrons, including Queen Victoria, Langham Place Society for the Employment of Women carried an air of respectability and promoted as its rationale the amelioration of the poverty of single, middle-class women, with little or no mention of the employment of married women.

In actual numbers, the society's achievements appear limited. In its first few years, it placed only forty-eight women in permanent jobs and forty-six in temporary positions. But its continuing efforts and the publicity of these efforts in pamphlets, books, and in the *English Woman's Journal* and its successor the *English Woman's Review* served to open awareness for the need and the right of women to work. Feminist Josephine Butler (1828-1906) played a major role in the nineteenth century in informing society of the problem. Butler recognized not only the apathy toward the millions of English women working for a subsistence, most of whom where single, but the general distaste of English society to effectively deal with the employment of women. The indifference, she wrote,

> resembles that of an indolent housewife who is aware of a certain chamber in her house which is full of accumulated dirt of years, but which she fears to look into, hopeless of any possible cleansing, and the door

> of which she keeps carefully closed,
> content so long as the rest of the
> dwelling is not fatally infected by the
> presence of the evil.

Part of her work would be to "constantly" remind the public of "this sorest of human griefs."[31]

Because of the dearth of options and society's sluggish responses, a number of organizations developed that encouraged women, especially single women, to emigrate. The majority of women in need of employment found little enthusiasm to venture to Australia or New Zealand, but a few courageous, enterprising individuals left the oppressive atmosphere of England and successfully implanted themselves abroad, opening businesses, and conducting commerce. Charlotte Brontë's good friend Mary Taylor (1817-1893) was one of the most successful of these independent women, operating a dry goods store in Wellington, New Zealand, for fifteen years.[32]

For a few intrepid women, leaving England was the only way of realizing their ambitions. A group of women, collectively known as "Victorian Lady Explorers," accomplished the "unthought of" by travelling, exploring, and working, usually alone, in Africa, the Orient, and the Middle East. Gertrude Bell (1868-1926), an alumna of Oxford's Lady Margaret Hall, stands out among these women. Travelling to the Middle East in the early twentieth century, she worked and coauthored with archaeologist Sir William Ramsay (1852-1916) and later served as Political Secretary in Baghdad and as Director of Archaeology at the museum there. In 1921 she helped mold the postwar administration of Iraq.[33]

Few women had the resources or the desire to sever all bonds and strike out alone across the globe. Feminists continued to agitate for more avenues within the country, recognizing that women's entry into full professional work was necessary for livelihood and self-fulfillment. But in England as well as America, the disparity between the number of women gaining a higher education and the number of women entering the higher professions was vast. Several reasons may be cited for this. First, the professions of law, medicine, the ministry, and college teaching were becoming more "learned," following a trend that had begun in the nineteenth century. Advanced degrees were now required to enter these fields. Often, however, women's ambitions to meet these new demands were thwarted by restrictive entrance policies and quotas on female admission to graduate and professional education.[34]

As Barbara Solomon notes, in America, "The undergraduate woman began collegiate study at the time when the Ph.D. was appearing dimly on the academic horizon."[35] For the next few decades, in what seemed a replay of the struggle for an undergraduate education, women had to prove that they were capable of completing a graduate program and that such was their rightful due. In response to closed doors, a number of American women, such as M. Carey Thomas, traveled abroad for graduate study, usually to France, Germany, or Switzerland.

Certain universities in America relented to accept women into graduate programs as "special students," but refused to grant them higher degrees even after the successful completion of their courses, examinations, and dissertations. Christine Ladd-Franklin, for example, was denied a Ph.D. in psychology from Johns Hopkins, even though she had accomplished all the requirements.[36] Only gradually did some of these institutions open graduate education to women. In 1891, Yale University, having occasionally made "special arrangements" for women graduate students, began officially to admit women, although denying them undergraduate admission until the 1970s. Slowly other graduate schools opened their doors, including Johns Hopkins in 1907 and the University of Virginia in 1920-21.

In the face of continuing obstacles, educated women began to work collectively to assure women's growing participation in graduate study. The Association of Collegiate Women, founded by Marion Talbot, Talbot's mother, and Ellen Swallow Richards in 1882, as part of its goal "to carry the college idea far and wide," began at the end of the decade to award fellowships to women scholars. Since most major American graduate schools were closed to women, many early ACA fellows studied abroad. Attorney Bessie Bradwell Helmer

(1858-1927), who served as chairman of the Committee on Fellowships, noted in 1907 that the first woman Ph.D. from Yale was an ACA fellow, as were the first American Ph.D.'s at the German universities of Gottingen and Heidelberg.[37]

In 1910, ten educated black women, including Mary Church Terrell, organized the College Alumnae Club. Adopting the same structure as the ACA, the CAC in 1919 initiated a scholarship program for black women.[38]

Similarly, in the early twentieth century, English women founded the Federation of University Women Graduates. With graduate opportunities even more limited in England than America, the Federation published lists of all the fellowships available throughout the British Isles and established an annual fellowship for women scholars who had already begun publishing.[39]

Despite these early efforts, women who chose to pursue graduate studies had little support, economic or otherwise. In both countries certain graduate and professional schools, as well as professional organizations, persisted in barring women altogether in the late nineteenth and early twentieth centuries, as the word *professional* became synonymous with a highly trained male in a specialized field.[40] Possibly the most famous instance of the exclusive policies of professional societies in England had been the refusal of the Royal Society of Great Britain to offer membership to Mary Somerville. Although she had won numerous awards and prizes, and even membership in the American Philosophical Society, the professional society of scientists in her own country denied her membership and recognition on the basis of her gender.[41] Such instances were common among educated women in the late nineteenth and early twentieth centuries in both countries. Now, having won the right to an undergraduate education, women faced new barriers blocking a smooth entry into professional life.

Among the "learned" professions, that of medicine became of greatest interest to women working to bridge the gulf between the separate spheres. There were a number of reasons for the attention given to medical careers for women. In England it had been Elizabeth Garrett's struggle for a medical education that ignited the movement for university education for women and raised the country's awareness of the issue. In addition, medicine was the first of the higher professions to become open to women. Elizabeth Blackwell and Elizabeth Garrett Anderson, through their efforts in nineteenth-century America and England, had forged a path that many talented, ambitious women would follow. Only ten years after Blackwell won her medical degree, there were around three hundred licensed women physicians in America.[42]

Blackwell, Garrett Anderson, and England's Sophia Jex-Blake, moreover, once their professional lives had been established, focused much of their energy on founding and administrating hospitals and schools of medicine for women and in assuring that newly opening medical schools would be coeducational. Other educated women joined this mission, as well. A classic case was the successful campaign to compel Johns Hopkins Medical School to admit women on the same terms as men. A handful of women scholars and activists, including M. Carey Thomas and her friend Mary Garrett (1854-1915), with personal money of Mary Garrett's as well as funds collected from women throughout the country, in essence bribed the newly forming medical school to accept women.[43]

In general, those who pushed for the further integration of women in the medical profession were at the forefront of those seeking to erase the line dividing women's work from men's. But the medical profession was not about to loosen the tightly drawn line without a fight. As Joyce Antler demonstrates, a woman's entry into medicine was unlike going into teaching or office work. Requiring extensive training, medicine was a lifetime commitment, and, as such, expanded the conventional boundaries of marriage and family life. The idea of a female physician, moreover, challenged the traditional view of male authority and female subjection.[44]

The story of England's Sophia Jex-Blake vividly illustrates Antler's points. In 1869, the year Elizabeth Garrett was awarded her medical degree by the University of Paris, Jex-Blake and four other women began their medical studies at the University of Edinburgh on a tentative basis. Proving that they could indeed master the material, the women were then granted admission to special segregated classes.

As they successfully completed their studies during their first six months at Edinburgh, a few professors and students, not unlike Elizabeth Garrett's male colleagues at Middlesex Hospital, began a desperate campaign to drive them from the university.

But the students at Edinburgh added violence to their methods. Like a preview of the women's suffrage "encounters" in the next century, they physically blocked the women from entering lecture halls, assaulted them with verbal abuse, and pelted Jex-Blake on one occasion with peas. Finally the university itself sought to deny the women their credentials and after four years of study and tuition payments, Jex-Blake and her colleagues left Edinburgh without their degrees.[45] Honnor Morten's response to Jex-Blake's experience reflected the outrage felt by many men and women in England and Scotland. Throughout history, she claimed, women have been subject to blame and ridicule, "but it remained to the humane followers of the healing art to show to what depths of defamation man can sink when his profession (and his pocket!) are attacked."[46] Sophia Jex-Blake ultimately won her degree in Dublin in 1877. Thereafter medical schools in England began slowly to admit women.[47]

While the practice of medicine might be justified as an extension of women's sphere, the legal profession was viewed as alien to feminine sensibilities and was thus more difficult for women to enter.[48] As one Wisconsin judge expressed it in 1875,

> It would be revolting to all female sense of innocence and sanctity of their sex . . . that woman should be permitted to mix professionally in all the nastiness of the world which finds its way into courts of justice; all the unclean issues, all the collateral questions, of sodomy, incest, rape, seduction, fornication, adultery, pregnancy, bastardy, legitimacy, prostitution . . . . Reverence for all womanhood would

suffer in the public spectacle of
woman so interested and so engaged
. . . .[49]

Furthermore, English common law forbade women's
reception to the bar, and women thus had to challenge the law in each
state to practice as attorneys.[50] Nineteenth-century America saw a
number of women, though, primarily in the West and Midwest where
educational opportunities were wider and where traditions were
slightly relaxed, struggle for admission to the bar. Iowa's record, in
particular, was one of flexibility in opening opportunities for women
lawyers. Iowa's Arabella Mansfield (1846-1911), for example,
acquired her legal education through self-directed reading and
apprenticeship and won admission to the bar in 1869. As law schools
began to replace apprenticeships in law offices as training grounds for
the profession in the late nineteenth century, women began to enter
the few law schools that would admit them, including Washington
University in St. Louis, Union College of Law in Chicago, Boston
University Law School, and the University of Michigan. The first
woman law graduate in the United States was Ada H. Kepley (b.
1847) from Illinois. Receiving her law degree in 1870 from Union
College of Law in Chicago, she was unable to practice in Illinois,
until finally, in 1881, the state admitted her to the bar.[51]

As more and more states allowed women admission to the bar
around the turn of the century, women found entry into law schools
difficult, especially in the older institutions in the Northeast. When a
young woman named Alice Jordan slipped through admissions and
obtained a degree from Yale University's School of Law in the 1880s,
Yale quickly changed its catalogue to explicitly read, "It is to be
understood that courses offered in this university are only open to the
male sex, unless otherwise specifically stated." The statement was
included, explained the Dean of the Law School, "to prevent a
repetition of the 'Jordan incident.'" By 1919 Yale began admitting
women to its law program.[52]

As Karen Berger Morello illustrates, black women who
aspired to practice law faced even greater obstacles. Should they

succeed in completing law school, as did Charlotte Ray (1850-1911) in 1872, the first woman law graduate of Howard University and the first black woman lawyer in the country, gaining clients and developing a practice were denied them. Although she was noted as "one of the best lawyers on corporations in the country," Ray was unable to establish herself in the profession. "The double impairment of being both black and female prevented Charlotte Ray from joining this professional class," explains Morello, since her clients, black as well as white, "simply would not retain her." Although initially resisting women law students (Ray having slipped through admissions by using her initials rather than her full name), Howard for a period remained the only law school in the District of Columbia that admitted women, black or white.[53]

Of the approximately one hundred twenty women lawyers in the United States in 1894, about one-third actually practiced law in the courtroom. Women attorneys followed other outlets, such as lecturing, writing, leading organizations concerned with suffrage and women's rights, and editing, sometimes anonymously. Illinois attorney Bessie Bradwell Helmer, for example, the daughter of attorney Myra Bradwell (1831-1894) and Judge James B. Bradwell, edited multiple volumes of the reports of the Appellate Court of Illinois, all bearing Judge Bradwell's name.[54]

English women had yet to enter the profession of law by 1920. Here the weight of tradition bolstered by the common law proved more formidable than the less rigid American system. Like many members of the profession in America, English lawyers did not relish the entry of women. "It is notable," stated Honnor Morten, "that English lawyers have so far stood firmly on the position that women and justice are incompatible, to which the obvious reply is that this is only natural, for women have had so little experience of justice."[55]

Only after Parliament passed the Sex Disqualification Removal Act in 1919 did the barrier to the legal profession come down in England. Traditionally English law students had prepared for their profession at the Inns of Court in London and only gradually were the universities beginning to create faculties of law in the early twentieth century. In 1921 Phoebe Sheavyn reported a "considerable number" of women preparing to be solicitors or barristers in these relatively new law faculties. None had yet, though, to be "called to the bar."[56]

Women in academic life in England and America faced rising obstacles, as well. In England the number of women in university positions were few, the majority being in the women's colleges. Here though, unlike women faculty in the separate American women's colleges, women academics had to compete actively with men for jobs, and the "number of women holding professorships could be counted almost on one hand."[57] Most of the women faculty held the lower positions of lecturer, assistant lecturer, and demonstrator. Relegated to these lesser positions, women, Edith Morley complained, are "swallowed up in the vortex of teaching and routine work," with little time left for independent writing and research, the key to their professional advancement.[58]

Although they were members of the Association of University Teachers, an organization founded by A. J. Clough for teachers with university training, women dons did not form a professional association and by 1920 had yet to develop a collective identity.[59]

In late nineteenth-century America, with the growth of quality women's colleges in the Northeast and the South, women academics enjoyed visibility and status as they filled the majority of faculty positions in these institutions. These colleges were especially important for women scholars in traditionally and predominantly male disciplines. In 1921, for example, women's colleges hired 40 percent of the women scientists in America.[60] Women Ph.D.'s, moreover, were found in these colleges in leading administrative positions, as presidents, academic deans, and registrars. As Geraldine Jonçich Clifford underscores, "the well-being of academic women in the nineteenth and twentieth centuries was closely tied to the fate of the women's colleges."[61]

After enjoying a prominent role in women's education in the late nineteenth century, women's colleges began slowly to decline in number at the turn of the century as coeducation became predominant. As positions declined, women academics more and more had to seek avenues in coeducation.[62] But here, their situation, analogous in so many ways to that of their female students, was tenuous.[63] Viewed initially by the traditional academic community as trespassers, women academics slowly entered coeducation through the doors that in essence spelled "Ladies only," taking them directly to feminized areas of specialization, especially, as we have seen, that of home economics.

As they one-by-one advanced to coeducational faculties, women often found their presence unwanted. Dr. Mary Bennet Ritter, who as medical examiner was the first professional woman at the University of California at Berkeley, found herself, when she took a part-time faculty position, "a sort of pariah in the University." Her course in health and home sanitation, which had been requested by Berkeley's "scarcely acceptable women students, caused some resentment in the faculty," she wrote in her autobiography.[64]

Although professors often welcomed and supported their women colleagues, others vented their "resentment" by continuing to isolate women faculty from both the academic and social mainstream. Seemingly insignificant, yet symbolic instances of ostracism may be cited across the country, as women were excluded from faculty clubs, faculty dining rooms, and even faculty meetings. Dr. Alice Hamilton's (1869-1970) experience as she joined the Harvard Medical School faculty is telling. The leading figure internationally in the field of industrial toxicology, Hamilton was told upon being hired that, as a woman, she could not march in the commencement procession.[65]

Paradoxically, while women professors were hidden from view, they were "extravisible."[66] Mirroring the awkward position of the early women college students, pioneer women faculty in coeducation were carefully scrutinized for inappropriate dress, mannerisms, or behavior. Those that did not conform to fashion dictates were quickly labeled eccentrics. The lifestyles of women faculty also provided occasions for gossip and innuendo. Although percentages were shifting in the first part of the twentieth century, most women professors were single.[67] Initially as women entered the professoriate, single status was incumbent, both in women's colleges and coeducational institutions, as women were expected to live with the students and monitor their behavior. As these extracurricular duties began to diminish, women professors, nonetheless, were expected, if not required, to remain single. Howard University's President Boyd, for example, in 1913 proposed "that any female teacher who thereafter married while teaching at the university would be considered as having resigned her position."[68] Similarly, the general rule in the women's colleges dictated that women "not only [be] single, but in no danger of marrying."[69]

Increasingly, though, women academics who remained single came to be viewed as abnormal and therefore as negative influences on female college students, more and more of whom were marrying after graduation. Cast in a light that rendered them as unfortunate spinsters leading dull, gloomy lives, women scholars, like single women in other professions, were often stereotyped, pitied, and derided.[70]

The either\or dichotomy of personal life versus professional life raised serious obstacles, not only for women faculty members, but for all educated women. As late as the early twentieth century, American and English women often had to relinquish the option of marriage in order to pursue a career. The choice posed an unenviable dilemma for bright, aspiring women who envisioned a place in the community at large. Familial and social pressure to marry remained strong, and the majority chose to marry and forsake a profession.[71]

Emma Goldman (1869-1940) addressed this issue when she spoke of "the tragedy of woman's emancipation." Few professional women, she acknowledged, succeeded in reaching equality with their male peers in either remuneration or status. Nonetheless, those that sought a professional life paid dearly, reaching their positions "at the expense of their physical and psychical well-being." This is why, she concluded, that "we find many emancipated women who prefer marriage, with all its deficiencies, to the narrowness of an unmarried life."[72] Feminist and social scientist Jessie Taft (1882-1960) put the predicament educated women faced more bluntly as "a choice between a crippled life in the home or an unfulfilled one out of it."[73]

Most married women in America who chose to work outside the home usually entered the female occupations of teaching, nursing, office work, or the newer and very popular field of social work.[74] And these women rarely viewed their work as a profession. Since historically many of these women in traditionally feminine fields worked only to occupy and support themselves before marriage, they viewed their work as temporary, of secondary importance. Tragically, then, they did not develop a professional identity, what Joyce Antler describes as "a self-conception as members of a highly trained professional discipline."[75]

This was not the same in England. Here school teaching in the prestigious new girls' schools was primarily accomplished by highly educated women, who, with virtually no options in the higher professions, chose teaching as the most intellectually gratifying career open to them. Having matriculated through universities and teacher-training programs, these women, in essence, the descendants of the doleful, ignorant Victorian governess, now formed an erudite, professional elite.[76] English schoolteachers, through professional societies, worked to raise their sights, their status, and their salaries, as well as to found and endow schools and to improve existing ones.[77] The Teachers' Training and Registration Society, in connection with the Women's Education Union, for example, opened the Maria Grey Training College, named in honor of the society's founder. In 1885 the Cambridge Training College for Women was founded for Newnham and Girton women, who after taking their Tripos, could gain professional training. Women teachers in England continued to form associations, strengthening their professional identity.[78]

Thanks to the elevation of teaching and nursing as professions for educated women, Clara Collet (1860-1948) of the University of London stated in 1902 that women no longer had to preoccupy themselves with an obsession to marry; their professions alone, she claimed, were "absorbing enough in themselves to be worth living for." Marriage, she added, should be regarded as a "possibility which may someday call them away from the path they are pursuing, but which should not be allowed to interfere with their plans in the meantime."[79]

By 1920, though, educated women in both countries began to seriously challenge the either\or imperative. The members of the Fabian's Women's Group in England were the most prolific and outspoken advocates of the economic independence of women, both unmarried and married. In a series of speeches and pamphlets, the group voiced opposition to efforts that sought to bar married women from certain occupations. Teachers and women in the civil service were the most susceptible to the "marriage bar" in England. As feminist Mabel Atkinson wrote, "Most women . . . can only continue to preserve that economic independence, so keenly appreciated and won by such fierce struggles, on condition of compulsory celibacy and, what to many women is far worse, compulsory childlessness."[80]

A combination of marriage and career was not an option for most English women before World War II, and only a few exceptions can be identified. In contrast to England's secondary teachers, university lecturers and professors faced no marriage bar. In 1914 Edith Morley urged lecturers to help shape a precedent and not allow governing bodies to interfere in what should remain a personal decision.[81] Elizabeth Garrett Anderson stands out in this regard by example and by entreaty as a woman well ahead of her era. "The woman question will never be solved in any complete way so long as marriage is thought to be incompatible with freedom and independent career," she emphasized.[82]

Similarly, a Smith College student in America wrote, "We cannot believe that it is fixed in the nature of things that a woman must choose between a home and her work, when a man may have both. There must be a way out and it is the problem of our generation to find the way."[83] During the decade of the twenties a number of books and publications in America addressed the question of combining career and family, as more and more college graduates married.[84] These books reflected a growing optimism that women indeed could "have it all." Career women were not all unanimous in this assessment and some warned women that it was still too difficult to have both.[85]

Having attained intellectual fulfillment in what amounted to a revolution in education in both countries, collegiate women for the most part chose to follow the time-honored way of domesticity rather than pursue the less worn path leading to professional fulfillment. One discerns, then, the power of the argument, so often used to mollify opposition, that education for women should be different, directing them toward a more intelligent, "professionalized" approach to wifehood, motherhood, and feminine work. Educated women, internalizing this prescriptive formula, continued to step into the traditional roles of women rather than aiming for new directions. In America institutions of higher learning, through systems of separation, helped to maintain this status quo. In England it was primarily the older universities that sought to keep women separate by withholding degrees, without which women's entry into professional work was hindered.

In spite of the difficulties, a number of early twentieth-century women forged ahead in professional life, making notable contributions in disciplines that only a few decades before were exclusively male. Some of these women, moreover, notably the Americans, were wives and mothers, and though their domestic lives did not fit the prescribed mold of the conventional Victorian/Edwardian family, these women managed to answer the family claim as well as the professional.

In America sociologist, anthropologist, and folklorist Elsie Clews Parsons (1875-1941) was a professional woman who sought to break the societal bonds that limited the self-realization of women. Born into a prominent New York family, Elsie Clews overruled her family's objection to a higher education and entered Barnard College in 1891. Here she studied the newly rising field of social sciences and in 1899 earned her Ph.D. in sociology at Columbia University. A year later Elsie Clews married Herbert Parsons, a young lawyer who shared his wife's ideas concerning women's position in family and society. Elsie Clews Parsons then returned to Barnard College as professor of sociology. Unusual in her determination to combine career and marriage, Parsons broke more unwritten rules by becoming a mother during her years on the faculty at Barnard.

In 1905 Parsons left teaching when her husband was elected to Congress. Finding herself in a social milieu alien to her interests and tastes, she detached herself from it and began examining and documenting Washington social behavior from a scientist's point of view. At the same time Parsons was encouraged and influenced by Columbia's Franz Boas (1858-1942), one of the founders of modern anthropology. As one of the first to distinguish anthropology from sociology, Boas inspired Parsons to pursue field work in the research of primitive peoples. From the parlors of Washington to the villages of Mexico, the American Southwest, and the West Indies, Parsons' observations and recordings of the customs and rituals of diverse cultures marked a vital achievement in anthropology and folklore.

As a highly educated woman and a keen, well-trained observer of the relationships between human behavior and cultural constructs, Elsie Clews Parsons thought deeply and perceptively about the position of women in American society and the importance of their education. The higher education of a woman, she affirmed, should lead directly, as it did for a man, to a professional career. The emphasis on the unique qualities of educated women and their roles as intelligent mothers and consumers was misdirected. A liberal arts education, she believed, was only the first step in the educational process whose goal should be professionalization. "Self-culture is incomplete," she claimed, "unless taking in is followed by giving out, unless production follows consumption."[86] Not as educated mothers and consumers, but as educated professionals, would intelligent women gain dignity and independence, which would ultimately lead both the family and society to a more advanced evolutionary stage. Rather than deprive themselves of family life, professional women should claim the right to rejoin the family. The future of the family, she argued, depended "on the fight of the professional women to get back into the family."[87]

Elsie Clews Parsons' arguments concerning women and the family, spelled out in books and numerous journals, were unsettling for her time, especially her endorsement of trial marriages and the sexual expression of women. Her life, too, was not free from controversy as she ignored propriety, lived ruggedly and uninhibitedly among different ethnic groups, and passionately pursued her work. Mother of six (two died in infancy), scholar, and author, Parsons represents, as biographer Peter Hare illustrates, a "forerunner of contemporary lifestyles."[88] Parsons represents, as well, an example of a woman whose education reached its logical conclusion in professional achievement. President of the American Folklore Society, editor of its journal for over two decades, treasurer and president of the American Ethnological Society, and finally in 1940, the first woman president of the American Anthropological Association, Parsons flung wide the doors that intellectually gifted women had struggled for so long to enter.[89]

Notes

1.   Ellsworth, 147.
2.   F.H. Sykes, "The Social Basis of the New Education for Women," *Teachers College Record* (May 1917): 229-230, quoted in Goodsell, 30.
3.   Maria Grey, quoted in Ellsworth, 145.
4.   Constance Maynard, *Between College Terms* (London: James Nisbet, 1910), 182-183.
5.   George Eliot to Emily Davies, 19 November 1869, Stephen, 227.
6.   Quoted in Peacock, 49.
7.   Quoted in Peacock, 49-50.
8.   Vicinus, *Independent Women*, 150-151.
9.   Victoria Glendinning, *A Suppressed Cry: Life and Death of a Quaker Daughter* (London: Routledge and Kegan Paul, 1969), 54, quoted in Vicinus, *Independent Women*, 151.
10. Letter from "V," in 25 May 192?, Jane Ellen Harrison Papers, Newnham College Archives, quoted in Vicinus, *Independent Women*, 155.
11. Quoted in Solomon, 94.
12. Burstall, *The Education of Girls in the United States*, 114.
13. Clifford, 54.
14. Solomon, 88-89.
15. At Mount Holyoke, for example, Emma Perry Carr, who in 1937 was the first woman to win an award from the American Chemical Society, traced her academic "lineage" back to Mary Lyon a century earlier. See Rossiter, 18-22.
16. M. Carey Thomas, "The Future of Woman's Higher Education," *Mount Holyoke College: The Seventy-Fifth Anniversary* (South Hadley, Mass., 1913), 100-104, in Cross, 170.
17. Ibid., 171.
18. Vicinus, *Independent Women*, 135.
19. Burstall, *The Education of Girls*, 61.
20. Ibid.

21.   Newcomer, 49.
22.   Alice Zimmern, *The Renaissance of Girls' Education* (London: A. D. Innes, 1898), 103.
23.   Ellen Fitzpatrick, *Endless Crusade: Women Social Scientists and Progressive Reform* (New York and Oxford: Oxford University Press, 1990), 8.
24.   Charles W. Eliot, *North American Review* (August 1882): 146-61, quoted in Woody, 437.
25.   Barbara J. Harris, *Beyond Her Sphere: Women and the Professions in American History* (Westport, Conn.: Greenwood Press, 1978), 115-121 and Burstyn, 62-63. Emil Reich's judgments concerning American women are especially piercing: "In spite of the most extraordinary measures and institutes for the development of the intellectual or artistic faculties of women in America; in spite of numberless colleges, universities . . . woman has in America done none of those remarkable deeds of a literary, scientific, or artistic character for which the Somervilles, Fawcetts, Brontës, George Eliots, Madame de Staël, George Sand . . . are famous in Europe." From *Woman Through the Ages,* Vol. 2 (London: n.p., 1908), 253-255, quoted in Woody, 2: 385.
26.   Antler, 66-71.
27.   As M. Jeanne Peterson illustrates, English aristocratic women often served actively as "helpmeets" to their husbands in charity, mission, and settlement work. Philanthropic activities provided a mutual sphere for both men and women. See Peterson, 162-164.
28.   Philippa Levine, *Victorian Feminism 1850-1900* (Tallahassee: The Florida State University Press, 1987), 92-96.
29.   Quoted in Levine, 85.
30.   Jane Lewis, *Women in England 1870-1950: Sexual Divisions and Social Change* (Bloomington: Indiana University Press, 1984), 3.

31. Josephine E. Butler, ed., *Woman's Work and Woman's Culture* (London: MacMillan and Co., 1869), xvi-xvii.

32. Hammerton, 71-91.

33. Despite their exploration, discoveries, and generally productive work, women explorers were refused entry in the Royal Geographical Society until 1913. Dea Birkett, *Spinsters Abroad: Victorian Lady Explorers* (Oxford: Basil Blackwell, 1989), 171, 214.

34. Harris, 117.

35. Solomon, 134.

36. Rossiter, 31, 44-45.

37. Marion Talbot and Lois Kimball Matthews Rosenberry, *The History of the American Association of University Women 1881-1931* (Boston and New York: Houghton Mifflin Co., 1931), 156-157.

38. Cynthia Neverdon-Morton, "The Black Woman's Struggle for Equality in the South, 1895-1925," in Sharon Harley and Rosalyn Terborg-Penn, eds., *The Afro-American Woman: Struggle and Images* (Port Washington, N.Y.: Kennikat Press, 1978), 52.

39. Edith J. Morley, *Women Workers in Seven Professions: A Survey of Their Economic Conditions and Prospects* (London: George Routledge and Sons, Ltd., 1914), 15.

40. Rossiter, 29-50, 73-99. Rossiter's exposé on the obstacles erected to bar women scientists from professional ranks reflects the problems of all professional women in America during this period.

41. Helsinger, Sheets, Veeder, 2: 78-79. For other problems of English women, see Burstyn, 121-132.

42. Antler, 207.

43. Mary Garrett, whose father was a Baltimore and Ohio Railroad magnate, used her fortune to benefit women's education, not only at Johns Hopkins, but also at Bryn Mawr. "Knowledge is power and I, for one, am going to do my best to gain it," she emphasized. See Dobkin, 20, 127.

44. Antler, 209-210.

45. Sophia Jex-Blake, *Medical Women: A Thesis and A History* (Edinburgh: Oliphant, Anderson, and Ferrier, 1886), 71-147.

46. Honnor Morten, *Questions for Women* (London: Adam and Charles Black, 1899), 43. For the sympathetic responses to Jex-Blake's dilemma, see Jex-Blake, 96-97.

47. Strachey, 255.

48. Harris, 110.

49. Quoted in Karen Berger Morello, *The Invisible Bar: The Woman Lawyer in America 1638 to the Present* (New York: Random House, 1986), 25.

50. Harris, 110.

51. Morello, 49-50.

52. Ibid., 88-94.

53. Ibid., 73, 145-147.

54. "Women at the Bar," in *The Woman's Book* (New York: Scribner's, 1894), 53-54.

55. Morten, 46.

56. Sheavyn, 14.

57. Holcombe, 66.

58. Morley, 16.

59. Holcombe, 51.

60. Rossiter, 172, 174.

61. Clifford, 4.

62. Simultaneously, as coeducation continued to grow in popularity, some women's colleges, to offset the decline in enrollment, hired more men, placing them in top academic positions. See Clifford, 4.

63. For some first-hand testimonies of the multiple problems facing women who had studied many hard years for their doctoral degrees and were now facing additional discrimination, see Antler, 386-389.

64. Ibid., 12.

65. Ibid., 29. Graham, 765-766.

66. Clifford, 29.

67. A study of women who earned their doctoral degree from 1877 to 1924 reported that one-fourth were married. See Clifford, 30.
68. Quoted in Clifford, 31.
69. Rossiter, 15-16. This was also the condition of being a teacher in the public schools in the United States until after World War II.
70. Clifford, 30-31.
71. Harris, 117.
72. Emma Goldman, "The Tragedy of Woman's Emancipation," in *The Feminist Papers,* 510, 513.
73. Quoted in Degler, 411. Some of the highest achievers of the early twentieth century indeed faced terrible choices. Journalist Rheta Dorr, for example, gave her son to relatives to raise; likewise writer Charlotte Perkins Gilman gave custody of her child to her first husband in order to pursue her career. See Antler, 11.
74. Harris, 118 and Ellsworth, 287.
75. Antler, 412.
76. Gorham, 28.
77. Bryant, 109-111.
78. Lee Holcombe, *Victorian Ladies at Work: Middle Class Working Women in England and Wales* (Hamden, Conn.: Archon Books, 1973), 49-51.
79. Clara Collet, *Educated Working Women: Essays on the Economic Position of Women Workers in the Middle Classes* (London: P.S. King and Son, 1902), 138-139.
80. Quoted in Carol Dyhouse, *Feminism and the Family in England* (Oxford and New York: Basil Blackwell, 1989), 78.
81. Ibid., 23.
82. Manton, 279.
83. Quoted in Degler, 412.
84. "Over 80 percent of graduates from women's colleges were marrying in the 1920s as compared with 50 percent thirty years before." See Degler, 412-413.

85.   As women Ph.D.'s, for example, tried to combine marriage and career, many found this impossible and in a major study advised women not to take the doctoral degree. See Clifford, 24.

86.   Rosenberg, 159-160.

87.   Quoted in Rosenberg, 160.

88.   Peter Hare, *A Woman's Quest for Science: Portrait of Anthropologist Elsie Clews Parsons* (Buffalo: Prometheus Books, 1985), 7. As Rosalind Rosenberg discerns, Parsons' unconventional lifestyle might never have been realized had she not had wealth and servants. See Rosenberg, 154.

89.   Hare, 20-21.

EPILOGUE

Muriel St. Clare Byrne and Catherine Hope Mansfield wrote that October 14, 1920, "will always be a memorable day in the history of women's education, the day of the first women's degree ceremony at Oxford."[1] While women had participated in college graduation ceremonies for many decades in universities throughout England and America, this day at Oxford was especially notable. As the oldest institution of higher learning in the English-speaking world, and the symbol of the highest intellectual achievement throughout the entire world, the integration of men and women within its venerable walls marked a new era in history. In retrospect, St. Clare Byrne found that "forty years had not seemed long to wait for the full privilege of membership of a university in itself seven or eight centuries old."[2]

In a similar ceremony, women of Cambridge, including some of the early pioneers, returned to their university to be awarded the degree title that they had earned but had not been granted as many as fifty years earlier. The year was 1921 and Emily Davies died shortly thereafter at the age of ninety-one.

The moment seemed auspicious. The treaty ending "the war to end all wars" had been signed, national women's suffrage had been gained in England and America, and alumnae in both countries looked forward to greater advances, intellectually and professionally. Indeed, during the decade of the 1920s American women reached their highest proportion in undergraduate, graduate, and faculty populations until the 1970s. In England even the struggle for Oxford and Cambridge degrees had triumphed. Finally, collegiate women in England and America had gained visibility, strength, and status. From their perspective, "the promise of the educated woman had just begun," notes Barbara Solomon.[3]

And so it probably seemed to the heirs of the pioneers of Girton and Newnham gathering to hear Virginia Woolf in 1928. They must have believed that they indeed had it now in their power to resurrect Shakespeare's sister and give voice to her long silent poetry. American women too felt empowered to create new lives for themselves and to shape a new world for all men and women.

But in America the reality would not match the expectation. The dialectic of success and disappointment would continue to characterize the struggle of equal education. The collegiate experience, for one, would be transformed during the next few decades, for changes were at work altering the nature of the American university which, in turn, would affect women's position in academic life. After a fifty-year period (1875-1925) during which higher education in America was notable for its diversity and democratization, the university became increasingly an institution devoted to research. Since the diversity of American institutions between 1875 and 1925 was a factor in aiding the arrival of American women in the halls of higher learning, one indirect but significant result of this change was that women would now look forward to a time of dwindling options in higher education and fewer of them would be found among the professoriate. As America's heterogeneous institutions, devoted previously to the ideal of teaching, began to follow the lead of the top research universities and emphasize instead the pursuit of knowledge and hence the doctorate or terminal degree, new problems emerged in higher education that future generations of women would struggle to overcome.[4]

This was not apparent, though, in the 1920s. In both countries the struggle to gain a higher education had been a record of achievement. Although further changes lay ahead which would present women with both new opportunities and, unfortunately, new obstacles, for the present, educated women could feel justly proud of their efforts. With each step, intelligent women had sought to put "an end to all this distracting talk," as Maria Grey had once said, "about this education being good for a man, that for a woman." Rather, they had worked and would continue to work towards the ideal Grey had articulated in England in 1871:

> The true meaning of education is the kindling and the strengthening of the love of knowledge, of beauty, of goodness, till they become governing motives of action. This alone is education, to be begun in the first twenty years of life, to be carried on through time, and as I trust through eternity; and this is the education which should be given, or at any rate aimed at, in the case of every human being.[5]

Notes

1.   St. Clare Byrne, 69.
2.   Ibid., 69-70.
3.   Solomon, 140.
4.   For an account of the changing university and its effect on academic women during the twentieth century, see Graham, 759-773.
5.   Grey, 25.

BIBLIOGRAPHY

PRIMARY SOURCES:

"American University for Women." *English Woman's Journal* (September 1864): 45.

Anderson, Elizabeth Garrett. "Sex in Mind and Education: A Reply." *Fortnightly Review,* May 1874, 582-94.

Astell, Mary. *A Serious Proposal to the Ladies for the Advancement of their True and Greatest Interest.* New York: Source Book Press, 1970.

Beecher, Catherine Esther. *Educational Reminiscences and Suggestions.* New York: J.B. Ford, 1874.

Blackwell, Elizabeth. *Pioneer Work in Opening the Medical Profession to Women.* London: Longmans, Green, and Co., 1895.

Bremner, Christina Sinclair. *Education of Girls and Women in Great Britain.* London: Swan Sonnenschein and Co., 1897.

Burstall, Sara, *The Education of Girls in the United States.* London: Swan Sonnenschein and Co., 1894.

Butler, Josephine, ed. *Woman's Work and Woman's Culture.* London: MacMillan and Co., 1869.

Chapone, Hester Mulso. *Letters on the Improvement of the Mind Addressed to a Young Lady.* London: H. Hughs for J. Walter, 1773.

Chesnut, Mary Boykin. *Mary Chesnut's Civil War.* Edited by C. Vann Woodward. New Haven: Yale University Press, 1981.

Claghorn, Kate Holladay. *College Training for Women.* New York: Thomas Y. Crowell, 1897.

Clarke, Edward H. *Sex in Education; or a Fair Chance for the Girls.* Boston: James R. Osgood and Co., 1873; reprint, New York: Arno Press, 1874.

Cobbe, Frances Power. "The Education of Women, and How it Would be Affected by University Examinations." In *Essays on the Pursuits of Women.* London: Emily Faithfull, 1863.

Coeducation at Colby. Waterville, Maine: Colby, 1890.

Collet, Clara. *Educated Working Women: Essays on the Economic Position of Women Workers in the Middle Classes.* London: P.S. King and Son, 1902.

Coolidge, Mary Roberts. *Why Women Are So.* New York: Henry Holt and Co., 1912; reprint, New York: Arno Press, Inc., 1972.

Cooper, Anna Julia. *A Voice from the South by a Black Woman of the South.* Ohio: Aldine Printing House, 1892; reprint, New York: Negro Universities Press, 1969.

Coppin, Fannie Jackson. "Training to Become an Educator." In *Black Women in White America: A Documentary History,* ed. Gerda Lerner, 89. New York: Vintage Books, 1973.

Courtney, Janet E. *The Women of My Time.* London: Lovat Dickson, Ltd., 1934.

Crawford, Mary Caroline. *The College Girl of America and the Institutions Which Make Her What She Is.* Boston: L.C. Page and Co., 1905.

Cross, Barbara, ed. *The Educated Woman in America: Selected Writings of Catharine Beecher, Margaret Fuller, and M. Carey Thomas.* Classics in Education, no. 25. New York: Teachers College Press, 1965.

Dall, Caroline. *The College, the Market, and the Court; or Woman's Relationship to Education, Labor, and Law.* Boston: Lee and Shepard, 1868; reprint, New York: Arno Press, 1972.

Darwin, Erasmus. *A Plan for the Conduct of Female Education in Boarding Schools.* Derby, 1797; reprint, New York: Johnson Reprint Corporation, 1968.

Davenport Adams, W. H. *Woman's Work and Worth in Girlhood, Maidenhood, and Wifehood.* London: John Hogg, 1880.

Davies, Emily. *Thoughts on Some Questions Relating to Women, 1860-1908.* Cambridge, England: Bowes and Bowes, 1910.

Dawson, Sarah Morgan. *A Confederate Girl's Diary.* Edited by James I. Robertson, Jr. Bloomington: Indiana University Press, 1960; reprint, Westport, Conn.: Greenwood Press, Inc., 1972.

Defoe, Daniel. "Essay on Projects." In *Daniel Defoe.* Edited by James T. Boulton. New York: Schocken Books, 1965.

Dike, Samuel Warren. "Sociology in the Higher Education of Women." *Atlantic Monthly* (November 1892); 673-75.

Dobkin, Marjorie Housepian, ed. *The Making of a Feminist: Early Journals and Letters of M. Carey Thomas.* Kent State University Press, 1979.

"The Education of Girls: Their Admissibility to Universities." *Westminster Review* 109 (January 1878): 56-90.

Fairchild, James Harris. *The Coeducation of the Sexes as Pursued in Oberlin College.* Hartford Conn.: Camp, 1868.

Fawcett, Millicent Garrett. "The Education of Women of the Middle and Upper Classes." *MacMillan's Magazine,* April 1868, 511-17.

_____. "The Medical and General Education of Women." *Fortnightly Review,* November 1868, 554-63.

_____. *What I Remember.* London: T. Fisher Unwin Ltd., 1925; reprint, Westport Conn.: Hyperion, 1976.

Foakes, Grace, "A London Schooling." In Janet Horowitz Murray, *Strong-Minded Women and Other Lost Voices from Nineteenth-Century England.* New York: Pantheon Books, 1982.

Gardener, Helen Hamilton. *Facts and Fictions of Life.* Boston: Arena Publishing Co., 1895.

Goldman, Emma. "The Tragedy of Woman's Emancipation." In *The Feminist Papers: From Adams to de Beauvoir,* ed. Alice S. Rossi, 506-08. New York: Columbia University Press, 1973.

Gregory, Dr. John. *A Father's Legacy to His Daughters.* New York: Garland, 1974.

Grey, Maria Georgina. *On the Education of Women.* London: W. Ridgway, 1871.

Halifax, Lord. *The Lady's New Year's Gift, or, Advice to a Daughter.* London: R. and J. Dodsley, 1756.

Hall, G. Stanley and Theodore L. Smith. "Marriage and Fecundity of College Men and Women." *The Pedagogical Seminary* (10 September 1903): 375-414.

Howe, Julia Ward, ed. *Sex and Education: A Reply to Dr. E. H. Clarke's "Sex in Education."* Boston: Roberts Brothers, 1874; reprint, New York: Arno Press, 1972.

Jex-Blake, Sophia. *Medical Women: A Thesis and A History.* Edinburgh: Oliphant, Anderson, and Ferrier, 1886.

The Joint Education of the Sexes. A Report Presented at a Meeting of the Ohio Teacher's College Association, Sandusky City, July 8th. Oberlin, 1852.

Maynard, Constance. *Between College Terms.* London: James Nisbet, 1910.

Mayo, A.D. *Southern Women in the Recent Educational Movement in the South.* Edited by Dan T. Carter and Amy Friedlander. Washington: U.S. Bureau of Education, Circular of Information, 1892, no. 1; reprint, London and Baton Rouge: Louisiana State University Press, 1978.

Meyer, Annie Nathan. *Barnard Beginnings.* Boston and New York: Houghton Mifflin Co., 1935.

_____, ed. *Woman's Work in America.* New York: Henry Holt and Co., 1891; reprint, New York: Arno Press, 1972.

More, Hannah. *Strictures on the Modern System of Female Education.* New York: Garland, 1974.

Morley, Edith J. *Women Workers in Seven Professions: A Survey of Their Economic Conditions and Prospects.* London: George Routledge and Sons, Ltd., 1914.

Morten, Honnor. *Questions for Women.* London: Adam and Charles Black, 1899.

Murray, Judith Sargent. "Desultory Thoughts upon the Utility of Encouraging a Degree of Self-Complacency, Especially in Female Bosoms." *Gentleman and Lady's Town and Country Magazine* 1 (1784): 253.

_____. *The Gleaner, A Miscellaneous Production, Vol. 3.* Boston: I. Thomas and E. T. Andrews, 1798.

_____. "On the Equality of the Sexes." In *The Feminist Papers: From Adams to de Beauvoir,* ed. Alice S. Rossi, 18-24. New York: Columbia University Press, 1973.

Papers on the Relations of Wesleyan University to the Higher Education of Women. N.p.: Pelton and King Print, 1900.

Pennington, Lady Sarah. *An Unfortunate Mother's Advice to her Absent Daughters; in a Letter to Miss Pennington.* London: 1761; reprint, New York, Samuel Marks, 1827.

Ravenel, Harriott Horry. *Eliza Pinckney.* New York: Charles Scribner's Sons, 1909.

Reeve, Clara. *Plans of Education with Remarks on the Systems of Other Writers.* New York: Garland, 1974.

Richards, Ellen Henrietta Swallow. *The Relation of College Women to Progress in Domestic Science.* Publications of the Association of Collegiate Alumnae, Series 2, no. 27, 1890.

Rousseau, Jean Jacques. *Emilius; or a Treatise of Education.* Edinburgh: N.p., 1763.

Rush, Benjamin. *Essays, Literary, Moral and Philosophical.* Philadelphia: Thomas and William Bradford, 1798.

_____. *Thoughts Upon Female Education, Accommodated to the Present State of Society, Manners, and Government in the United States of America.* In *Essays on Education in the Early Republic,* ed. Frederick Rudolph. Cambridge, Mass.: Belknap Press, 1965.

Ruskin, John, "Of Queen's Gardens." In Janet Horowitz Murray, *Strong-Minded Women and Other Lost Voices from Nineteenth-Century England.* New York: Pantheon Books, 1982.

Sheavyn, Phoebe. *The Higher Education for Women in Great Britain.* London: International Federation of Women, Pamphlet no. 2, 1921.

Shirreff, Emily. "College Education for Women." *Contemporary Review* 15 (Fall 1870): 55-66.

"Should University Degrees be Given to Women?" *Westminster Review* 115 (April 1881): 493-503.

Sidgwick, Arthur and Eleanor. *Henry Sidgwick: A Memoir.* London: MacMillan and Co., 1906.

Smedley, Menella B. "The English Girl's Education." *Contemporary Review* 14 (Spring 1870): 28-41.

Smith, Goldwin. "University Education." *Journal of Social Science* 1 (June 1869): 22-55.

Somerville, Mary. *Personal Recollections from Early Life to Old Age of Mary Somerville.* Edited by Martha Somerville. Boston: Roberts Brothers, 1874.

Talbot, Marion. *The Education of Women.* Chicago: University of Chicago Press, 1910.

The *Times* (London). 19-22 May 1897.

Tyler, William S. "The Higher Education of Women." *Scribner's Monthly,* February 1874, 456-62.

Vanderpoel, Emily Noyes. *Chronicles of a Pioneer School From 1792 to 1833.* Cambridge Mass.: University Press, 1903.

Webster, Noah. "On the Education of Youth in America." In *Essays on Education in the Early Republic,* ed. Frederick Rudolph. Cambridge, Mass.: Belknap Press, 1965.

Willard, Emma. *A Plan for Improving Female Education.* Middlebury, Vt.: J. W. Copeland, 1819; reprint, Middlebury College, 1918.

Wollstonecraft, Mary. *Thoughts on the Education of Daughters with Reflections on Female Conduct in the More Important Duties of Life.* London: J. Johnson, 1787; reprint, New York and London: Garland, 1974.

_____. *Vindication of the Rights of Woman (the 1792 Text).* Edited by Miriam Brody Dramnick. New York: Penguin Books, 1978.

The Woman's Book. New York: Scribner's, 1894.

Woolf, Virginia. *A Room of One's Own.* New York: Harcourt Brace Jovanovich, 1929.

Wordsworth, Elizabeth. *Glimpses of the Past.* London: A.R. Mowbray and Co., 1912.

Zimmern, Alice. *The Renaissance of Girls" Education.* London: A.D. Innes, 1898.

SECONDARY SOURCES:

Alic, Margaret. *Hypatia's Heritage: A History of Women in Science from Antiquity through the Nineteenth Century.* Boston: Beacon Press, 1986.

Anderson, Bonnie S. and Judith P. Zinsser. *A History of Their Own: Women in Europe from Prehistory to the Present.* New York: Harper and Row, 1988.

Anderson, Louisa Garrett. *Elizabeth Garrett Anderson 1836-1917.* London: Faber and Faber Ltd., 1939.

Antler, Joyce. *The Educated Woman and Professionalization: The Struggle for a New Feminine Identity 1890-1920.* New York and London: Garland Publishing Inc., 1987.

Banks, Olive. *Faces of Feminism: A Study of Feminism as a Social Movement.* New York: St. Martin's Press, 1981.

Battiscombe, Georgina. *Reluctant Pioneer: A Life of Elizabeth Wordworth.* London: Constable, 1978.

Birkett, Dea. *Spinsters Abroad: Victorian Lady Explorers.* Oxford: Basil Blackwell, 1989.

Blease, W. Lyon. *The Emancipation of English Women.* London: 1910; reprint, New York: Arno Press, 1977.

Boas, Louise Schutz. *Woman's Education Begins: The Rise of the Women's Colleges.* Norton, Mass.: Wheaton College Press, 1935; reprint, New York: Arno Press, 1971.

Bradbrook, M. C. *That Infidel Place: A Short History of Girton College, 1869-1969.* London: Chatto and Windus, 1969.

Branca, Patricia. "Image and Reality: The Myth of the Idle Victorian Woman." In *Clio's Consciousness Raised: New Perspectives on the History of Women,* eds. Mary S. Hartman and Lois Banner, 179-189. New York: Harper and Row, 1979.

Brink, J. R., ed. *Female Scholars: A Tradition of Learned Women Before 1800.* Montreal: Eden Press Women's Publications, 1980.

Brittain, Vera. *The Women of Oxford: A Fragment of History.* London: George G. Harrap and Co., Ltd., 1960.

Browne, Alice. *The Eighteenth Century Feminist Mind.* Detroit: Wayne State University Press, 1987.

Bryant, Margaret. *The Unexpected Revolution: A Study in the History of Education of Women and Girls in the Nineteenth Century.* London: University of London Institute of Education, 1979.

Burstall, Sara. *Frances Mary Buss.* London: Society for Promoting Christian Knowledge, 1938.

Burstyn, Joan. *Victorian Education and the Ideal of Womanhood.* London: Croom Helm, 1980.

Cash, W.J. *The Mind of the South.* New York: Alfred Knopf, 1941.

Clifford, Geraldine Jonçich, ed. *Lone Voyagers: Academic Women in Coeducational Universities 1870-1937.* New York: The Feminist Press at the City University of New York, 1989.

Clinton, Catherine. *The Plantation Mistress: Woman's World in the Old South.* New York: Pantheon Books, 1982.

Conable, Charlotte Williams. *Women at Cornell: The Myth of Equal Education.* Ithaca and London: Cornell University Press, 1977.

Conway, Jill. "Perspectives in the History of Women's Education in the United States." *History of Education Quarterly* 14 (Spring, 1974): 1-12.

Cooper, William J. and Thomas E. Terrill. *The American South: A History.* New York: Alfred A. Knopf, 1990.

Corgan, James X. "Toward a History of Higher Education in Antebellum East Tennessee." *The East Tennessee Historical Society's Publications* 60 (1988): 39-66.

Cornelius, Roberta D. *The History of Randolph-Macon Woman's College.* Chapel Hill: University of North Carolina Press, 1951.

Cott, Nancy. *The Bonds of Womanhood.* New Haven: Yale University Press, 1977.

Dabney, Charles William. *Universal Education in the South.* Chapel Hill: University of North Carolina Press, 1936.

Degler, Carl. *At Odds: Women and the Family from the Revolution to the Present.* New York: Oxford University Press, 1980.

Delamont, Sara and Lorna Duffin, ed. *The Nineteenth Century Woman: Her Cultural and Physical World.* London: Croom Helm, 1978.

Dixon, Brandt V. B. *A Brief History of H. Sophie Newcomb Memorial College 1887-1919.* New Orleans: Hauser Printing Co., 1928.

Dyhouse, Carol. *Feminism and the Family in England.* Oxford and New York: Basil Blackwell, 1989.

_____. "Social Darwinistic Ideas and the Development of Women's Education in England, 1880-1920." *History of Education* 5 (1976): 41-58.

Ellsworth, Edward W. *Liberators of the Female Mind: The Shirreff Sisters, Educational Reform, and the Women's Movement.* Westport, Conn.: Greenwood Press, 1979.

Finch, Edith. *Carey Thomas of Bryn Mawr.* New York: Harper and Bros., 1947.

Finley, Ruth E. *The Lady of Godey's: Sarah Josepha Hale.* New York: Arno Press, 1974.

Fischer, David Hackett. *Albion's Seed: Four British Folkways in America.* New York and Oxford: Oxford University Press, 1989.

Fitzpatrick, Ellen. *Endless Crusade: Women Social Scientists and Progressive Reform.* New York and Oxford: Oxford University Press, 1990.

Fox-Genovese, Elizabeth. *Within the Plantation Household: Black and White Women of the Old South.* Chapel Hill and London: The University of North Carolina Press, 1988.

Frankfort, Roberta. *Collegiate Women: Domesticity and Career in Turn-of-the-Century America.* New York: New York University Press, 1977.

Gaines, F.H. *The Story of Agnes Scott College 1889-1921.* N.p., n.d.

Gardiner, Dorothy. *English Girlhood at School: A Study of Women's Education Through Twelve Centuries.* London: Oxford University Press, 1929.

Gay, Peter. *The Bourgeois Experience: Victoria to Freud.* Vol. 1, *Education of the Senses.* New York: Oxford University Press, 1984.

Giddings, Paula. *When and Where I Enter: The Impact of Black Women on Race and Sex in America.* New York: William Morrow and Co., 1984.

Glazer, Penina Migdal and Miriam Slater. *Unequal Colleagues: The Entrance of Women into the Professions, 1890-1940.* New Brunswick and London: Rutgers University Press, 1987.

Goodsell, Willystine. *The Education of Women; Its Social Background and Problems.* New York: MacMillan, 1924.

Gordon, Ann D. "The Young Ladies Academy of Philadelphia." In *Women of America: A History,* eds. Carol Ruther Berkin and Mary Beth Norton. Boston: Houghton Mifflin Co., 1979.

Gorham, Deborah. *The Victorian Girl and the Feminine Ideal.* Bloomington: Indiana University Press, 1982.

Graham, Patricia Albjerg. "Expansion and Exclusion: A History of Women in American Higher Education." *Signs: Journal of Women in Culture and Society* 3 (1978): 759-773.

Green, Elizabeth Alden. *Mary Lyon and Mount Holyoke: Opening the Gates.* Hanover, N.H.: University Press of New England, 1979.

Green, Fletcher Melvin. "Higher Education of Women in the South Prior to 1860." In *Democracy in the Old South and Other Essays,* ed. J. Isaac Copeland. Nashville: Vanderbilt University Press, 1969.

Green, Mary Elizabeth. "Elizabeth Elstob: The Saxon Nymph." In *Female Scholars: A Tradition of Learned Women Before 1800,* ed. J.R. Brink, 137-160. Montreal: Eden Press Women's Publications, 1980.

Grylls, Rosalie Glynn. *Queen's College 1848-1948.* London: George Routledge and Sons Ltd., 1948.

Hammerton, A. James. *Emigrant Gentlewomen: Genteel Poverty and Female Emigration 1830-1914.* London: Croom Helm, 1979.

Hare, Peter. *A Woman's Quest for Science: Portrait of Anthropologist Elsie Clews Parsons*. Buffalo: Prometheus Books, 1985.

Harris, Barbara J. *Beyond Her Sphere: Women and the Professions in American History*. Westport, Conn.: Greenwood Press, 1978.

Helsinger, Elizabeth K., Robin Lauterbach Sheets, and William Veeder. *The Woman Question: Defining Voices, 1837-1883*. Vol. 1, *The Woman Question: Society and Literature in Britain and America, 1837-1883*. New York and London: Garland Publishing, Inc., 1983.

Herstein, Sheila R. *A Mid-Victorian Feminist, Barbara Leigh Smith Bodichon*. New Haven: Yale University Press, 1985.

Hogeland, Ronald W. "Coeducation of the Sexes at Oberlin College." *Journal of Social History* (1972-73): 160-176.

Holcombe, Lee. *Victorian Ladies at Work: Middle-Class Working Women in England and Wales*. Hamden, Conn.: Archon Books, 1973.

Holt, Rackham. *Mary McLeod Bethune: A Biography*. Garden City, N.Y.: Doubleday and Co., Inc., 1964.

Irwin, Inez Haynes. *Angels and Amazons: A Hundred Years of American Women*. Garden City, N.Y.: Doubleday, Doran, and Co., Inc., 1933; reprint, New York: Arno Press, 1974.

James, Janet. *Changing Ideas About Women in the United States, 1776-1825*. New York and London: Garland Publishing, Inc., 1981.

Johnson, Mary Lynch. *Elizabeth Avery Colton: An Educational Pioneer in the South*. Issued by the North Carolina Division of the South Atlantic Section of the American Association of University Women, n.d.

Kaledin, Eugenia. *The Education of Mrs. Henry Adams*. Philadelphia: Temple University Press, 1981.

Kamm, Josephine. *Hope Deferred: Girls" Education in English History*. London: Methuen, 1965.

Kelley, Mary. *Private Woman, Public Stage: Literary Domesticity in Nineteenth Century America.* New York and Oxford: Oxford University Press, 1984.

Kelly, Thomas. *For Advancement of Learning: The University of Liverpool 1881-1981.* Liverpool: Liverpool University Press, 1981.

Kendall, Elaine. *"Peculiar Institutions," An Informal History of the Seven Sisters Colleges.* New York: G. P. Putnam's Sons, 1976.

Kerber, Linda. *Women of the Republic: Intellect and Ideology in Revolutionary America.* Chapel Hill: University of North Carolina Press, 1980.

Leach, William. *True Love and Perfect Union: The Feminist Reform of Sex and Society.* New York: Basic Books, Inc., 1980.

Lerner, Gerda. *The Female Experience: An American Documentary.* Indianapolis: Bobbs-Merrill Co., 1977.

_____. *The Grimké Sisters from South Carolina: Pioneers for Woman's Rights and Abolition.* New York: Schocken Books, 1975.

Levine, Philippa. *Victorian Feminism 1850-1900.* Tallahassee: Florida State University Press, 1987.

Lewis, Jane. *Women in England 1870-1950: Sexual Divisions and Social Change.* Bloomington: Indiana University Press, 1984.

Logan, Rayford W. *Howard University: The First Hundred Years 1867-1967.* New York: New York University Press, 1969.

Lutz, Alma. *Emma Willard: Daughter of Democracy.* Boston: Houghton Mifflin, 1929; reprint, Washington D.C.: Zenger Publishing Co., n.d.

_____. Emma Willard. *Pioneer Educator of American Women.* Boston: Beacon Press, 1964.

Manton, Jo. *Elizabeth Garrett Anderson.* New York: E. P. Putnam and Co., 1965.

Martin, Theodora Penny. *The Sound of Our Own Voices: Women's Study Clubs 1860-1910.* Boston: Beacon Press, 1987.

McNair, Walter Edward. *Lest We Forget.* Atlanta: Tucker-Castleberry Printing, Inc., 1983.

McWilliams-Tullberg, Rita. "Women and Degrees at Cambridge University, 1862-1897." In *A Widening Sphere: Changing Roles of Victorian Women,* ed. Martha Vicinus, 117-145. Bloomington: Indiana University Press, 1977.

_____. *Women at Cambridge: A Men's University--Though of a Mixed Type.* London: Victor Gollancz, 1975.

Montgomery, Robert. *Examinations: An Account of their Evolution as Administrative Devices in England.* University of Pittsburgh Studies in Comparative Education, no. 6. Pittsburgh: University of Pittsburgh Press, 1967.

Morello, Karen Berger. *The Invisible Bar: The Woman Lawyer in America 1638 to the Present.* New York: Random House, 1986.

Neff, Wanda Fraiken. *Victorian Working Women: An Historical and Literary Study of Women in British Industries and Professions, 1832-1850.* New York: AMS Press, Inc., 1966.

Neverdon-Morton, Cynthia. *Afro-American Women of the South and the Advancement of the Race 1895-1925.* Knoxville: University of Tennessee Press, 1989.

_____. "The Black Woman's Struggle for Equality in the South, 1895-1925." In *The Afro-American Woman: Struggle and Images,* eds. Sharon Harley and Rosalyn Terborg-Penn, 43-57. Port Washington, N.Y.: Kennikat Press, 1978.

Newcomer, Mabel. *A Century of Higher Education for American Women.* New York: Harper and Row, 1959; reprint, Washington, D.C.: Zenger Publishing Co., 1975.

Newell, Mary Gathright. "Mary Munford and Higher Education for Women in Virginia." In *Stepping Off the Pedestal: Academic Women in the South,* eds. Patricia A. Stringer and Irene Thompson, 26-38. New York: Modern Language Association of America, 1982.

Noble, Jeanne L. *The Negro Woman's College Education.* New York: Bureau of Publications, Teachers College, Columbia University, 1956.

Norton, Mary Beth. *Liberty's Daughters: The Revolutionary Experience of American Women, 1750-1800.* Boston and Toronto: Little Brown and Co., 1980.

Notable American Women 1607-1950: A Biographical Dictionary. Cambridge, Mass.: Belknap Press, 1971.

Peacock, Sandra J. *Jane Ellen Harrison: The Mask and the Self.* New Haven and London: Yale University Press, 1988.

Perkins, Linda M. "The Education of Black Women in the Nineteenth Century." In *Women and Higher Education in American History,* eds. John Mack Farragher and Florence Howe, 64-86. New York and London: W.W. Norton and Co., 1988.

Peterson, M. Jeanne. *Family, Love, and Work in the Lives of Victorian Gentlewomen.* Bloomington and Indianapolis: Indiana University Press, 1989.

Rogers, Annie M.A.H. *Degree by Degrees: The Story of the Admission of Oxford Women Students to Membership of the University.* London: Oxford University Press, 1938.

Rogers, Katherine. *Feminism in Eighteenth Century England.* Urbana, Chicago, and London: University of Illinois Press, 1982.

Rosenberg, Rosalind. *Beyond Separate Spheres: Intellectual Roots of Modern Feminism.* New Haven and London: Yale University Press, 1982.

Rossiter, Margaret. *Women Scientists in America: Struggle and Strategies to 1940.* Baltimore and London: Johns Hopkins University Press, 1982.

Rothblatt, Sheldon. *The Revolution of the Dons: Cambridge and Society in Victorian England.* New York: Basic Books, Inc., 1968.

Rury, John and Glenn Harper. "The Trouble with Coeducation: Mann and Women at Antioch, 1853-1860." *History of Education Quarterly* 26 (Winter, 1986): 481-502.

Rubinstein, David. *Before the Suffragettes: Women's Emancipation in the 1890s.* New York: St. Martin's Press, 1986.

St. Clare Byrne, Muriel and Catherine Hope Mansfield. *Somerville College 1879-1921*. London: Oxford University Press, 1922.

Sanchez, Regina Morantz. "The Female Student Has Arrived, The Rise of the Women's Medical Movement." In *"Send Us A Lady Physician:" Women Doctors in America, 1835-1920*, ed. Ruth J. Abram, 59-69. New York: W.W. Norton and Co., 1985.

Scott, Anne Firor. "The Ever Widening Circle: The Diffusion of Feminist Values from Troy Female Seminary, 1822-1872." *History of Education Quarterly* 19 (1979): 3-25.

_____. *The Southern Lady: From Pedestal to Politics 1830-1930*. Chicago and London: The University of Chicago Press, 1970.

Seelye, Clark L. *The Early History of Smith College*. Boston: Houghton Mifflin Co., 1923.

Sklar, Kathryn Kish. *Catharine Beecher: A Study in American Domesticity*. New Haven: Yale University Press, 1973.

_____. "The Founding of Mount Holyoke College." In *Women of America: A History*, eds. Carol Ruth Berkin and Mary Beth Norton, 177-201. Boston: Houghton Mifflin Co., 1979.

Solomon, Barbara Miller. *In the Company of Educated Women: A History of Women and Higher Education in America*. New Haven: Yale University Press, 1985.

Spruill, Julia Cherry. *Women's Life and Work in the Southern Colonies*. New York: W.W. Norton and Co., Inc. 1972.

Stephen, Barbara. *Emily Davies and Girton College*. London: Constable and Co., 1927; reprint, Westport, Conn.: Hyperion, 1976.

Strachey, Ray. *"The Cause": A Short History of the Women's Movement in Great Britain*. Port Washington, N.Y.: Kennikat Press, Inc., 1928; reprint, 1969.

Talbot, Marion and Lois Kimball Rosenberry. *The History of the American Association of University Women 1881-1931*. Boston and New York: Houghton Mifflin Co., 1931.

Tarbell, Ida M. *The Business of Being a Woman*. New York: The MacMillan Co., 1912.

Taylor, James Monroe. *Before Vassar Opened: A Contribution to the History of Higher Education in America.* Boston and New York: Houghton Mifflin Co., 1914; reprint, Freeport, N.Y.: Books for Libraries Press, 1972.

Tuke, Margaret. *A History of Bedford College for Women.* London: Oxford University Press, 1939.

Tylecote, Mabel. *The Education of Women at Manchester University 1883 to 1933.* Manchester: Manchester University Press, 1941.

Veysey, Laurence R. *The Emergence of the American University.* Chicago and London: The University of Chicago Press, 1965.

Vicinus, Martha. *Independent Women: Work and Community for Single Women 1850-1920.* Chicago and London: The University of Chicago Press, 1985.

Vickery, Dorothy Scovil. *Hollins College 1842-1942: An Historical Sketch.* Hollins College, Va., 1942.

Wells, Robert V. "Women's Lives Transformed: Demographic and Family Patterns in America, 1600-1970." In *Women of America: A History,* eds. Carol Ruth Berkin and Mary Beth Norton, 16-33. Boston: Houghton Mifflin Co., 1979.

Williams, Frances Leigh. *A Founding Family: The Pinckneys of South Carolina.* New York and London: Harcourt, Brace, Jovanovich, 1978.

Woloch, Nancy. *Women and the American Experience.* New York: Alfred A. Knopf, 1984.

Wood, Ann Douglas. "'The Fashionable Diseases': Women's Complaints and Their Treatment in Nineteenth-Century America." In *Clio's Consciousness Raised: New Perspectives on the History of Women,* eds., Mary S. Hartmann and Lois Banner, 1-22. New York: Harper and Row, 1974.

Woody, Thomas. *A History of Women's Education in the United States.* New York: Science Press, 1929; reprint, New York: Octagon Books, Inc., 1966.

Young, Elizabeth Barber. *A Study of the Curricula of Seven Selected Women's Colleges of the Southern States.* New

York: Teachers College, Columbia University Bureau of Publications, 1972.

Zophy, Angela Howard. *For the Improvement of My Sex: Sarah Josepha Hale's Editorship of Godey's Lady's Book, 1837-1877.* Ph.D. Dissertation, Ohio State University, 1978.

INDEX

Clarke, Dr. Edward H., 83-86, 95
  (n. 11), 113
Clough, A.J., 93, 97 (n. 92), 195
Cobbe, Frances Power, 51
Coeducation in America, xiii, xiv,
  43-44, 56-57 (n. 32), 99-109,
  111, 113, 114-115, 120, 156-
  159, 165-170, 184-185, 196,
  206 (n. 62); and separation of
  women, 44, 102-109, 115, 116
  (n. 11), 156-159
Colby College, 107
College Alumnae Club, 190
College and university teaching, 189,
  195-197, 199, 239
Collet, Clara, 198
Colton, Elizabeth Avery, 151-152
Columbia University, 110, 151
Cooper, Anna Julia, 157
Coordinate Colleges, 109-110
Cornell University, 105-107, 113,
  117 (n. 29), 158, 170
Crandall, Prudence, 37, 153
Curzon, Lord George, 127-128
Dall, Caroline, 82
Darwin, Erasmus, 23
Davies, Emily, 42, 48, 51-53, 59
  (n. 69), 65-75, 91, 92, 111,
  115, 122, 126, 181, 209
Dawson, Sarah Morgan, ix, 142-143
Defoe, Daniel, 10
Degrees, university, in America, 44,
  60-61, 77, 120; in England, 51,
  77, 120-135, 172-173, 176; at
  Cambridge, 66, 70, 128-135,
  172-173, 176, 183, 210-211;
  Oxford, 125, 126-128, 129,
  172, 176, 210-211

Dike, Samuel, 170
Discontent, from lack of education,
  ix; Eighteenth century, 9-10, 16;
  in the South, 142-143, 161
  (n. 26)
Domestic Science, 117 (n. 29), 154-
  155, 166-171, 173-176, 196
Domesticity, Eighteenth century, 9;
  Nineteenth century, 38-42, 75,
  87, 155-156; Twentieth century,
  169-171, 174-176, 199-201
Douglass, Frederick, 153
Dubois, W.E.B., 155
Eliot, Charles, 109, 171, 185
Eliot, George, 67, 68, 181, 204
  (n. 25)
Elstob, Elizabeth, 23-24
Emerson, Joseph, 34
Endowed Schools Act, 65-66
English Reform Movement, 58
  (n. 50)
English Woman's Journal, 52, 61,
  187
Equal Education, Ideal of, xiv-xv,
  10, 14, 17, 20-21, 53, 60-81,
  83-86, 93, 99-119, 149-150,
  159, 183-184, 210-211
Fabian's Women's Group, 199
Faithfull, Lillian, 174
Fawcett, Henry, 73
Fawcett, Millicent Garrett, 73, 121,
  126
Fawcett, Philippa, 126
Federation of University Women
  Graduates, 190
Fisher, Sally Logan, 9
Fisk University, 116 (n. 11), 155,
  157